CUMBERLAND ISLAND
Strong Women, Wild Horses

John F. Blair, Publisher
Winston-Salem, North Carolina

CUMBERLAND ISLAND
Strong Women, Wild Horses

CHARLES SEABROOK

Published by John F. Blair, Publisher

Copyright © 2002 by Charles Seabrook
All rights reserved under International and
Pan American Copyright Conventions
Sixth Printing, 2013

The paper in this book meets the guidelines
for permanence and durability of the
Committee on Production Guidelines for
Book Longevity of the Council on Library Resources

Library of Congress Cataloging-in-Publication Data
Seabrook, Charles.
Cumberland Island : strong women, wild horses / by Charles Seabrook.
p.   cm.
Includes bibliographical references and index.
ISBN 0-89587-267-6 (alk. paper)
1. Cumberland Island (Ga.)—History. I. Title.
F292.C94 .S43 2002
975.8'746—dc21
2002007853
ISBN 978-0-89587-305-7 (Paperback Edition, 2004)

Cover photograph © Fred Whitehead
Map by Chuck Blevins / Sources: U.S. Census Bureau. ESRI, National Park Service
Book design by Debra Long Hampton

To

Laura, Mildred, Cynthia, Vivian, Doris, Caroline, and Vola, strong women all

In

loving memory
of my mother, Rosa Jeanette Garvin Seabrook, an exceptionally strong woman

Contents

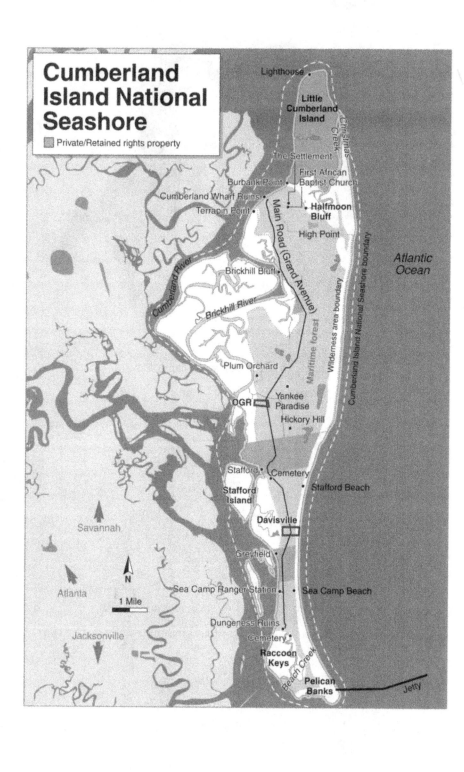

Cumberland Island National Seashore

Private/Retained rights property

Lighthouse

Little Cumberland Island

Christmas Creek

The Settlement

First African Baptist Church

Burbank Point

Cumberland Wharf Ruins

Terrapin Point

Halfmoon Bluff

High Point

Main Road (Grand Avenue)

Cumberland River

Brickhill Bluff

Brickhill River

Maritime forest

Wilderness area boundary

Cumberland Island National Seashore boundary

Atlantic Ocean

Plum Orchard

OGR

Yankee Paradise

Hickory Hill

Stafford

Cemetery

Stafford Beach

Stafford Island

Davisville

Savannah

Greyfield

Atlanta

N

1 Mile

Sea Camp Ranger Station

Sea Camp Beach

Jacksonville

Dungeness Ruins

Cemetery

Raccoon Keys

Beach Creek

Pelican Banks

Jetty

CUMBERLAND ISLAND
Strong Women, Wild Horses

PROLOGUE

I AM A PASSENGER in a battered Ford pickup truck eighteen years old, jouncing over what is called Grand Avenue on Cumberland Island National Seashore off the coast of Georgia. Driving is Whit Foster, a great-great-grandson of Thomas Carnegie, who helped his brother Andrew amass one of the world's great fortunes in steel well over a century ago. Whit's ancestors once owned nearly all of Cumberland, a lush barrier island now cherished by multitudes for its great natural beauty and serenity.

Like a jungle thick and wild, clumps of spiky saw palmettos hem in the narrow dirt road. They scratch the old truck's fenders and make my skin crawl. Massive live oaks dripping with gray Spanish moss form a cathedral-like canopy over the avenue.

Then, around a curve, a mansion appears, grand, white, elegant. It takes my breath away. It is Plum Orchard, built by the Carnegies a century ago. Rising from a broad green lawn, nearly the length of a football

3

field, it is graced with balustrades, railed verandas, ornate terraces, French doors, and arched floor-to-ceiling windows. Four sturdy Ionic columns support a gabled roof two stories high. It has thirty-five rooms, an indoor swimming pool, a squash court, and an elevator, Whit says.

As I stare, it seems incongruous that this great Neoclassical Revival mansion would rise in a subtropical maritime forest on an island forty-five minutes by boat from the mainland.

I'm dying to see inside, but there's nobody to let us in, so we go back to the truck. As we drive on, wild horses, their ribs poking out like the ridges on a washboard, clop across in front of us, taking their sweet time while we wait patiently for them to move along.

We stop at a huge grove of giant, low-hanging oaks, where we stroll among lichen-covered chimneys of former slave cabins. They are ghostly reminders of when an oddball plantation owner named Robert Stafford chased off his freed servants after the Civil War and burned down their cabins—or so the story goes.

Eight miles south of Plum Orchard, we come upon the stark remains of its mother mansion, Dungeness. In the early 1900s, Dungeness was one of the most ostentatious residences on the East Coast and the hub of a social whirl unmatched south of Newport. Now, standing in dignified repose, the crumbling brick walls stab at the sky. In my mind, they are as awe-inspiring as the Anasazi ruins in Mesa Verde.

"We've got it all on Cumberland," says Whit, a trim, sandy-haired, forty-four-year-old oil and gas broker whose permanent address is Baltimore. "We've got history, beauty, nature, and some of the most remarkable women you'll find anywhere."

———————

We come into another clearing, bounded by spreading oaks and tall pines. In the sunny space is a weathered, tin-roofed cabin. A small, equally seasoned barn squats behind it. A Rhode Island Red rooster crows lustily.

A sense of loneliness pervades the place. It is called the Settlement, where once lived former slaves and their descendants. No African-American lives here now.

What we have come to see is the tiny, whitewashed First African Baptist Church on the edge of the old village. In September 1996, this sturdy little chapel no bigger than a corncrib was more famous than Notre Dame in Paris. It was where John Kennedy, Jr., and Carolyn Bessette came to be married in an ultrasecret ceremony that threw the paparazzi for a loop. For weeks after the remarkable event, flotillas of writers and photographers from tabloids and the mainstream press alike came here to ponder why a man like Kennedy would be wed in such a tick-infested place.

A rusty padlock secures the church's red double doors. I peer through a window, but I can't see much because the panes are stained. I do make out rough wooden pews and a white wooden table with an open Bible on it.

"We might as well stop by Carol's," Whit suggests.

She is Carol Ruckdeschel, who lives close by in the cabin with the barn in back. The crowing rooster is hers. I have known her for years. She is a naturalist who came to the island in the early 1970s and never left. During the Kennedy-Bessette wedding, she sat on an upturned milk crate in her barn's doorway, sipped a beer, and watched the hubbub.

She is in her corral tending her two horses and her blue-eyed Abyssinian cats when she spies us. "Wow, what a surprise. It's been a long time," she says as she hugs me. Her brownish hair is in long braids, as it always is, and she's wearing bib overalls and a T-shirt, as she usually is. Her research partner, with whom she shares her cabin, walks from behind it and greets us heartily. He is Bob Shoop, a retired marine biologist from the University of Rhode Island. His head is shaved bald, and he's wearing a blue T-shirt and stained khaki pants.

On the cabin's back porch, we sit among hip boots, firewood, empty jars, deer antlers, rusting pieces of machinery, nets, driftwood, and other jetsam. An unseen hog grunts nearby. Birds chirp. A male painted bunting, whose stunning red, green, blue, and yellow feathers look like a parrot's, pecks at something in a homemade feeder. A bright red cardinal perches amid a clump of moss. A mallard duck waddles in a pen, being fattened for Thanksgiving.

The screen door scrapes opens, and Carol emerges with Margaritas, cold and blended just right. Bob follows with a bowl of assorted nuts and popcorn and a plate of cut-up sausage. "I got it in Missouri," he says of the meat.

"Eat up," says Carol.

I hesitate. This is the woman John McPhee profiled in the *New Yorker* in 1974, describing her proclivity for picking up snakes, possums, and other assorted creatures run over on the highway, then sometimes boiling or roasting them for supper. Nonetheless, I plunge in. The sausage is tasty, the Margarita refreshing. In this remote place, the cocktail hour is sacrosanct.

"A lot of things are happening on this island, and they're not good," Carol says. "The sea turtles are still in big trouble, the wild horses and hogs are ruining the place, and some people want the Park Service to haul loads of tourists all over the island."

———————

Cumberland's natural splendor, its unsullied beach nearly eighteen miles long, its big houses, its unfettered horses, its ruins of mansions and slave cabins, its little white church—all cast a mystique, an aura, over the island.

They also, amazingly, breed discontent. They embroil this dolphin-shaped strip of sand, maritime forest, and salt marsh in some of the bitterest turmoil you'll find anywhere in America. Historic preservationists, environmentalists, politicians, the National Park Service, former landowners—all have conflicting desires for the island. All want control. Few of America's other national parks are beset by such strife.

It has triggered lawsuits, political retaliation, public outcries, and berating newspaper editorials. People who were once good friends and neighbors have stopped speaking to each other. Peyton Place was never this crazy. In vituperative exchanges bordering on slander, the factions blame each other for letting the island's old mansions and horse stables and indoor pools crumble. They sue each other over who can drive cars on the beach or along Grand Avenue or through the forest of spreading oaks and wild grapevines thick as a man's leg. They even feud over the island's 250 wild horses, solemn-eyed and unapproachable. The free-running animals thrill visitors, but they also denude swaths of fragile vegetation. Biologists say they should be rounded up and hauled off, or their numbers at least thinned. Politicians say the horses are what tourists come to see, so they should be left alone.

Some of the battlers are rich and famous. Some live in shacks. Some are tree-huggers. Some hate tree-huggers. Some are the inevitable lawyers, politicians, and government bureaucrats.

In the thick of it are the Carnegie descendants and the heirs of Asa Griggs Candler, the Atlanta pharmacist who introduced Coca-Cola to the world. The Carnegies once owned 90 percent of Cumberland. The Candlers owned most of the rest.

Carnegie and Candler progeny still live on the island at least part of the year through retained-estate agreements with the National Park Service. The government dangled the privileges in front of them in the 1970s as inducements to sell their property to create the national seashore. Under the agreements, the heirs have exclusive use of their old island homes for periods ranging from forty years to lifetimes. Some of the agreements are up as early as 2010. Others won't run out until the grandchildren of some of the estate holders are dead.

Some Carnegies never made a pact with the government, stubbornly refusing to sell. Some—the so-called inholders—still own their island property outright. The Park Service has the authority to condemn their land, pay them fair market price for it, and run them off the island. But that's unlikely to happen because condemnation could set off bitter court battles. The Park Service already is gun-shy from a land-taking squabble in the late 1970s, when a Carnegie heir who also was a Rockefeller took the agency to court. The jury said the government should have paid him three times more than what the Park Service said was fair market value for his land. The agency was aghast over the jury's decision. "After that, they didn't talk much about condemnation," said James S. "Pebble" Rockefeller, Jr.

Instead, the government decided to wait patiently for the landowners' deaths, then step in and make an offer to their children or grandchildren. Of course, someone else could outbid the government, and that worries the Park Service and conservation activists to no end.

Meanwhile, in another war of words, the inholders and retained-estate holders demand essentially the same rights their ancestors had before Cumberland became a national park. The government promised them that, they say. They want to drive their cars on the island's sandy roads and its wind-swept beach, activities taboo for ordinary park visitors. Whit tells me that his ancestors preserved and cherished Cumberland long before the government had designs on it, so the present generation deserves favored status.

He's right about the Carnegies and Candlers rallying against would-be spoilers. If it were not for their vigilance, Cumberland might well have become another place like Hilton Head Island in South Carolina, top-heavy with golf courses, strip malls, and subdivisions of cedar-sided homes with three-car garages.

Charles Fraser, the cocky developer of Hilton Head's exclusive Sea Pines Plantation, bought thirty-one hundred unspoiled acres on Cumberland in 1968 from two financially strapped Carnegie brothers. Almost immediately, he began laying out golf courses, streets, and an airport. When irate Carnegies and Candlers learned of the scheme, they pooled their resources, jerked strings in Washington, and ran him off the island.

"The most stubborn people I ever dealt with," Fraser said of them.

To me, it seems reasonable that the government should grant some lifetime concessions to landowners who donate their land or sell it at less than face value for the public good. A vast portion of America's unspoiled lands came into the public domain that way. Without the promise of retained rights for the former owners, hundreds of thousands, maybe millions, of acres of our protected green space would be outside public ownership, perhaps buried under concrete and asphalt.

But on Cumberland, environmentalists resent any special treatment for anybody. It's been forgotten, they say, that Cumberland is a national park, owned by all the people. They want the privileges already granted the families reined in.

"It's not the Carnegie National Park," opines Norman Owen, who keeps watch over Cumberland for the Sierra Club. "It's Cumberland Island National Seashore. It's supposed to be managed for the benefit of all, not for a select few who believe they are entitled to special favors."

The irony is that all the people fighting, litigating, and vilifying each other over the island profess deep love for it. Like a couple in a nasty divorce case, each demanding custody of a cherished child, they all think they know what's best.

———•·•———

Caught up in the maelstrom is the twenty-two-thousand-square-foot Plum Orchard, the embodiment of a time—the robber baron era, the time of Jay Gatsby—when the very rich erected fabulous mansions in grandiose displays of their wealth. Plum Orchard sits on the backside of Cumberland along the winding Brickhill River overlooking a vast salt marsh with twisting tidal creeks. It is one of five opulent mansions built by the Carnegies on Cumberland a century ago. Now, it's like a once-beautiful dowager grown old yet trying to keep up appearances, her fortune petered out, her gowns threadbare, her larder empty, her once-curvaceous body shrunken and wrinkled.

Plum Orchard appears palatial from a distance, but on closer inspection, I see paint peeling in big flakes, structural support beams rusting through, the roof leaking, graceful balconies nearing collapse, banisters rotting.

This was not supposed to happen, the Carnegies say. When they sold or donated Cumberland to the Park Service, they entrusted Plum Orchard and twenty-five other historic structures to the government's custody. They contend that it is the government's duty to restore and maintain the mansions, the stables, the barns, the servant cottages, the greenhouses, the laundry rooms, the potting sheds, the private gymnasiums, and the indoor swimming pools that supported their ancestors' extravagance. Plum Orchard's seediness is a prime example of the government's dereliction of duty, they complain.

"I've watched so much of my heritage fall in on Cumberland. That was never the intent of our family," says Janet "Gogo" Ferguson, a great-great-granddaughter of Thomas Carnegie. "I've watched some of the structures being torn down. I've watched most of them fall in through demolition by neglect. And it just very much disheartens me. It makes me so angry."

She is one of the inholders. She inhabits a swath of land in the middle section of the island, where five generations of her family once lived, acreage that the National Park Service covets but has been unable to get. In a studio attached to her home, she makes fine jewelry from bones, shells, and other bits of nature picked up on the island. When John Kennedy, Jr., married Carolyn Bessette, she arranged the extraordinary event and designed their wedding rings.

Park Service bigwigs tell me that they lament letting the mansions and other buildings go to rot. But they say Congress metes out little money for saving and maintaining the structures. Most of Cumberland's $1.9 million annual budget goes for administrative services and for maintaining campgrounds, hiking trails, picnic areas, restrooms, and ferryboat docks that serve forty-eight thousand visitors per year. Little is left for historic preservation.

Some Park Service workers once confided to me that Plum Orchard really isn't of much historic importance anyway. A former park ranger who once had to care for Plum Orchard told me this: "It is an enormous spavined and gut-rotted white elephant that the Carnegie heirs foisted off on tax-payers. The best thing that could happen to it would be a providential lightning strike that burned it to the ground."

———•◦•———

Stoking the uproar are eighty-four hundred acres of maritime forest, beach, and salt marsh that Congress designated an official wilderness area on the island, and that the United Nations named a Global Biosphere Reserve for its rare ecology and beauty and for its sea turtles, wood storks, and other endangered creatures.

By federal law, federally designated wilderness areas are supposed to be free of human intrusion except for occasional hikers and campers. In wilderness areas, no power equipment is allowed: no cars, ATVs, chain saws, bulldozers. Yet Cumberland's wilderness has houses in the midst of it. Running through it are underground utilities and Grand Avenue. To get to Plum Orchard by land, you must go through the wilderness. The Carnegies, the Candlers, and their historic-preservation allies say that, given so many human alterations, Congress never should have declared the island a wilderness area in the first place. Over the past twenty years, they have campaigned passionately to repeal the wilderness designation. To Denis Davis, Cumberland Island National Seashore's embattled superintendent in the late 1990s, Gogo once wrote, "We are sympathetic to your plight and impossible task of managing a wilderness which does not, and cannot exist."

To the great aggravation of wilderness boosters, the retained-rights agreements allow the Carnegie and Candler heirs and a handful of other people who also struck deals with the government to drive their Jeeps, ride their bicycles, and run their whining chain saws in the wilderness. They are the only people who have those rights. Run-of-the-mill tourists don't have them. I have seen visitors wax furious when the National Park Service told them they couldn't pedal in the wilderness, while others can.

The Park Service people say they don't have such rights either.

Instead, they have to walk, go by boat, or ride horses when they cross the boundary into the wilderness. They can't use a chain saw. Trucks can be used only in emergencies or for carrying heavy equipment. All-terrain vehicles may be used only during hurricane warnings, fires, and turtle patrols and research.

"For us to be the principal agency for upholding the Wilderness Act, we cannot violate the act," Cumberland's superintendent, Art Frederick, told me.

The Wilderness Society, a watchdog group dedicated to keeping machines out of refuges, demands that Frederick do what he already has done for ordinary visitors and for his own personnel—yank driving-in-the wilderness privileges from the inholders and retained-estate holders.

The inholders beg to differ.

When he was Cumberland's superintendent, Denis Davis warned his bosses in Washington that although the retained-rights residents indeed had certain privileges on the island, "they have exceeded their rights in many cases." For his pains, his superiors pulled him off the island in early 2000 and dispatched him out west.

Another group gave him an award. The National Parks and Conservation Association, a Washington-based advocacy group for the park system, conferred upon him in 1998 its highest award, given to persons who muster the courage to protect parks under assault. "He remains undaunted by island residents with names like Carnegie and Candler, who feared they would have diminishing rights and privileges," said Carol Aten, the group's vice president. "He put the welfare of the park above his career and fought for the wilderness area against strong opposition."

It is great irony that this serene place whose natural splendor uplifts the human spirit and refreshes weary minds is the center of great upheaval. To understand the quarreling, one must understand the island, its people, its incredible history.

Primitive hunters and gatherers existed harmoniously on Cumberland thousands of years before Europeans arrived. Then the Spanish, the French, and the English waged deadly battles over it. Spanish Franciscan monks established a mission with a huge church to save the souls of the Indians, who would die out within a century and a half from diseases caught from the Europeans. After the Revolutionary War, entrepreneurs came with broadaxes and crosscut saws to fell giant live oaks for the fledgling nation's tall ships. Before the Civil War, cotton planter Robert Stafford had a memorable affair with his mulatto slave.

Former president Jimmy Carter once said this was one of his favorite places on earth. John Kennedy, Jr., said it was one of the very few places where he could escape the pressing throngs and the paparazzi's flashing lights.

But what shaped Cumberland's amazing past more than anything else was the cadre of domineering women who watched over and protected the island for two centuries as if it were their feudal fiefdom.

And someday, historians may look back on the twenty-first century as the time when two very strong women—Gogo Ferguson and Carol Ruckdeschel—tugged in opposite directions over Cumberland's soul.

Carol Ruckdeschel on her ATV
Courtesy of *Atlanta Journal-Constitution*

Janet "Gogo" Ferguson at her home on Cumberland Island
Courtesy of Atlanta Journal-Constitution

CHAPTER ONE

GOGO AND CAROL live only a few miles from each other on Cumberland. Once, they were great friends. Carol said she loved Gogo like a sister. Now, they don't speak to each other.

A few years ago, Gogo wanted to turn Plum Orchard into a haven for artists. Putting the derelict mansion to good use, she said, would save it from ruin.

Carol retorted that an artists' retreat in the midst of a wilderness area would ruin the island's peacefulness. "The government should be working to reduce the number of people and vehicles on the island, to enhance wilderness values," she told the government. "The impact of people can only increase with this plan."

Gogo then blamed Carol for killing the colony before it ever welcomed its first poet or screenwriter. Carol made no bones about being dead-set against the scheme, but she denied responsibility for its demise.

Their quarrel reached all the way to Congress, where a tough old senator and an ambitious young congressman got into their own bitter set-to over Plum Orchard.

Carol was twenty-nine in 1973 when she came to live on Cumberland with John Pennington, a former writer and city editor for the *Atlanta Journal* who said he was burned out by the big-city grind. "I left my newspaper job [and wife and three kids] and paid the price in lost income to get away from the contrived environment of the city," he wrote in *National Geographic* in 1977. "I wanted to feel the touch of a clean breeze, the wet kiss of the rain in a natural setting, to hear the ocean's roar instead of the freeway's, the trumpeting call of the pileated woodpecker instead of the jackhammer's chatter."

His crowning journalistic feat was rescuing the political career of a future president of the United States. Jimmy Carter, then a little-known peanut farmer from Plains, Georgia, was running for the State Senate in the 1960s when his opponent seemed to eke out a hair-thin victory. In an investigative report, Pennington wrote that a hundred citizens apparently had crawled out of local cemeteries to vote for Carter's adversary. The revelation prompted a recount, which gave Carter the win. "Had it not been for Pennington's courage and skillful reporting, I never would have run for political office again," Carter recalled.

Pennington and Carol came to Cumberland as caretakers for the property of the Candler family on the island's remote north end. Pennington, tall, handsome, his jet-black hair streaked with gray, wanted to take advantage of the quiet and beauty to write a novel. But after a couple of years, his romance with Carol fizzled. He met a woman who worked at the island's Greyfield Inn and married her. He died of cancer in October 1980 in a Florida hospital, his novel unfinished.

Carol, who grew up in Atlanta, saw living on the island as an opportunity to pursue her self-taught career as a naturalist.

Before coming to Cumberland, she reaped national notoriety through John McPhee's vivid *New Yorker* profile. Readers were enthralled by his account of Carol's picking up road-killed possums, snakes, and other creatures for scientific study—and occasionally cooking and eating them. She recounted how she sometimes spent the night in a sleeping bag in a graveyard because she felt safe there. No one ventured into a cemetery at night, she mused. "She was trim and supple and tan from a life in the open," McPhee wrote. In one memorable scene, she held aloft a large water snake "like a piece of television cable moving with great vigor."

Another writer, William L. Howarth, described her as young, free, handsome, and wild, a woman whose life and work habits defied most labels. He said she didn't fear serpents, could live without men, and took things apart to see how they were made. She would dare touch and taste anything, he wrote.

She also was the subject of a less-flattering piece by Robert Coram in 1981 in the now-defunct *Atlanta Weekly* magazine. "Because of Carol, serious men have done silly things," he wrote. In one scene, Coram, a former Cumberland park ranger, said that, while visiting Pennington on the island, "we heard the rolling thunder of a herd of wild horses coming through the compound. . . . Astride a horse in the middle of the herd was Carol, knees gripping the horse's bare back, one hand tangled in the mane, the other holding aloft a bottle of Jack Daniel's."

After splitting with Pennington, Carol became the lover of a divorced Orange Park, Florida, surveyor named Louis McKee. With his help, she worked out a deal with the grandchildren of an ex-slave to get a three-room cabin of her own in the Settlement, near the Candler property. She then sold the cabin to the Park Service and was granted a lifetime estate on the island.

It was at that rustic dwelling on April 17, 1980, that she shot and killed McKee. In a statement to police, she said that McKee, wielding a canoe paddle and screaming and cursing, had tried to break down her cabin's locked door. Apparently, he was enraged that she had made friends with a backpacker she had met on the island. Frightened out of her wits, Carol raised her twelve-gauge shotgun—the one McKee had given her for protection—and fired point blank through the disintegrating door. He died instantly.

A Camden County coroner's jury ruled that Carol shot McKee in self-defense, making it a justifiable homicide. She walked out of the courtroom a free woman.

Not surprisingly, she doesn't like to discuss the unpleasant event. She prefers to dwell on her passion, Cumberland Island. "You can fall in love with this island, and it will still be there in the morning," she says.

———————

It was on the beach at Cumberland that Carol found her calling—to save from extinction the big sea turtles that nest here each year. She would clean toilets and polish silverware for the wealthy residents during the day so that she could be up all night monitoring turtle nests on the beach.

On moonlit nights from May through early August, barnacle-encrusted loggerhead turtles—and occasionally a rare leatherback—struggle ashore in a cumbersome, lurching gait to lay their eggs in the powdery sand beyond the tide's reach. Weighing as much as 350 pounds, the ponderous animals are a threatened species—that is, they're not yet on the brink of extinction, but they soon could be.

The eggs are the size, roundness, and whiteness of Ping-Pong balls. A female turtle laboriously scoops out the sand with her hind flippers, lays as many as two hundred eggs, covers the nest, and drags herself back into the sea, leaving bulldozer-like tracks in the sand. About sixty days later, if the nest survives the ghost crabs, raccoons, and wild hogs that find turtle eggs delectable, the hatchlings claw out of their sandy incubator and scurry into the surf. Temperature and instinct dictate that the baby turtles, no bigger than a half dollar, emerge from their nest at night and crawl toward the stars hovering over the sea's horizon.

Cumberland's beach is ideal for them. Only a precious few miles of Atlantic and Gulf coast beaches are like Cumberland's, still dark and wild enough for the creatures. On other beaches, lights from condos and hotels confuse the tiny turtles, beckoning them inland, where they surely will die.

Jimmy Carter tells a remarkable story: "Once, we happened to witness on a Fourth of July weekend a sea turtle laying her eggs on Cumberland. We happened to be back down there on Labor Day and went to look at the nest, and as we were looking at it, the little turtles emerged. We watched them and guarded them as they entered the ocean for the first time in their lives."

———————

Carol has seen something else with great regularity—dead loggerheads washing up on the sand. The toll has abated little over the years. She still finds scores of the big reptiles belly up each summer. "At this rate, they won't survive as a species," she says.

When she first got to Cumberland, she didn't have a project lined up to satisfy her budding naturalist urges. But when she saw turtle after turtle dead on the beach, she knew what she should do. "I realized we needed to know the magnitude of the deaths because nobody, it seemed, was doing anything about it," she says. "So I started the Sea Turtle Stranding Network in Georgia. I wrote as many people as I could on the other islands to get them to voluntarily keep a count.

"Well, it wasn't long before you could see that turtle strandings was a serious problem. The Georgia Department of Natural Resources started paying attention. And ultimately, our network came to be run by the National Marine Fisheries.

"So I found myself looking for sea turtles, whales, dolphins on a weekly basis on Cumberland. I figured I might as well look for all vertebrates. A dead animal could go unreported for weeks or months—or not at all—if you didn't make a regular survey.

"We've got a better database because of this beach. It's the regularity of the beach survey that counts. Once you can document, you're a step ahead. If you just arbitrarily go out and find an animal one day and then next year find two more, you can't say much about it. But with this weekly survey, we've got quality baseline data, and probably the best on the East Coast for the longest period of time regarding vertebrates.

"So that's what I've been doing since '79. I do necropsies on the turtles and the marine mammals and save parts of them for the database."

Since beginning her studies, she has found more than seventeen hundred sea turtles dead on the beach. Her accumulated data is some of the most extensive in the country. Researchers drool over it.

"I study death to better understand life," she explains.

———•—•———

On a hot, sunny day in June 1999, she has come to the beach on her ATV to examine still another dead loggerhead. Beach patrollers radioed her this morning with the location.

"Hello, young fellow," she says as she approaches the turtle, a male juvenile sprawled in the sand. "I'm so sorry this happened to you." Except for its missing eyes, pecked out by vultures, the animal seems free of blemishes. The saddest part, Carol says, is that it never had a chance to mate, never had a chance to contribute its genetic material to the survival and diversity of its species.

She shoos away black flies swarming around the carcass and pays no attention to the putrid odor wafting from it. She makes a quick black-ink drawing of it. Wielding her razor-sharp hunting knife, she slits open the craw in its throat. Out spill small rocks, shells, and a black mass of decomposing shrimp. Carol says a dead turtle with a craw full of shrimp and no obvious signs of illness or injury likely got tangled in a shrimp net and drowned.

She takes some of the craw's gloppy material, dribbles it into plastic zip-lock bags, and carefully labels them. Then, grunting and straining, she flips the animal over and cuts open its gut. A thick, smelly black liquid oozes on to the powdery white sand. With her bare hands, she probes inside. Her hands make sucking, squishing sounds as they feel around. Some of the gut contents and the flesh she slices from the gut are placed in other bags and labeled. The stuff will be analyzed in her laboratory. The gut exam, she says, can give insight into the animal's eating habits and other behavior that may reveal something about its ocean sojourn.

Then she goes back to the front of the carcass. With a few deft cuts, she removes the eyeless head and places it in a labeled container strapped to the back of the ATV. The head is destined for one of the big maceration buckets in her yard to remove the flesh. When that's completed, the skull will become part of her collection. One day, she hopes a scientist will do genetic studies on the heads.

Her chore on the beach completed, she jots down some notes. Finally, she drags the heavy carcass behind a sand dune and leaves it for vultures, insects, and other creatures to feast on. Before departing, she walks down to the surf and washes her hands in the sea.

———•◦•———

She blames many of the turtle deaths on offshore shrimpers, whose big nets sometimes entrap the animals and drown them. Turtles are air breathers, although they are able to stay underwater for hours. But when they are entangled in nets, struggling to escape, they quickly use up their oxygen and give up the fight.

Carol's detailed documentation of turtle strandings over the years helped convince the government to require that shrimpers install turtle excluder devices, or TEDs, in their nets. The devices are supposed to let trapped turtles escape through trap doors in the nets. But lifeless turtles continue to roll up on the beaches—sixty-seven one summer, eighty-nine another summer, sixty the next summer, on Cumberland alone. On a single Saturday one July, Carol found twenty-seven dead turtles.

Thus, TEDs are not the only answer to saving the creatures, she concludes.

"I wouldn't say that TEDs are having no effect at all," she says. "They might be. They also might be lulling us into a false sense of security, in that turtles that escape from the nets die anyway, maybe eight to ten hours later, from the stress of trying to escape. So we don't think TEDs is the final answer, even though millions of dollars and many years have been spent pursuing this one single method.

"We would rather see some diversity, in addition to TEDs. Try other approaches and see what works. The best thing, as a minimum, we should have areas that are off-limits to trawling. We should have established wilderness areas in or near shore areas. People are calling for turtle-safe shrimp like dolphin-safe tuna. That means farm-reared shrimp. We're really beyond hunters and gatherers. We need to be farming."

———————

Carol may know more about Cumberland's ecology than any other living soul. She has been described as one of the most gifted naturalists ever to work in Georgia. In addition to her study of sea turtles, she has cataloged every plant species on Cumberland in carefully crafted notebooks replete with detailed drawings.

The sun has seasoned the skin covering her wiry frame since the days of the *New Yorker* profile. Her loose-fitting Levis, rubber boots, belt, and knife scabbard are weathered as well. She zips about the island on her battered ATV, her long braids often tied down by yarn. The battered felt hat atop her head holds clothespins that she uses to keep her hair out of her face while she dissects dead creatures.

Her cabin is the only occupied structure in the Settlement. She has a cell phone, but it can't receive incoming calls. She rarely calls out because she has to find a high spot—up a tree or on a roof—to get the signal beamed out.

Around the place are piles of boards to be recycled and odd bits of machinery. In the cluttered yard are a chicken coop, a vegetable garden, a pen in which she raises the Abyssinian cats, and a small corral for her two horses.

Hers is a simple life. Island living offers few temptations to the pocketbook. Her clothes may be castoffs found on the beach. She has no qualms about slicing choice cuts from a dead horse stuck in the mud or from a shark stranded on the beach and roasting the flesh and eating it. She does require that it be fresh and disease-free. She makes a tasty armadillo pâté and one Christmas made bobcat Burgundy for Bob Shoop and herself.

"But if I have to eat beans and rice for a week, that's fine," she says. "You can always go catch fish. I have a garden. So I don't focus on food, [although] I dearly love to eat. I love good wine, good cheese—everything that costs money. I don't have it very often. The creek has everything—fish, clams, oysters, shrimp. Just throw in a cast net, and the sea will provide. I've got pigs in a pen and more pork than I ever want. I do go to town once in a while if I want coffee or whatever minor. I don't like to go off the island unless I absolutely have to. I didn't ever mind leaving Atlanta."

She supplements her meats and greens with grapefruit from old plantation sites. She makes tea from holly leaves, gets honey from wild beehives, and harvests edible berries, plums, persimmons, and nuts. She rarely passes up edible mushrooms spied in the woods.

In the summer, an aroma of decaying flesh pervades her compound. It emanates from rotting porpoises, sea turtles, and other creatures picked up on the beach. The animal parts are kept in buckets filled with water, in which they macerate to remove the flesh. "Maceration is the best way to skeletonize marine mammals," Carol says.

The odor lures black vultures, which perch on her cabin's roof or hang around the back porch like lazy hounds for most of the day. Sometimes, she feeds them the remains of the creatures she dissects. "You get to where you don't even notice them most of the time," she says. When she has dinner on the porch, she tosses tidbits from her plate to them. They rush pell-mell, wings flapping, to snatch up the handouts. "They eat everything except beef from a certain supermarket chain," she says.

In her kitchen is a wood-burning stove. In the refrigerator might be tissue specimens in plastic bags next to jars of jelly and pickle relish. She keeps the specimens refrigerated until she's ready to study them.

The cabin's decor consists largely of jetsam washed up on the beach and crafted into items of art by Carol. The kitchen countertop is made from sturdy three-by-ten boards that were once part of a dock; they still bear traces of barnacles. In the living room, varnished turtle shells decorate the cypress walls. A mobile of animal ribs and vertebrae hangs from the ceiling. A lamp made from the leg of a horse sits on a table.

Fifty feet from the cabin is Carol's guest house, remodeled from an old shed. It has two beds and a flush toilet. Her "wake-up call" is tossing a handful of hickory nuts on the galvanized tin roof, which to a guest sounds like a surprise battlefield attack. The shower is outside, next to her cabin. Jimmy Carter, with whom she once canoed on Georgia's Chattahoochee River, stops by to see her when he's on Cumberland, but he doesn't stay at the guest house.

The compound's most significant structure is identified only by a small wooden sign tacked near the door. "Cumberland Island Museum," it reads. The museum is the culmination of Carol's more than twenty-five years of research.

The crude, twenty-by-forty-foot, plywood-covered building, which she and Shoop designed and built, serves as their research facility. "We had a roof-raising party, and many of the people on the island came up and helped finish it one weekend," Carol says.

It is a place few people outside academia know about and even fewer people have visited. "It's not a tourist destination point, that's for sure," says Carol.

The structure sits off the ground on trees stumps. Nailed over its entrance is the curved spine of a porpoise. Inside, where temperature and humidity are controlled, lie stacks of sea-turtle shells and countless bones.

Bones by the barrelful. Bones bagged and boxed ten feet high. In fact, the museum houses one of the world's largest collections of sea-turtle skulls, shells, and other remains. On plywood shelves and in secondhand specimen cases, some of them from the Smithsonian, is a compendium of Cumberland wildlife—snakes, salamanders, and fish in jars of formaldehyde; bones of birds, alligators, porpoises, moles, squirrels, and mice. There is a preserved baby sperm whale and a box labeled "cheloid gut remains." Some bottles hold the gut contents of long-dead birds. A jar that once held pickles now contains parasites from the cranial sinus of a dwarf sperm whale. In the attic are horse skulls and other bones galore.

Researchers who make their way to the museum stand slack-jawed when they first see the collection. No one has anything like this.

The specimens may help researchers figure out, for instance, how climate change affects sea turtles, or if certain animals are a new subspecies. "This is not an ooh-aah collection. It's for research," Carol says.

She and Bob may spend much of their day in the museum, rising as early as three in the morning, organizing and sketching the specimens, jotting notes, reading scientific journals, and writing to scientific colleagues and environmental groups. Because Carol has no telephone, she has no e-mail. The museum's surprisingly large library holds dozens of books on the natural history of Georgia and the South. Carol sometimes plans her rare trips to Atlanta to coincide with used-book sales at the city's malls, where she may pick up dozens of volumes for a few dollars.

Next to the museum is a crude laboratory. There, she and Bob, wielding razor-sharp scalpels, dissect, clean, and prepare the specimens for the museum.

And only a horse-chip throw away is the First African Baptist Church, where tourists occasionally come. Many of them think Carol's compound is part of the show.

———————

Gogo Ferguson, the slight, raven-haired great-great-granddaughter of Lucy and Thomas Carnegie, who bought most of Cumberland in the late 1880s, describes herself as a poor relation who regularly visited the island as a child. Her parents divorced when she was about four, and she and her two brothers "got sort of shipped down here" for the summers to stay with her grandparents, Robert and Lucy Ferguson. The Fergusons lived at Greyfield, one of the four great mansions Lucy Carnegie built on Cumberland for her children.

"Usually, there were lots of cousins," Gogo recalls. "We'd go out sea-turtle hunting on the beach at night. And back then, before the park was here, we had dirt bikes, motorcycles, and [we could] race up and down the roads. It was a haven for kids. It was like *Lord of the Flies*. We had the run of the island."

Later, in 1965, the Fergusons turned Greyfield into an inn. In 1978, "Miss Lucy," as everyone called her, asked Gogo to manage the establishment, which by then had become one of the most select inns in the country. Men wore black ties for dinner; women wore evening dresses.

Miss Lucy, one of the strongest women ever to dominate Cumberland, ran the inn like a near tyrant. She refused to buy a dishwasher, and she held bra checks to see if female workers were wearing the undergarment.

"Her idea of managing was to work me to the bone and do exactly as she told me," Gogo recalls. "It was just Louise [a lifelong friend] and myself and a boat captain. We did everything. Louise was cooking a hunters' breakfast at four in the morning, and then she'd go on to cook regular breakfast and lunch and dinner. I did the house, and I'd drop the vacuum cleaner and run out and do the tours. And then I'd wait on tables at night. It was unbelievable. I don't know how we got through it."

After years of that, she took a vacation—a hike along a ninety-five-mile trail in Scotland. "When I came back, my grandmother had replaced me," she says. "I was devastated because it was the first real time off I had in about seven years, more than three or four days at a time. It was a hard lesson for me because I'd put so much time into it. I was so hurt that I took a job in Washington."

It was there that she married and gave birth to her daughter, Hannah. The marriage ended in divorce after about two years. She decided to bring Hannah to Cumberland with her.

Gogo had attended the Rhode Island School of Design and had majored in art at the University of Massachusetts, where she received instruction in jewelry design. But it was only after returning to Cumberland and seeing how she could combine her artistic talent with her love for the island that the idea of bone jewelry evolved.

Her jewelry is based on seashells and bones from rattlesnakes, sharks, alligators, armadillos, raccoons, and other island denizens. Some pieces are mixed with turquoise, jade, and onyx; some are cast in silver or fourteen-karat gold.

"My favorite class was physiology because I loved drawing the muscle tissue and the bones and everything," says Gogo. "And I was always designing things for myself when I was running the inn. People were always commissioning me to do a necklace."

But even for a Carnegie descendant, starting a new business was a rocky path.

"When I got back here, I was scraping bottom," Gogo says. "I cooked at the inn. I worked. I did anything I had to do to make money and start this business. I wanted to design a business where I could base myself here."

She asked an Atlanta bank for a loan. "I spread out all of these bones," she says, "and I convinced these poor guys, these very straight-laced Southern bankers, that I was going to pay back this loan. They gave me eight thousand dollars and two years to pay it back. And I paid it back in six months.

"And I was so naive. I went bombing up to every accessories writer in New York and spread my bones out again and told my story. And they were fascinated that I had grown up on this island. And my designs were so unique. They still really are. I don't know of too many people who are designing out of bones or natural items. It was a fresh idea.

"I think they could see how naive I was. But it was the fact of living on Cumberland and my whole history that intrigued them. And they came down and were just absolutely mesmerized by the whole story. And consequently, it sort of snowballed. I just started selling more and more. Now, we do almost a quarter of a million a year in sales."

There's a ring made from rattlesnake ribs, a pendant from alligator vertebrae, and earrings cast from raccoon penis bones. The raccoon, Gogo explains, is one of the few animals that has such a bone.

To collect her materials, she traipses around the island barefoot, her long hair windblown and tangled. When it's too far to walk, she drives an old Ford Bronco with the top torn off, a Pekingese named Puppy by her side.

She has two stores on Martha's Vineyard in Massachusetts open June through October. Isabella Rossellini, Goldie Hawn, Mike Wallace, Art Buchwald, and Hillary Clinton are some of the collectors of her work. Her wedding-band designs for John Kennedy, Jr., and Carolyn Bessette are a matter of privacy, she says.

Through her inheritance, she got a small plot of land on Cumberland near Greyfield and built her house on it. She does most of her jewelry work in a studio attached to the house.

The nine-room whitewashed-pine dwelling is U-shaped, built around a deck overlooking the salt marsh. She and husband David Sayre, a pilot and builder, patterned it after a stable house on her family's summer property in South Dartmouth, Massachusetts. "I always wanted to live in a place that I could nail anything to the walls," she says.

An eye-grabbing collection of alligator, horse, and wild boar skulls crowds the shelves. In the hallway leading to her bedroom is a photograph of her grandmother with a pet buzzard. In back of the house is a vegetable garden.

"This house is a dream," she says. "I always dreamed of having my own place. We sort of recycled everything. All our windows are from the dump or from the junkyards. David and I sort of drew a house. Then we started building it. Some rooms got shorter and longer, but we knew we wanted one central living room. Everyone congregates here. It's a place where we can sit by the fire and have breakfast or dinner, and we can cook at the same time and be a part of it. All my belongings and bottle collections and arrowhead collections and pottery collections surround me."

She is fond of entertaining guests and hosting small dinner parties on the deck. Her brother Mitty Ferguson, who helps manage the inn, comes over and roasts oysters on the grill. The meat course often is roasted Cumberland pork, a superb dish.

The island is her soul. "It's gut-wrenching every time I leave, almost like cutting the umbilical cord all over," she says.

Her passion for its historic structures, most of them built by her Carnegie forebears, is just as deep. The most elegant mansion by far is Plum Orchard, constructed in 1898 for George, the fifth son of Lucy and Thomas Carnegie, and his wife, Margaret. To Gogo, Plum Orchard is sacred ground. "Coming there as a child, when it was all lit up, it was a magical place," she says.

Alarmed that Plum Orchard was falling apart before her eyes and that the Park Service had little wherewithal to halt the deterioration, let alone to restore the mansion, Gogo formed the Plum Orchard Center for the Arts in 1994. Through that foundation and an agreement with the Park Service, she would make the house a retreat for painters, writers, and dancers. Moreover, using the mansion on a daily basis would help preserve it. "I realize that these huge structures have to be lived in," she says. "They have to be open and breathing or they can't be maintained. I thought it would be such a low-impact use of Plum Orchard, with fifteen artists coming there to work."

The retreat would enable the artists to work in total isolation, "which is so rare for them," she notes. "It affords them the opportunity to come and be funded for a month or two and work on whatever projects they're working on. They basically close their doors. They have breakfast, they're delivered a picnic lunch, and you never see them.

"People have a total misconception of artist retreats. They sort of visualize Sedona or some huge artist fairground or something."

She sought commitments for more than $10 million in outside dona-
tions. On her board of directors were luminaries like John Kennedy, Jr.,
CBS newsman Forrest Sawyer, poet and journalist Rose Styron, writer
George Plimpton, and dancer Mikhail Baryshnikov. She spent a considerable amount of her own money on the effort.

She did not expect the bitter, negative reaction from environmentalists. Plans for the retreat collapsed, and she pointed her finger at Carol,
among others, for the defeat.

Carol and Gogo became friends soon after Carol came to
Cumberland. They were on voluntary firefighting crews together. Together,
they went through Gogo's grandmother's diaries, looking for significant
bits of natural history.

Then, in 1995, Carol came across a copy of a confidential memorandum stating that the Park Service would allow the Plum Orchard Center
for the Arts to use the old mansion for up to seventy-five years. "What's
this?" she asked. As she read it, she decided that the Park Service "was
shoving this thing under the rug."

When the agency appeared likely to approve the venture without
first studying the impact on the adjacent wilderness area, a hastily formed
group of activists who called themselves the Defenders of Wild Cumberland
filed a lawsuit. Carol helped found the group, although, strangely, she never
joined it.

The artists' colony, Carol claims, likely would have doubled the
island's population—to a grand total of sixty. "An artist colony or corporate retreat all add up to a residential community because you have to
have permanent staff and on and on," she says. "That is not insignificant.
Sixty people don't sound like much when you're talking about Manhattan
Island, but on Cumberland, it's a lot."

The group's executive director, a lawyer named Hal Wright, labeled the proposed artists' retreat "just a bed-and-breakfast for the rich and fa-mous, who will want a lot of conveniences and other stuff." He said Carol was unfairly being picked on, since she was not a member of the Defend-ers of Wild Cumberland.

The Wilderness Society, the Georgia Conservancy, and other en-vironmental groups equally scorned the proposal, saying it would increase truck, car, and van traffic through the island's wilderness area. They in-sisted that federal law be obeyed—that there be no mechanical contrap-tions whatsoever in the wildernesses.

Gogo argued that you couldn't get to Plum Orchard by car without going through the preserve. Grand Avenue, the only land route to the mansion, slices through the heart of the wilderness. Vehicular access was necessary to haul in supplies, staff, and guests, she said.

Her opponents shot back that people and supplies could be brought to Plum Orchard by boat, thereby circumventing the wilderness area. The mansion is only five hundred feet from a dock on the Brickhill River. Make people walk from the dock to the house, they said.

Gogo insisted cars were still needed. Out of exasperation, one of her cousins called the enviros "militants who go snooping about."

In the end, the Park Service said the lawsuit didn't matter. The real reason for quashing the artists' retreat was bureaucratic red tape, since the memorandum of agreement was not in compliance with the agency's rules for leasing historic structures. "They should have used a long-term his-toric-lease agreement," Denis Davis said. "A memorandum of agreement is for a short period. A long-term historic lease is for a longer period, and that's what the Park Service prefers."

The hard feelings between the two island neighbors lingered. Carol referred to Cumberland as "the Carnegie National Monument." Gogo criti-cized Carol for her "extremism and growing isolation." The Carnegie de-scendants stopped letting Carol ride their private ferryboat back and forth to the mainland. And she couldn't get her mail at Greyfield Inn anymore.

In 1998, an ultraconservative Republican congressman named Jack Kingston drove the wedge between Carol and Gogo even deeper.

Kingston, who represents Georgia's coastal district, claimed he was appalled that ordinary taxpayers had no access to genteel Plum Orchard or the Settlement unless they were able to make an arduous trek of several miles by foot in one day—an impossible task for most people. The only way to get to the island was by boat, he explained. The vast majority of visitors were day-trippers, who had to catch the last departing ferry to the Georgia mainland at four-thirty. Plum Orchard and the Settlement were eight and fifteen miles, respectively, from the ferry docks on the island, much too far for a day hike. And Grand Avenue, the only road leading to them, ran through the wilderness area, where ordinary taxpayers couldn't drive a car, ride a bike, or travel by anything else mechanical.

"It's equivalent to going to Yellowstone and not having access to Old Faithful because you're not allowed to drive there," Kingston said. "I want it so that the common person who punches a time clock can go to Cumberland and look at the Plum Orchard mansion and the Settlement."

In particular, he pointed out that the descendants of slaves once lived in the Settlement and built the little church there. Therefore, it was part of their African-American heritage and should be more publicly accessible, he opined. "If John Kennedy, Jr., and his entourage can drive up there for a wedding, African-American families and their children should be able to drive up there, too," he said.

He introduced a bill in Congress in an attempt to quell the dissension among Gogo and Carol and their allies. The legislation, he declared, would expand Cumberland's wilderness, help restore Plum Orchard to its former glory, and allow more sightseers to eyeball the old mansion. It also would allow tourists to go by car, bicycle, or golf cart to the north end and gaze at the Settlement.

Gogo and her historic-preservation friends thought the bill a wonderful idea. The Candlers on Cumberland's north end loved it, too, since one of its provisions would allow them to take back a portion of the national-park land they had sold to the government in 1982 for the seashore.

But it threw Carol, the Sierra Club, the Wilderness Society, and their supporters into a tizzy. They questioned Kingston's motives and said unpleasant things about his ancestry. They had little doubt that he introduced the bill more at the behest of the Carnegies and the Candlers than from any heartfelt feelings for black Americans and average citizens.

Kingston claimed to be surprised by the virulence. His bill failed, but not because of the enviros. The National Park Service opposed it. The agency said that if it had to restore public land to the Candlers, the move would cause turmoil throughout the park system because other former landowners would want their property back, too.

Then Kingston tried another tactic. Until he got his way, he would persuade his congressional comrades to withhold federal money earmarked for buying more of Cumberland from the Carnegies. But that scheme only triggered more bitterness. It made Max Cleland, Georgia's senior United States senator, mad as hell. He was trying to make political hay by helping the Park Service acquire more of the Carnegie land. He said Kingston was single-handedly ruining the plan.

In the end, Kingston's friends said he got in over his head. He should have bowed out of the Cumberland mess altogether. One thing he didn't count on was some unyielding and very formidable women. "It's like negotiating peace in the Middle East," he said. He tried to find a face-saving way of extricating himself. Perhaps if he had better understood Cumberland's remarkable history and its inhabitants' reverence for the island's unparalleled beauty, he indeed might have opted out.

C H A P T E R   T W O

Tacatacura o Tan ot d...

C UMBERLAND I SLAND is not spectacular. It doesn't have jagged mountains or craggy seacoasts. Its natural beauty is in its mellowness, its sweeping salt marshes, its sun-spangled beach, and its verdant maritime forest.

A subtropical climate and a stirring azure sea form the serene environment. Sweet-singing songbirds build their nests in summer in the dense foliage. Tall palmettos and tangles of wild grapevines that are themselves intertwined with sparkleberry and Virginia creeper give the feel of a tropical paradise. Even in the dead of winter, wildflowers bloom on Cumberland. The tiny, lemon-yellow, trumpet-shaped jasmine appears as early as January.

Cumberland is the largest and southernmost of Georgia's barrier islands, which form an archipelago hugging the coastline. Geologists call them barrier islands because they sit like stoic sentinels protecting the mainland from sea storms. Most of them remain un-

Grand Avenue in the early 1900s
Courtesy of the National Park Service

spoiled because, over a century ago, it was fashionable among the mega-rich to own a Georgia island. They built fabulous mansions on the islands but otherwise left them mostly wild.

Comprising some thirty-six thousand acres, Cumberland is a third larger than Manhattan. Eighteen miles long, it ranges from three miles to a half-mile in width.

Ask visitors and residents what their favorite part is, and most emphatically say the beach. Empty and wild, the shell-flecked swath of fine sand is a couple of hundred yards wide. It is also the longest expanse of undeveloped beach on the Atlantic coast—so long that one cannot see from one end to the other, due to the earth's curvature.

Astir on the beach are mixed flocks of shorebirds—gulls, terns, willets, oystercatchers, sandpipers, sanderlings, plovers, and, occasionally, an endangered piping plover. The sandpipers run back and forth in front of the advancing and retreating waves. The sanderlings scurry like little ghosts across the sand.

The flocks probe the wet sand for tiny mole crabs and multicolored coquina clams, which burrow in the sand and extract algae and plankton from incoming waves. As the tides advance and recede across the sand twice daily, the crabs and clams shift higher or lower on the beach in mass movements. The shorebirds follow the procession.

The tide sweeps numerous sea creatures on to the beach. When it retreats, marine snails, hermit crabs, blue crabs, fingerling fish, starfish, jellyfish, and other denizens of the ocean may be trapped in the beach's long, shallow tidal pools, where they become easy prey for the birds.

Other ocean inhabitants—horseshoe crabs, sand dollars, sea cucumbers, sea lilies, sea urchins, burgundy-colored sea pansies, and magenta sea fans—also get washed up. Scavenging ghost crabs feast on the stranded creatures, picking them apart with sharp, tiny claws. The crabs get their name from their pasty white color and their amazing ability to vanish in the blink of an eye, dashing over the sand, then stopping and blending immediately into the background. They prey upon any small living creatures in the surf zone, especially newly hatched turtles scooting across the beach toward Mother Atlantic.

Facing the beach is a wall of young sand dunes sculpted by wind and waves, their faces raw and steep. These primary dunes are the island's first line of defense against the sea. On their inward side, sea oats, lavender-flowered morning glories, pennywort, and other hardy, deep-rooted plants anchor the dunes, keeping them stabilized.

Farther back stand older, larger, precipitous dunes, their sand as soft as talcum powder. They rise more than fifty feet to provide backup protection against wind and storms.

Nestled between the primary and rear dunes are meadows of waving grasses and sedges that attract seed-eating birds, rabbits, and other small animals. Thickets of scrawny wax myrtle produce copious quantities of bluish berries gobbled up by more than thirty bird species. Prickly pears, favored by raccoons, take root here. Growing also in the sandy soil are copses of seaside goldenrod, Spanish bayonet, and fragrant red cedars, which islanders once chopped down for Christmas trees.

Pocketed behind the dunes in long, slender depressions are freshwater ponds called sloughs. The largest is Lake Whitney. It's gradually filling in with sand, and much of its sapphire-blue water is thick with aquatic weeds. Nevertheless, it is still a good fishing place. Ten-foot-long alligators live in the sloughs. In the spring, scores of long-legged egrets, herons, black skimmers, and ibises come here to feed. In the winter, ducks arrive.

Beyond the dunes and sloughs, the great maritime forest begins. Marvelous live oaks form dense, almost continuous canopies and lord it over the other trees—palmettos, pines, Southern magnolias, laurel oaks, American hollies, sassafras, red bays, sweet gums—which, in turn, tower over the shrubby understory of yaupon hollies, staggerbush, devil's-walking-stick, and saw palmettos.

The live oaks' character changes remarkably as the forest moves inland. Nearest the beach, the limbs have been so pruned, shaped, twisted, and stunted by the wind and salt spray that they look like a Japanese garden. Away from the wind and briny spume, they take on the traditional, more graceful pattern of live oaks—massive trunks four to seven feet in diameter and broad, spreading limbs arching out horizontally forty feet or more. Some of the more ponderous limbs sink to the ground for support.

A Cumberland oak is an island in itself. Dust and leaf mold accumulate in the bark's deep grooves, creating a rich growth medium for seeds and tiny plants blown among the branches. Flourishing in the fertile humus are resurrection ferns, whose leaves turn brown and curl during drought, but unfurl and turn a minty green with the next rain. Dangling in long gray tendrils from nearly every limb, Spanish moss lends a mellow, dignified charm.

After the Revolutionary War, live oak was in great demand. Its strength and resistance to rot and woodborers, as well as its naturally curved limbs, made it ideal for building tall ships—frigates, men-of-war, brigantines, packets, whalers, merchantmen. The dense wood doesn't float, even when fresh. Some said it surpassed the teak of India as the best timber for the greatest variety of naval purposes. Cannonballs hitting live-oak planking zinged back into the water.

In the late 1700s, shipwrights from Maine, Connecticut, Massachusetts, New York, and Pennsylvania set sail for Cumberland and the other coastal islands of Georgia, South Carolina, and Florida in search of live oak. They found entire forests of it. Thousands of "live oakers," as the men who cut and hauled the timber called themselves, were dispatched south to saw and hack in the oak groves. Ships hauled the felled timber to shipyards in New England.

Many of the huge live oaks on Cumberland today sprouted from the rotted stumps of trees harvested in the shipbuilding days. The live oak has little commercial use now, but its beauty and ecological value are unsurpassed. It is, in fact, Georgia's official state tree. Georgians say the tree takes a hundred years to grow, another hundred to live, and a hundred more to die.

The forest marches down to the edge of Cumberland's backside, where the steep bluffs tumble to the Cumberland River and its tributary, the Brickhill River. The splendid salt marsh begins there, stretching as if never-ending. The vast wetland is one of the most extensive salt marshes south of Chesapeake Bay.

Dominating it is *Spartina alterniflora*, or cordgrass—gold and glowing in fall and winter, a waving expanse of green in spring and summer, like a tall-grass prairie. Little seaside sparrows and marsh wrens build their dainty nests in it. The sun setting over it can be one of Mother Nature's most exquisite shows. The marsh smells of *Spartina*—a clean, fresh smell to those who have lived by the sea all their lives, but strange and not altogether pleasing to those sniffing it for the first time.

As on the beach, the tides rise and ebb twice daily in the marsh, bringing in phosphorus, calcium, and nitrogen from the ocean and rich sediments from the rivers that begin in Georgia's gently rolling Piedmont. The nutrients and sediments make the marsh one of the most biologically productive systems on the planet, more fertile than the richest Iowa farmland. An acre of salt marsh might produce five to ten tons of organic matter, while the most fertile farm acre produces only half that much.

Spartina flourishes in the black muck because it is tolerant of the tidal fluctuations and the saltiness. Its roots reach into the muck and mine the nutrients there. When *Spartina* dies, it decomposes into a protein-rich detritus. The detritus, nutrients, and sediments brew a veritable bouillabaisse that forms the base of an intricate food web supporting diverse creatures—oysters, clams, shrimp, periwinkles, fiddler crabs, flounder, anchovies, menhaden, croakers, squid, butterfish. A single acre of marsh can support a million fiddler crabs, which, like ghost crabs, munch on almost any dead fish, plant, or animal coming their way. Ultimately, Cumberland's salt marsh is part of the vast East Coast marsh that nourishes an estimated 70 percent of all commercially important fish and shellfish.

Gentle tidal creeks snake through the marsh. The best time to be in the creeks, preferably in a flat-bottomed johnboat, is at low tide just after sunrise, when a cool mist hovers over the *Spartina* and the early-morning rays give it a golden glow. Cautious raccoons, frisky otters, and sometimes a nervous mink come to the water's edge. Egrets and the day herons—great blues, little blues, Louisiana herons—lazily flap their long wings over the marsh looking for fishing spots along the creeks. Fidgety clapper rails probe the soft mud for edibles. Fiddler crabs zigzag all over the place.

Christmas Creek, on Cumberland's north end, is the best known of the island's tidal streams. It winds through the marsh stretching between Cumberland and a smaller neighboring island. At low tide, it empties directly into the ocean. At high tide, it pulls seawater into the marsh and smaller creeks. Supposedly, Christmas Creek got its name because of the many gifts of food that come from it—shrimp, crabs, clams, oysters, a variety of fish.

For thousands of years, humans and nature coexisted harmoniously on Cumberland. Long before the Europeans, the slave owners, the Carnegies, and the Park Service arrived, the Indians were here. No one knows exactly when the first ones came.

The first Europeans were feisty French Huguenots who arrived in 1562. At that time, Cumberland was the sanctuary of the peaceful and remarkably handsome Timucuans. They spoke a different tongue from their neighbors, the Guale Indians, who inhabited Georgia's islands to the north. Cumberland, in fact, was the Timucuan-Guale dividing line. The Timucuans and other natives knew Cumberland variously as Wissoe, meaning "beautiful"; Missoe, meaning "sassafras"; and Tacatacuru, meaning "beautiful island."

The French were amazed at the Timucuans' stature—some men were over seven feet tall and some women over six feet. Many of the men and some women covered most of their bodies with elaborate, maze-like tattoos made by slicing their dark skin and rubbing soot in the bleeding wounds. They worshiped the sun and the moon and sometimes wore only Spanish moss for clothing. They ate mostly oysters, acorns, and roots. Deer and fish occasionally provided meat. In rituals, the men gulped a bitter-tasting black drink brewed from roasted yaupon holly leaves. The vomiting it caused purified their bodies, they believed. Much more palatable was a root-beer-like concoction made from the sassafras tree. It was pleasing to everyone, including the French, who intended to ship great bundles of sassafras back to France, where it commanded a high price as a remedy for human ills.

But the Spaniards regarded Georgia's islands and Florida as their territory and didn't take kindly to the French intrusion. In the early 1560s, the ruthless Spanish governor of Florida, Pedro Menendez de Aviles, ordered his men to herd hundreds of captured French settlers and soldiers to a spot near what is now St. Augustine and put them to the sword. The bloody slaughter strengthened and consolidated Spanish power over its claims, including Tacatacuru, although the French continued to be pests.

In obedience to King Philip II of Spain, Menendez then turned to saving the Indians' souls. Pious Jesuit priests, who took vows of poverty and chastity, first tried converting the Timucuans, but they failed miserably. Tacatacuru's Timucuans killed three of them. The conniving French probably put them up to it. To subdue the natives and keep the French at bay, Menendez established a Spanish garrison and ordered construction of an earth-and-log fort on Tacatacuru, which he renamed San Pedro.

In the late 1580s, zealous Franciscans subsidized by the Spanish Crown came to San Pedro to try their hand at converting the Indians. Unlike the Jesuits, they were accepted by the Timucuans. On San Pedro's south end, the good friars established a big mission, San Pedro de Mocama, on the site of a Timucuan village. When more gray-clad Franciscans arrived, a second mission was opened on a high bluff on the north end.

But the violence-prone Guales to the north didn't like the Franciscans. In 1597, a friar heaped a tongue-lashing upon a proud Guale chief for practicing polygamy. To the celibate Franciscans, a man who had many wives was a terrible sinner. For the Guales, that was the last straw. In an uprising along the Georgia coast, they made a last-ditch effort to wipe out the Franciscans and Christianity.

When forty canoe loads of Guales tried to attack San Pedro, the island's Timucuan chief, Don Juan, stood by the Franciscans, who trembled and prayed earnestly for safe deliverance. Their prayers were answered. The Timucuans repelled the attack and saved the terrified monks and their missions. As a reward for the Timucuans, Florida's new governor, Mendez de Canzo, ordered a new church—a cavernous sanctuary with a shingled roof—to be built at the island's main mission. It was as large as St. Augustine's main church.

It was about then that the island's first strong woman—or a least the first we know about—emerged. She was Dona Maria Melendez, a Timucuan who married a Spanish soldier. The Spaniards praised her strength, called her a "good Christian," and took great delight when she proselytized the other Indians. She was named princess of San Pedro, and she tolerated no disobedience from lesser chiefs in her domain.

They were not apt to disobey anyway. San Pedro's Indians had by then become devout Catholics. They also took easily to reading and writing. They raised corn, beans, and pumpkins in the sandy soil and depended less on hunting than did the tribes on neighboring islands and the mainland. Their docile nature and their relatively stationary life on San Pedro probably accounted for their loyalty to the missions.

But while imparting their religion and technical know-how to the natives, the Europeans also shared something else—deadly maladies like smallpox, measles, syphilis, and influenza. More than anything else, the white man's diseases were responsible for the extinction of the Guales and the Timucuans. A single measles epidemic killed thousands of coastal Indians in Georgia and Florida in the 1650s.

The native depopulation alone would have doomed the missions, but the establishment of British colonies on the eastern seaboard hastened their end. Beginning in the 1660s and increasing in the 1680s, fiery raids on Timucuan and Guale missions by Carolina mercenaries, sometimes aided by the nearly lawless Carolina militia, were regular occurrences. The Indians fled in terror. Many were captured, and their villages were abandoned. The Spanish missions' last days came between 1702 and 1705, when several such raids destroyed the remaining outposts. The surviving Timucuans rushed to refugee towns close to St. Augustine, where Franciscan friars continued caring for them.

The natives' numbers continued spiraling downward. A 1717 census listed three wretched villages housing only 250 Timucuans. By 1726, the number was down to 157. Two years later, it was 70. In 1752, only 29 remained, all living in a single pestilence-plagued town. A decade later, only a single Timucuan Indian—a wizened old man named Juan Alonso Cabal—was alive to accompany the Spaniards when they withdrew from Florida to Cuba. He died there in 1767.

Creek Indians then moved in, occupying what the Timucuans had deserted.

By the early 1700s, nearly all vestiges of Spain's influence had vanished from Georgia's Golden Isles. Now, it was Great Britain's turn.

Colonel James Oglethorpe—a God-fearing, rigid moralist and strict disciplinarian—founded Savannah in 1733. That done, he set about strengthening his defenses against the hateful Spaniards, who still controlled Florida. To create a buffer between the Spaniards and the good people of Savannah, he founded a settlement called Darien down the coast from Savannah. In 1736, even farther down the coast, he established Fort Frederica on St. Simons Island. Then, poring over crude maps of the Georgia coast, he concluded that San Pedro, just south of St. Simons, was an ideal place for repulsing the Spaniards, should they sail up the rivers and sounds behind the barrier islands for a sneak invasion of Georgia.

On a sunny day in March 1736, Oglethorpe, accompanied by his Scottish Highlanders and about forty Creek Indians, landed on San Pedro as part of what he said was an expedition "to see where His Majesties and the Spaniards dominions joyn." Leading the Indians was their proud chief, Tomochichi, and his young nephew, Toonahowi. Toonahowi was among those Oglethorpe had taken with him to England the year before to show the royal court some of Georgia's aborigines. In London, Toonahowi had been formally introduced to the courtly fifteen-year-old prince, William Augustus, the duke of Cumberland. Toonahowi especially enjoyed watching His Highness take daily riding lessons. The two boys—"the dark-eyed, black-haired child of the wilderness and the fair-haired, blue-eyed child of generations of royalty," as one writer put it—became such close friends that Prince William presented Toonahowi a gold watch when the visit ended.

Remembering that gift, Toonahowi, shortly after stepping onto San Pedro, asked Oglethorpe to rename the island Cumberland in honor of his blue-blooded friend. Oglethorpe happily complied.

On Cumberland, Oglethorpe's entourage found scattered remnants of the missions and rotting huts abandoned by the Timucuans. Otherwise, only the rolling surf, noisome bugs, and twittering birds greeted them.

As Oglethorpe scanned the island, he quickly made up his mind what should be done. He ordered the Highlanders to erect a star-shaped fort at Cumberland's north end on the sandy "high point" where the second Spanish mission had stood. Named Fort St. Andrews, it was intended to intercept any Spanish force approaching through the inland waterway and hold it in check until word was relayed to Fort Frederica, the main base of defense.

Pressed by warnings of Spanish warmongering, Oglethorpe ordered some of his British regulars, who recently had seen service at Gibraltar, to occupy and fortify Fort St. Andrews. The garrison became the center of a little village dubbed Barrimacke. Lots were assigned to married soldiers, who cultivated and improved their acreage. By 1740, the town boasted twenty-four families.

But Fort St. Andrews was not an orderly place. The soldiers had gotten used to the relatively easy life of Gibraltar. They had no love for this wild, lonely, miasma-plagued land. Mutiny, duels, and court-martials were frequent. One mutinying soldier even shot at Oglethorpe, but the bullet only grazed the colonel. Loyal officers and men quickly put down the uprising.

A second fort was built on Cumberland's south end—Fort Prince William, named for the young prince. Defended by high log walls, it was intended for the same purpose as Fort St. Andrews, although it became the stronger of the two.

But the fortifications did nothing to deter the Spaniards from their single-minded aim—to run the upstart English out of Georgia. War was inevitable.

It came in 1739—the War of Jenkins' Ear, as it was known in America. A Spanish armada of fifty ships and two thousand soldiers sailed from Havana in the spring of 1742, bound for Georgia. It attacked and destroyed Fort St. Andrews, then headed north to take on the main British force on St. Simons. In what became known as the Battle of Bloody Marsh, the two forces clashed on St. Simons on June 28. Oglethorpe, with little more than seven hundred men, repulsed the enemy in a decisive battle.

The Spaniards then sailed south and tried to land again on Cumberland. This time, Fort Prince William's troops valiantly fended them off. When Oglethorpe's troops arrived, the Spaniards turned tail and headed back to Cuba. They never returned. Thus ended the Spanish attempt to conquer Georgia. Cumberland Island and its fortifications had proven pivotal.

Oglethorpe, though, lost the battle at home. His rigid management caused great dissension among the settlers. One reason for the furor: he banned rum and slavery in the colony. The trustees in London recalled him. With the Spanish threat diminished, Cumberland's two forts were decommissioned, and Barrimacke was abandoned.

Then, in 1763, an Englishman named Denys Rolle had a brilliant idea. He applied to the English Board of Trade to found what he envisioned would be a society of women from London's rowdy streets. The colony would occupy the old town and the forts on Cumberland. The women would turn from a less-virtuous life to raising silk, flax, and indigo. Perhaps Rolle thought an island would be the best location for such a colony. But the Board of Trade thought not and turned him down.

When botanist William Bartram visited Cumberland during his famous travels in 1774, he found a scarecrow-thin river pilot living hermit-like in old Fort Prince William.

Eventually, the ravages of time erased all trace of the forts and of Barrimacke. Their remains have never been found.

"Lots of people have said, 'Well, we know where they are,' and they would take us to where they thought they were," said John Ehrenhard, a National Park Service historian. "And either they couldn't remember when they got there or we could never find anything."

Another Cumberland locale associated with Oglethorpe was a place on the south end called Dungeness. Legend says that he built a hunting lodge there on a plateau created by a mound of white shells built up over the centuries by the Indians. He named it after Castle Dungeness on the cape of Dungeness in the county of Kent in England. By 1790, maps of Cumberland labeled the area as Dungeness.

Dungeness would become a well-used moniker. Two of Cumberland's strongest women picked it for the magnificent mansions erected for them on the island. The first was a Rhode Island-born Yankee, Catharine Greene Miller.

CHAPTER THREE

MEN OF GREAT POWER and influence scurried like smitten teen-
agers to indulge Catharine Littlefield Greene, "Caty" to her friends.
She aroused desires in men. No doubt, some of them would have
risked careers, families, dignity, and self-respect for a fling with her.

She was a small woman with flossy black hair, soft white skin,
a snapping pair of dark eyes, and a vivacious expression. She wore
fashions that accentuated her ample bosom.

"She was one of the most brilliant and entertaining of women,"
an admirer wrote. "In addition to beauty, she possessed personal
charm, intuitive perception and a very acquisitive intellect."

She is remembered for holding sway over some very important men—her husband, General Nathanael Greene, commander of
the Continental Army in the South during the Revolution; George
Washington, commander in chief; General Anthony Wayne, her
husband's hotheaded fellow officer, called "Mad Anthony" because

Catharine "Caty" Greene Miller
Courtesy of the National Park Service

of his dazzling military exploits; and Eli Whitney, the cotton gin inventor.

She was born on wind-swept Block Island, Rhode Island, and lived there until age eight, when her mother died. She went to live with her benevolent aunt, also named Catharine, in the quaint village of East Greenwich on the mainland. She was nearing her eighteenth birthday when she met the ruggedly handsome Nathanael Greene, twelve years her senior. He was the fourth of eight sons of a Quaker preacher who owned a large farm and several forges and gristmills. Within a year, he and Caty married.

Despite his Quaker upbringing and its antiwar sentiment, Nathanael joined the colonists' uprising against Mother England and in short order was commissioned a brigadier general. When the thirteen colonies declared themselves free of Great Britain, Nathanael Greene, George Washington, Mad Anthony, and their comrade Light Horse Harry Lee became household names in the fledgling nation.

The Revolution was a stirring time. Even when pregnant, Caty spent weeks in austere military camps with Nathanael, close to the fighting. Between the battles were jaunty military balls at which swashbuckling officers strutted and dainty ladies flirted. When Caty walked into the room, men and women craned to get a look. On one occasion, George Washington danced four hours with her without once sitting down. Caty, in fact, always preferred the company of men to women, which sparked whispering among the ladies, who worried she might lure their heroes into affairs.

When American independence was won, several states presented General Greene with real estate—seized from British loyalists—in appreciation of his service to the new nation. Georgia bestowed upon him Mulberry Grove, a rice plantation on the Savannah River eight miles upstream of the city by that name. Before the Revolution, it had belonged to John Graham, a staunch British supporter. It was named for the mulberry trees planted there to provide food for silkworms when colonial Georgia went all-out for the silk industry. With the plantation came a retinue of slaves and a large, two-story house about a hundred yards from the river.

Nathanael chose Mulberry Grove as his family's new home after selling a plantation given him by South Carolina. Money from that sale went to cover some of the personal debts he had run up in the war to clothe, feed, and equip his ragged soldiers when the government couldn't afford it.

He proceeded to revive Mulberry Grove's rice cultivation, put on hold because of the war. Caty pledged her utmost help. But what Nathanael really needed was more manpower. The slaves who had come with the plantation were not enough. He needed more slaves to produce vast quantities of rice, and he borrowed heavily to get them. To do so, he had to swallow his lofty principles on slavery. As a Quaker, he was not a believer in the inevitability of black enslavement. During the war, he had promised emancipation to any slave who fought for the Continental Army. But at Mulberry Grove, rice growing made slave labor a necessity.

Caty had no problem with owning slaves. Her Rhode Island grand-father had made a tidy sum from the "Triangular Trade," in which rum was shipped to Africa and traded for slaves, slaves were transported to the West Indies and traded for sugar and molasses, and sugar and molasses were brought back home and made into rum. Each leg was immensely profitable for the investors.

But the party-loving Caty found existence on a Georgia plantation a bit dull. She was accustomed to the swirling social life of Northern cities and the lascivious eyes of handsome men at fancy balls.

At that time, Anthony Wayne lived farther up the Savannah River at Richmond and Kew Plantations—his gifts from a grateful Georgia. Like Nathanael Greene, he also intended to make his fortune in rice. He was a frequent guest at Mulberry Grove, and historians say Caty fell in love with him. There is little doubt of Anthony's affections for her. His wife refused to move to Georgia from up north. In the humid, tangled landscape of coastal Georgia, Caty was Mad Anthony's oasis in an intellectual desert. They often rode together in the afternoons and worked elbow to elbow in their gardens, doting over favorite flowers and herbs.

Rumors whispered in Savannah's parlors hinted that Anthony paid nocturnal visits to Mulberry Grove when Nathanael was away. One item even had it that Caty and Anthony planned to murder Nathanael with a butcher knife and blame it on a runaway slave. Some of the sordid reports caught up with Nathanael. He reportedly was on the verge of going after Mad Anthony—perhaps calling out his old comrade to a duel—when, on June 11, 1786, during a visit to a neighboring rice plantation, he toppled over from sunstroke. Muttering feverishly of soldiers and lovers, he died eight days later.

With the general gone, men jockeyed for his beautiful widow's affec-tion. Mad Anthony was first in line. Caty, though, grew indifferent to him. His estrangement from his wife and the rumors of his affairs with other sweethearts along the Savannah River made it awkward for Caty and Anthony to be lovers in proper society. Her feelings cooled further after he was disgraced by a fraudulent election that got him seated illegally in the United States House of Representatives. For that transgression, he was impeached and removed from Congress.

President George Washington, who visited Caty twice at Mulberry Grove after Nathanael's death, later gave Mad Anthony an appointment to fight the Indians. Anthony went out of Caty's life forever. He once again became a military hero, defeating the outmanned Indians in the Great Lakes region and opening up the vast territory for settlement. He died at his post in 1795.

Other men of power ached for Caty, but she only strung them along. Most of her energy went into trying to turn a profit on her plantation. The first thing she did was to make her children's tutor, Phineas Miller, the plantation manager. Caty and Nathanael had hired him to come to Mulberry Grove when he was twenty-one and freshly graduated from Yale to teach their five children—George, Martha, Cornelia, Nat, and Louisa. Caty and Nathanael were following the custom of the day, in which a planter's children received basic instruction from a private tutor and then went to school in the East to round out their education.

Manly and reserved, Phineas was a person of culture and manners. He was also well versed in the classics and an avid conversationalist. Though he was ten years Caty's junior, she had liked him from the start. He had loved her immediately.

When Caty promoted him, tongues in Savannah wagged that she and Phineas were cohabiting without benefit of marriage. Even George Washington delicately pointed out that their unmarried state was not good.

She and Phineas certainly acted like a couple. Still unwed in 1792, they agreed as a favor to a plantation family across the river to ask Phineas's friend Ezra Stiles, Yale's president, about a tutor for the family's children. Stiles recommended a twenty-seven-year-old Yalie named Eli Whitney. Caty made arrangements by letter, suggesting that Whitney meet her and Phineas in New York and sail back to Savannah with them. After an arduous, storm-tossed journey to Georgia during which he was seasick, Whitney agreed to stay a short spell at Mulberry Grove before taking up the tutoring job across the river.

The job never happened. From the start, Whitney was disinclined to be the family's tutor. The money was not good. "Instead of a hundred, I found I could get only fifty guineas a year," he complained. And Caty's charm and beauty captivated him. Like so many other men, he fell under her spell.

Whitney was not handsome. He was tall, long-nosed, and delicate of mouth. His intelligence, though, glowed in his black eyes. He was puzzled over Phineas's role in Caty's life—she and Phineas were not married, but they acted as if they were.

At Caty's urging, Whitney sojourned at Mulberry Grove as a handyman and a tutor to her younger children. Like a mother hen, she suggested he study law in his spare time.

He impressed her in another way—he had a knack for fixing gadgets around the plantation. He perfected a frame for her embroidery and repaired her watch. Delighted, she suggested he put his mind to inventing a greatly needed contraption—a machine to separate cotton seeds from lint.

This was a time when sea-island cotton was of little importance in the global market because of the slow, laborious task of removing the seeds by hand. Ten hours of work were needed to separate one pound of lint from three pounds of small, tough seeds. Until a machine could be devised to do the work, cotton was little better than a weed, unable to compete with wool and flax.

Intrigued, Whitney set to work. He watched the hand movements of slaves cleaning cotton. One hand held the seed while the other teased out the short strands of lint. The plans he drew up in his room were for a machine that duplicated the manual process. Then he began tinkering in one of the outbuildings.

On an evening in September 1793, he triumphantly toted a working model of his cotton gin into the parlor of the plantation house and placed it on a mahogany table for a demonstration before Caty, Phineas, and some of their friends. He placed some fluffy cotton bolls in the hopper and turned the handle. To the amazement of his audience, out came seeds on one side and cleaned, white fiber on the other. But there was still a problem. Some of the cleaned fibers clung to the cylinder teeth and clogged up the slots through which the seeds dropped.

"Why, Mr. Whitney, you want a brush," Caty said, and handed him a clothes brush to remove the lint.

"Madam, you have completed the cotton gin," he replied.

His machine, he told the astonished folks in the parlor, could turn out in one hour the full day's labor of several workers cleaning cotton by hand.

Within days, word zipped through coastal Georgia of the astounding development. Within months, plantation owners were making plans to plant vast fields of cotton.

To protect his invention until it was patented, Whitney closely guarded his model from outside inspection. Ladies, though, were allowed a peek. One historical account says a young man named Edward Lyon, dressed in skirts and passing as a woman, took an extra close look. The result was that he and a brother came out with a rival machine.

Phineas became Whitney's financial partner, forming the Miller and Whitney Company to market the cotton gin. The company was financed in part by some of the forty-seven thousand dollars Caty finally received from the government as an indemnity for her late husband's out-of-pocket expenses during the Revolution.

Whitney returned to Connecticut to set up a factory to make cotton gins. Phineas remained in Georgia to arrange sales and contracts. A large ginning house was set up at Mulberry Grove to demonstrate the machine's practicality.

But by now, others had discovered the workings of the fantastic machine. Sixty drawn-out lawsuits were fought to sustain Whitney's patent. They were of little avail. Although historians recognize Whitney as the inventor of the cotton gin, neither he nor Miller derived any great financial return from the machine that ushered in King Cotton's long and prosperous reign.

———————

Caty and Phineas finally married on May 31, 1796, in Philadelphia in a ceremony witnessed only by George and Martha Washington and a few other close friends. It was so private that it didn't make the local papers. The couple simply knelt before a clergyman, who pronounced them man and wife.

Eli Whitney took it hard when he was told about the nuptials. He, too, was in love with Caty. As long as she lived, she was his only true emotional tie to womanhood.

Probably a reason she and Phineas did not marry sooner was that she was trying to get Congress to pay the money owed Nathanael for feeding and clothing his troops. Congress, she believed, might be more sympathetic to a widow. But even after she got the money, she and Phineas did not rush to the altar. Her closest friends speculated that she was enjoying the heady freedom of an unattached woman who could have flirtatious relationships with several men. Once she was married, those relationships would have to be reined in.

———————

Three years before his untimely death, Nathanael Greene had acquired a half interest in Cumberland Island. The heirs of the late planter Thomas Lynch of South Carolina, a signer of the Declaration of Independence, held the other half interest. The island's huge quantities of live oak influenced Nathanael's decision to invest. "The amount of timber is immense, the best in the world for ship-building," he remarked. He foresaw hefty profits in supplying oak to the navy and Northern shipyards. The income would help pay off his stack of debts.

His passing undid those plans, but it did not relieve his estate of its outstanding IOUs. His financial affairs were an intimidating mess. Caty's indemnity from the government erased only a portion of the debt. On top of that, Phineas added to the burden with the bills he ran up suing people over the cotton gin. Making matters even worse were several lousy rice crops at Mulberry Grove.

If this were not enough, Caty and Phineas got caught up in a colossal land scam in 1795. It was called the Yazoo Affair. Promoted by a group of New Englanders, the scheme's aim was to buy 35 million acres of undeveloped land from the Georgia legislature and then sell it, at great profit, to prospective cotton planters rushing into the state. The land comprised most of present-day Alabama and Mississippi.

One of the officers in the company was Caty's son-in-law John Clarke Nightingale, who had married her daughter Martha. Nightingale was also Phineas's cotton-planting partner. He urged Caty and Phineas to invest in the company, promising huge returns. Whitney also was asked to join, but he demurred, saying it sounded too good to be true. His refusal irritated Phineas.

In the deal approved by the Georgia legislature, the Yazoo Land Company would pay only $490,000 dollars for the land, a little more than a penny an acre. If ever a deal was lopsided, this was it. The good citizens of Georgia quickly found out why—dozens of lawmakers and other key officials had been bribed wholesale to approve the scam. When an angry, outraged citizenry yelled for justice, a newly elected legislature rescinded the corrupt deal the next year.

Like thousands of others, Caty and Phineas had invested all they could muster in the Yazoo debacle. Now, the money was gone. Facing a financial setback of bankrupting proportions, they decided in 1798 to sell Mulberry Grove and move to Nathanael's estate on Cumberland. Phineas would revive Nathanael's plan to chop down and sell live oak to the navy. But their biggest venture would be growing sea-island cotton. By now, factories in New England and Great Britain were clamoring for the prized fiber.

As Caty and Phineas contemplated their move, they faced another setback—no buyer for Mulberry Grove came forward. She and Phineas had to sell a dozen slaves to raise cash to go to Cumberland. To satisfy the unpaid bills, Camden County tax collectors finally put Mulberry Grove on the auction block in 1799, selling it for fifteen thousand dollars—far less than what Caty and Phineas expected to get.

By then, the two of them and Caty's surviving children—George had drowned in the Savannah River—already had moved to Cumberland. Dominant as she was at Mulberry Grove, Caty would become even stronger on Cumberland. Under her, Cumberland would become one of the South's first major cotton-growing areas.

———————

At that time, the island was uninhabited except for some slaves and white bosses at a small indigo plantation run by the Lynch family. Poachers and bootleg loggers slipped over from time to time to hunt or steal timber. Scofflaws hid out briefly in its deep woods to elude mainland authorities and debt collectors. An occasional military deserter or runaway slave used it as a way station.

Caty, of course, was no stranger to life on an island, having been born and having spent much of her girlhood on one. But there were big differences between Block Island, Rhode Island, and Cumberland Island, Georgia. Block was cold and wind battered. The few trees growing there were stunted by the fierce winds. Cumberland was redolent of the tropics, covered by a lush maritime forest that made portions of it impenetrable. And Cumberland had something else—rich soil that was ideal for growing cotton.

While Caty turned her attention to cotton, Phineas went after the live oaks. He had won a navy contract to supply oak frames for six big gun ships. By June 1800, his mosquito-plagued workers had felled two thousand oak pieces and sent them to New England shipyards. Some of the oak was used in the hull of the famed frigate USS *Constitution*, helping it win the nickname "Old Ironsides."

But live-oaking proved only marginally profitable. At one point, Phineas was near financial panic. Supplies and salaries for his men and food for his timber-hauling oxen were costing him plenty. He was quickly running through his government advance. Other seemingly insurmountable problems cropped up. "Am sorry to acknowledge," he wrote the navy in 1800, "that the further I advance in this perplexing contract for the timber, the greater do I find . . . the expense and the disappointments." He complained that the estimated quantity of live oak on Cumberland and on the mainland had been exaggerated, partly by General Greene.

Then there were the debts still pending on Nathanael's estate. Creditors' demands for payment reached the point in 1800 where a federal marshal had to sell portions of the dead hero's Cumberland land to pay the chits. One buyer was Lucy Stafford Spalding, a widow who purchased 125 acres. Her son, Robert Stafford, later would become Cumberland's biggest landowner and slave master.

Cotton saved the day for Caty and Phineas. While Phineas was felling live oaks, Caty was supervising the slashing and burning of Cumberland's thick woods for cotton fields. In short order, the fields were snowy white with ripened bolls.

With the promise of big money rolling in from cotton, Caty and Phineas were upbeat, certain that their financial woes would vanish. They made big plans, the most grandiose of which was building Caty's dream house, a mansion on Cumberland's south end at the place called Dungeness.

The headstrong Caty brought in architects and craftsmen to get construction under way. Slaves would provide most of the labor. For her superb new home, she chose to keep the Dungeness name.

A thirty-room mansion emerged in surprisingly short order. It had a tabby foundation six feet thick below ground and four feet thick above. Tabby, akin to concrete, was made from limestone, water, and oyster shells. Yielding the shells for Dungeness's tabby were the mounds that the Timucuan Indians had built up over the centuries. The mansion probably was the biggest house ever made of tabby.

The enormous, perfectly proportioned, ninety-foot-tall dwelling had four stories on a high basement. Servants lived in the basement. On the first and second floors were grand, lofty, tall-windowed rooms for sitting, dining, and playing music. On the third and fourth floors were bedchambers. Outside, six Doric-crowned pilasters ran from the top of the basement to the cornice of the roof. A massive flight of steps led to the front entrance, which was faced with hewn granite. The roof was sheathed in copper and crowned by four brick chimneys, two in each end wall, giving vent to sixteen fireplaces.

Caty wanted the grounds around Dungeness to be as palatial as the mansion and as exquisite as any in blue-blooded Charleston up the coast. At that time in America, an elegant garden was just as prestigious as an imposing house. Caty and Phineas skillfully laid out twelve acres of elaborate gardens enclosed by a tabby wall. Using shovels and mule-drawn wagons, slaves moved hundreds of tons of soil and built sturdy retaining walls to complete the terraces that descended to the salt marsh. Phineas supervised the planting of thousands of trees, shrubs, and flowers. He found that tropical fruits thrived in the steamy Georgia climate. "The garden and the grounds seem quite a paradise with hedges formed of lemon, groves of orange trees, roses and other flowers in full bloom, even though it is January," noted a visitor. Also gracing the grounds were date palms, sago palms, India-rubber trees, coffee plants, camphor trees, fig trees, lime trees, and pomegranate, citron, and guava trees. The olive grove had eight hundred trees.

Beyond the mansion, miles of roads were cut through the thick forest. The longest, Grand Avenue, ran clear from Dungeness all the way to the northern tip of the island, nearly eighteen miles distant.

To Caty's great delight, Dungeness was hailed as the most elegant residence on the Georgia coast when she and Phineas moved into it in 1803. Even then, some of the rooms were left undone. A family superstition may have been the reason: if the house were ever finished, it was feared, some misfortune would befall it and its occupants. The truth was

The ruins of Caty Miller's Dungeness, which burned shortly after the Civil War
Courtesy of the National Park Service

that they probably ran out of money.

The superstition certainly didn't apply to poor Phineas. Less than a year after moving into Dungeness, the gentle scholar punctured his finger on a thorn during a trip to Florida to purchase tropical plants. Within a week, he was dead of lockjaw at age thirty-nine.

Caty was brokenhearted. But within a few months, she dried her tears and took control. Bolstered by her years of coping with social upheaval and debt crises, she never doubted her ability to run Dungeness, supervise its scores of slaves, and oversee its cotton growing.

Her holdings included roughly half of Cumberland, which had been partitioned in 1802 between the Lynches and General Greene's estate. Since most of their money had gone to build Dungeness and its gardens, Caty and Phineas had been unable to buy the Lynch property or repurchase the acreage sold to pay off earlier debts. Neither was a good money manager. Caty would forever be in heavy debt.

Under her hand, Dungeness was typical of self-sufficient cotton plantations of the era. The orchards and gardens produced enormous quantities of fruits and vegetables. Fish and game abounded in the tidal creeks and woods. Kitchen servants made tasty gourmet soup from loggerhead turtles, which were flipped upside down on the beach and butchered there. Deer were so plentiful that venison was a staple.

Caty never lost her zest for gala balls. So it was no surprise that Dungeness became a center of social merrymaking equaled by few other plantations. Caty took advantage of every opportunity to have guests, many of them from up north. Her extravagant parties belied the notions that Cumberland was isolated and that she had many creditors. Old Savannah friends stayed for a season at a time. An occasional visitor was Eli Whitney, who found Dungeness handsome, roomy, and stoutly built but lacking in the elegance of Mulberry Grove.

Guests feasted on shrimp, crabs, oysters, and fish; turkeys, chickens, ducks, and geese; pork, mutton, beef, and venison; vegetables, fruits, preserves, and jellies. Watermelon-rind pickles and brandy-soaked peaches were two of Caty's specialties. An ample stock of Madeira always was available for dinner. At Christmas and other festive times, Madeira-flavored syllabub was consumed with great gusto. A keg of rum was kept for hot toddies at bedtime.

Guests hunted, fished, picnicked, rode horses, and went for carriage drives along the wooded trails or on the beach. The evenings were taken up with charades, cards, musical performances, and dancing.

Not all guests were welcomed. In 1804, Vice President Aaron Burr, a fugitive from justice because of his killing of Federalist Party leader Alexander Hamilton in a duel, sent word to Caty that he wanted to visit her on Cumberland. She and Burr were acquaintances, but she had been a close friend of Hamilton's, and her daughter Cornelia once had a teenage crush on him.

Caty did not want to see Burr, but it would have been ill-mannered to reject his request for a visit. On the other hand, she could not receive one whose hands were tainted with blood. So she told her servants that when Burr's boat hove into sight, she was to be informed immediately. When it indeed was spied crossing Cumberland Sound, she and her family hopped into waiting two-horse phaetons and sped down Grand Avenue into the island's interior. At Dungeness, Burr was met only by household servants. Thoroughly snubbed, he haughtily turned and left, and Caty and her family returned to their home. She never heard from him again.

In 1812, when America was again at war with Great Britain, United States troops were quartered at St. Marys on Georgia's mainland. Cumberland's residents were warned to leave, but the stubborn Caty refused.

She had a serious fight brewing in her own household. It had erupted between her and her children over the division of General Greene's slaves and land on Cumberland and in Tennessee. Fueling the schism was the breaking up of slave families to make sure each Greene heir got an equal share of the assets. Caty insisted she always had tried to avoid splitting up families, even though she had acquiesced to it when Mulberry's slaves were sold. Her children questioned her professed love for the slaves, suspecting it was a ploy to keep them for herself. They maintained she had never shown qualms over the slave trade. Indeed, one of her acquaintances, Robert MacKay, owned a big ship used for smuggling slaves into the United States after Congress banned their importation. With Caty's permission, MacKay occasionally used a Dungeness outbuilding as a holding place for his contraband slaves until places for them were available on the mainland.

Caty was even more perturbed when her two sons-in-law plotted against her. One was Ned Littlefield, her brother Billy's son, her own nephew. She despised him for what she called an unforgivable act—eloping with her daughter Cornelia, his own first cousin. Cornelia, whose first husband had died, was nine years older than Ned.

The rancor got so bad that Cornelia and Ned decided to leave Georgia. They would emigrate to the Greene family's Duck River plantation in Tennessee—a gift to Nathanael by the North Carolina legislature before Tennessee split off and gained statehood.

But before they left, they clashed again with Caty. While visiting friends in Savannah for a few days in August 1813, Caty spied them and their children driving down a back street in a wagon with seven slaves cowering in the back. Caty let out a scream. The slaves still belonged to her. Cornelia and Ned, taking advantage of her absence from Dungeness, had hand-picked them to bring to Tennessee. Cornelia and Ned were arrested and detained for several days until old family friends in Savannah signed bonds guaranteeing Caty the amount of money at which the slaves were valued. The entourage then was allowed to proceed to Tennessee. Caty never again saw Cornelia, who became a talented writer and raconteur.

The other son-in-law, Dr. Henry Turner of East Greenwich, Rhode Island, was Martha's new husband. Her first spouse, John Clarke Nightingale, the former officer in the Yazoo Land Company and an owner of a

Rhode Island slave ship, had succumbed to yellow fever in 1806.

Turner took his argument with Caty to the point of squabbling over who should get the late general's priceless medals and library. "I bore all pretty well until Turner demanded his proportion of the honors of General Greene," Caty wrote Eli Whitney. "This so put me out that I have been ill ever since."

She was so disgusted that she sliced both Cornelia and Martha from her will and vowed never again to let them pass through Dungeness's wrought-iron gates. Although each of her four surviving children had inherited a portion of Cumberland from their father, only daughter Louisa would inherit Dungeness.

In a move that gladdened Caty, son Nat transferred his swath of Cumberland to her. His deed was intended both to prop her up financially and to wash his hands of slavery, for which he had no stomach. Caty rewrote her will so that his children would inherit his old property, known as Rayfield, located in Cumberland's midsection.

Even then, Caty found little peace. Lawsuits were still pending against the estates of both Nathanael and Phineas. Phineas's business affairs were proving even more snarled than Nathanael's. She faced judgments against her totaling sixty thousand dollars, mostly because of Phineas's unpaid loans, legal fees incurred in the cotton-gin lawsuits, and the Yazoo scam.

In desperation, her lawyers advised that she sue her old friend and confidant Eli Whitney to force his return to Georgia to settle accounts. She recoiled at such a thought. "Never was any one so cheated and ill-used as I have been," she lamented in a letter to him.

In March 1814, she had a respite from the turmoil. Louisa, who had helped her run the plantation, married James Shaw, a Scot who had farmed with Caty. A month later, she had more good news: Congress appropriated $8 million for the relief of those investors hoodwinked by Yazoo nearly twenty years earlier.

But in late August, she caught bilious fever, which regularly plagued

Georgia in the summertime. The fever quickly worsened. Violent chills wracked her frail body. On September 2, 1814, she died in her sleep at age sixty.

She was buried in a little tabby-walled cemetery among stalwart oaks near the gentle tidal creek winding through the marsh next to Dungeness. "She possessed great talents and exalted virtue," her tombstone said.

———•◦•———

Four months later, Louisa and Martha invited some close friends from plantations on neighboring islands to a small house party at Dungeness. The guests stayed several days. It was the first social affair—albeit a small one, in order to stay within the bounds of decent mourning—at the mansion since Caty's death. In a twinge of sisterly love, Louisa had reopened Dungeness to Martha.

The males jested with a little bravado about a possible British invasion. Such an unpleasant occurrence seemed unlikely on remote Cumberland. So it was with considerable alarm—and more than a few frightened gasps—that the partygoers spied a British fleet's billowy white sails on the horizon. The warships dropped anchor off Cumberland, and landing boats manned by agile seamen in red-and-white-striped jerseys hauled detachments of red-coated marines to the beach. Some of Dungeness's gentlemen guests trudged warily to the beach, waving a white flag and asking the gun-toting marines to respect private property on the island. The British replied that indeed they would.

In command was Admiral George Cockburn, the same cocky commander whose men had set fire to Washington, D.C. He was not aware that the Treaty of Ghent ending the War of 1812 had been signed a few weeks earlier. His aim was to recruit slaves to the British flag. He and his officers tromped into Dungeness and announced they were commandeering it for their headquarters. The hostesses and their guests were banished to the upper floors.

A short while later, the British sent an invitation to those upstairs to come down and join the officers. The adults harrumphed and turned up their noses, but some of the girls were thrilled. Truth be known, they were titillated by the English gentlemen in their gold-braided regimental garb. One girl, a dark-eyed lass named Ann Couper of Cannon's Point Plantation on St. Simons Island, caught the eye of Lieutenant John Fraser, who immediately was smitten with her.

Outside, Cockburn's men, despite promising to protect private property, were seizing Dungeness's slaves and its bales of cotton, stored in a three-story barn. Some men wantonly wrecked orange groves to build fortified trenches. Others cut down shiploads of live oak to haul to Bermuda.

On Cumberland's north end, the British set up a staging area, from which slaves seized at Dungeness and other plantations were to be shipped to Bermuda and as far away as Halifax, Nova Scotia. More than twelve hundred slaves were brought to the island, where they were drilled in military protocol before being sent out to the British lands. Many a plantation owner was amazed at the quality and efficiency of British recruitment and drilling. One planter found it remarkable to see his slaves, who had been hoeing and chopping only a few days earlier, being transformed "into regular soldiers of good discipline and appearance."

Cockburn had been ensconced at Dungeness for well over a month—the partygoers having long since been permitted to return to their homes—when word of the treaty finally reached him. He and his men and their ships quickly departed. Many of the slaves and much of the cotton they had seized were returned to the plantations.

Within a year, Lieutenant Fraser returned. He came back to marry Ann Couper, whom he called "my pretty prisoner of Dungeness." The romance sparked during the house party turned into a lasting attachment that produced many children and grandchildren.

———•—•———

Louisa, the only Greene offspring to live continuously on Cumberland after Caty's death, assumed the role of mistress of Dungeness. She never had children, but she doted on her wiry nephew, Phineas Miller Nightingale, who visited her often.

Young Phineas was at the landing at Dungeness in early 1818 when a strange schooner dropped anchor in the river. Manning a longboat, the ship's sailors gingerly set ashore a hoary figure straight out of the American Revolution—an ailing Light Horse Harry Lee. A small, battered trunk and a cask of Madeira were his only possessions.

He had fought brilliantly under General Greene to defeat the British in the South, then served as a member of the Continental Congress, as governor of Virginia, and as a United States representative. When George Washington died in 1799, Lee penned the famous eulogy: "First in war, first in peace, first in the hearts of his countrymen."

Suffering from wounds incurred when he tried to defend a newspaper publisher friend from an angry Baltimore mob, the old soldier, age sixty-two, sought to regain his health and write his memoirs in the mild climate of the West Indies. The change didn't help. Wracked by pain, his body withered away, probably from cancer. Knowing that he was dying, he booked passage on the schooner to return to his beloved Virginia. But on the way, his suffering grew unbearable. Knowing he would not make it home, he asked the ship's captain to put him ashore at Cumberland.

Upon landing, the general—feeble, pale, emaciated, penniless—sent word by young Nightingale to Louisa: "Tell her that I am purposely come to die in the house and in the arms of the daughter of my old friend and compatriot, General Greene."

The boy returned to the dock with a horse-drawn carriage. With the ship's captain and first mate in escort, the general was carried to Dungeness. Louisa tried to pay the captain for the general's expenses, but he would not hear of it. "It was a special pleasure and privilege to minister to the comfort and respond to the wishes of so distinguished a hero of the Revolution," he said.

Louisa and her household made the old man welcome, despite his miserable crotchetiness. Everything possible was done for his comfort. For a time, he was able to take short walks around the fragrant garden, leaning on young Nightingale. But he became weaker and weaker and was finally unable to leave his room.

At that time, an American fleet was anchored in Cumberland Sound awaiting final negotiations to transfer Florida from Spanish control to the United States. When the fleet's commanders heard of the general's impending death, they called at Dungeness to pay their respects. Two navy physicians were sent to minister to him.

Two months after being put ashore, he died.

Wearing mourning crepe on their sidearms, army and navy officers went to Dungeness to escort the body to the burial ground half a mile away—the same plot that had received Caty Greene Miller's body four years earlier. Guns were fired from the *John Adams*, flagship of the fleet.

The hero of the Revolution in the South was buried in Georgia soil. His famous son, Robert E. Lee, commander of the Army of Northern Virginia, visited the cemetery in 1870 and solemnly laid a wreath on his father's grave.

———

Louisa worked diligently to make Dungeness a thriving plantation. Like her mother, she had the final say in all matters, her husband having died only a few years after they married. She became so expert at growing cotton, olives, and oranges that her name was prominent in coastal Georgia. She collected, identified, and drew specimens. "Her knowledge of botany exceeds that of any lady in America," said a fellow botanist.

She died in 1831 at age forty-five and was buried in Dungeness's olive grove. She left the plantation and most of her personal belongings—including General Greene's library and a portrait of George Washington—to nephew Phineas. She granted freedom to her personal slave, Aboo, and Aboo's infant child and gave them several of her belongings.

Thus ended the second generation of Greenes on Cumberland.

———

Life at Dungeness continued under Phineas Nightingale much as it had under Caty and Louisa. Visitors were welcome, and weddings were a familiar sight. There was no cessation of gay house parties. Tall Christmas trees touched the high ceilings. Groaning banquet boards were laid out whenever Phineas gathered prominent local men for marathon sessions of imbibing, feasting, and conversing. Those sessions began late in the afternoon and lasted far into the night.

He continued growing cotton and made an unsuccessful try at raising oranges. He purchased several tracts from his Cumberland neighbors, including most of the property once owned by the Lynches. He borrowed heavily and mortgaged his property to the hilt to finance the purchases. In this way, he got himself in a financial mess. He would have to fight desperately to keep Dungeness out of the hands of a ruthless man he abhorred, Robert Stafford.

But Phineas may have inspired abhorrence himself. Like his grandmother, he may have engaged in slave smuggling. Stories passed down by slaves to their children and grandchildren told of coming to America during Nightingale's era on a large boat that landed off Cumberland "on a big dock."

Today on Cumberland, Grand Avenue, the road cut by Phineas and Caty Miller, is still the island's main north-south thoroughfare. It still passes twisted, old live oaks, longleaf pines, palmettos, aromatic bayberries, magnolias, yaupons, and hollies, though it now slices through the congressionally designated wilderness area of Cumberland Island National Seashore.

Caty Miller's Dungeness is gone. Just after the Civil War, when Union soldiers occupied Cumberland, it caught fire one night while the troops drank and caroused with freed slaves. It burned all night. By morning, only a smoking shell of the once-great house remained.

The ruins inspired wonder. "It is to be hoped . . . that the vulnerable pile may remain for ages untouched and unchanged by man," an 1878 *Harper's Magazine* correspondent said of the remnants of Caty's Dungeness.

That was not to be. An even more regal structure took the place of her Dungeness. It was built by another domineering woman, Lucy Coleman Carnegie, on the same spot as Caty's old mansion. It also was called Dungeness.

But before there was a second Dungeness, there was another woman prominent in the annals of Cumberland—a beautiful mulatto slave named Zabette. A strong woman in her own right, she gave birth to four remarkable daughters who married admirals and artists and royalty. Her white master, Robert Stafford, Cumberland's biggest landholder and slave owner, fathered the children. Their strange affair inspired a three-act opera called *Zabette*, which premiered in Atlanta in April 1999. The librettist was Mary Bullard, a Cumberland historian and a Carnegie descendant.

One wonders what Robert Stafford, Zabette, and their progeny would have thought about all this—an opera about them, no less. Stafford, no doubt, never would have envisioned himself under a woman's sway. He was powerful, rich, and independent. Yet Cumberland also wrought its strange magic over the women in his life.

Robert Stafford
Courtesy of the National Park Service

CHAPTER FOUR
Slaves and Love

OTHER THAN THE CARNEGIES who came after him, Robert Stafford was Cumberland's biggest private landowner ever. He was a formidable man—tall, haughty, and strapping, with penetrating blue eyes and a thunderous voice. Driven by his unswerving desire for wealth, he amassed a fortune in cotton and real estate. His property included most of the land once owned by Nathanael Greene's heirs—and nearly 350 slaves.

Zabette was one of them. She birthed his four daughters and two sons.

He was born in December 1790 on the island's south end, where Caty Miller was to build Dungeness a decade later. His father and uncle worked first for General Greene and the Lynches, then for Caty and Phineas Miller. They oversaw the Millers' live-oaking, cotton growing, and other ventures and supervised the start of Dungeness's construction.

Stafford's father was not around for the mansion's completion, dying of yellow fever in 1800, when Robert was ten. Young Robert remained on the island with his mother, Lucy, and two sisters. A few months after her husband's death, Lucy bought 125 acres on Cumberland for $187 at the sale held to pay off General Greene's debts. Two years after that, she married Isham Spaulding, a friend of her late husband who was also a small landowner on Cumberland.

As a youngster, Robert Stafford was exceptionally bright, which did not go unnoticed by his beaming mother. She arranged for him to go to a Yankee boarding school in New London, Connecticut. Husband Isham would cover some of the cost, and Phineas Miller would kindly help. Aid also would come from a man named Daniel Copp, another of her late husband's friends. He was a Connecticut ship owner who came regularly to St. Marys on business and later bought a plantation near the town.

One of Copp's schooners carried young Stafford up north to begin his sojourn at the New London Grammar School. He boarded with the Copps in Groton, located just across the Thames River from New London. There, he became like an older brother to their son, Belton, six years his junior.

Stafford received what he later called a "right smart Yankee education." Perhaps more important were the lasting connections he made with the Copps and a handful of other Connecticut families, who decades later would help him pull off one of the most daring acts a white man in antebellum Georgia could attempt.

He came back to Georgia after completing school in 1806, when he turned sixteen. He and his sisters opened a dry-goods store in St. Marys. For a few years, they made decent money. But Georgia's financial condition was shaky at best. Banks were untrustworthy.

Stafford realized he might make more money as a private banker. He lent money at a hefty interest to borrowers, who put up their property as collateral. When they defaulted on the loans, he called in the debt. Through foreclosure and outright purchase, he accumulated large swaths of land, on which he grew rice and cotton.

In 1813, he and his sisters and mother made their first big land buy on Cumberland—nearly six hundred acres for three thousand dollars. That purchase was the nucleus of what is still known as Stafford Plantation today. The seller was Cornelia Greene Littlefield, Caty's daughter who had fled to Tennessee.

Stafford set about cultivating rice with newly purchased slaves. But he was hungry for more—he wanted the entire island for himself. He bought Rayfield Plantation from Nat Greene's children and much of the land held by Phineas Nightingale. The proud Nightingale grudgingly agreed to the sales. He had an icy disdain for Stafford, whose ruthless, greedy business ethics nauseated him. To him, Stafford was nothing more than an immigrant offspring who had the gall to think he was equal to the blue-blooded Greenes. He and his kin used every tactic they could devise to keep Stafford away, but their efforts mostly were for naught.

Stafford stuck to his plan in the 1830s and 1840s, loaning as much as eight thousand dollars at a time to borrowers, who put up land and slaves as security. When they couldn't pay, he lost no time in foreclosing. It bothered him little that people engaged in such business often are not the most beloved citizens in a community. He was getting rich, which was the thing that really mattered.

He acquired from the widow and children of a man named John Grey a five-hundred-acre tract just south of Stafford. Known then as Spring Plantation, it later was called Greyfield. Grey had put it up as security for a thirty-five-hundred-dollar loan. When he died, his family could not cover the debt. Stafford foreclosed. Quietly, sadly, the family moved to the mainland.

Stafford particularly profited from Phineas Nightingale's financial woes. Nightingale's misfortunes set the stage for Stafford's biggest land coup. In 1843, at a sheriff's sale in St. Marys for debt nonpayment,

Nightingale was forced to sell Stafford forty-two hundred acres on Cumberland. It brought Stafford to the very doorstep of Dungeness, where Nightingale still lived in genteel poverty.

Nightingale swore that "only over my dead carcass" would Stafford get the Greenes' ancestral home.

———◦•◦———

Stafford accumulated eight thousand acres altogether on Cumberland. His slaves' primary duties were planting, plowing, chopping, and picking the sea-island cotton that brought him a high price of seventy-five cents a pound. Factories in England and New England could not get enough of the strong fiber.

To produce superior crops, Stafford divided his acreage into two separately managed plantations, then encouraged rivalry between them. The competition was fierce. So much of Cumberland was cleared for cotton that a person standing in the middle of it could look eastward and get a clear view of the ocean or westward and see the river and salt marsh beyond. The marsh's nutrient-rich black muck was spread on the fields as fertilizer.

Not satisfied just with cotton production and money lending, Stafford pursued other ventures. He sold the island's wild ponies, or marsh tackies, for five dollars apiece to anyone gutsy enough to try to break them. His slave "cowboys" rounded them up. Accompanied by fierce, growling "horse dogs," they drove the horses to a place on Cumberland still known today as Horse Landing. From there, the horses were forced to swim to the mainland. If a stallion tried to turn the herd, the snarling dogs pounced on his back and sunk their yellow teeth into his flesh.

Stafford trained his stoutest slaves to row a barge in festive races against other slave-powered vessels. The races, held at St. Marys, across from Cumberland, attracted big crowds, who bet huge stakes. Stafford's rowers won often and made him a pot of money.

His wealth and success brought him acclaim and influence, enabling him to wield considerable clout in coastal Georgia, especially on the mainland. Fellow planters there often called on him to help settle business and legal disputes.

His mother, Lucy, a widow again after her second husband died, and his sister Susannah, also a widow, lived with him at Stafford Place, as his first Cumberland plantation was called. He never married. Flush with success in the 1820s, he built them a stately new plantation home—a large, pleasant, simple frame building with two stories over a ground floor.

When Lucy and Susannah turned deathly ill from yellow fever in 1836, Stafford's nearest neighbor, Marguerite Bernardey, sent over her young mulatto slave, Zabette, to help nurse them. Marguerite and Zabette lived at Plum Orchard, a Cumberland plantation named for the profusion of wild plums growing there.

Zabette was light-skinned, tall, and slim. Her high cheekbones and large brown eyes endowed her with a haunting beauty. Marguerite had carefully raised her, training her well in nursing and managing household affairs.

Probably the reason Marguerite was so protective was because Zabette was her granddaughter—the daughter of her late son, Peter Bernardey, and his slave Mary. The Bernardeys were of French descent and had lived in a French community on Jekyll Island before Peter bought Plum Orchard. He died of consumption in 1827, when Zabette was seven years old, and was buried at Plum.

Stafford aided Marguerite considerably after her son died. He prepared legal papers for her, advised her on crop planting, and offered tips on slave management. In repaying his neighborly kindness, Marguerite sent him Zabette.

His mother and sister died within two months of one another. Weeping for his loss, he buried them in a tabby-walled cemetery next to one of his cotton fields. They left a tremendous void—they had run his household and nursed his slaves. Now, he was all alone and in desperate need of someone to fill the gap.

Robert Stafford's plantation house, circa 1888. Built originally for Stafford's mother and sister, Lucy Carnegie gave the house to her son Bill and his wife Gertrude. It later burned.

Courtesy of the National Park Service

That someone was Zabette. He formally leased her from Marguerite to minister to his slaves and manage his household.

She also fulfilled another need. In 1839, at age nineteen, she quietly submitted to him in his spacious bed. Nine months later, she bore a baby girl, whom she named Mary, after her mother. "Having my baby is a sign of my respect and fidelity for you," Stafford told her. When they learned of the birth, the other plantation hands whispered in the fields and their shut cabins that Zabette was just another "yellow gal" currying Master's favor through sexual liaison.

For reasons history has not made clear, Marguerite two years later fully conveyed Zabette and two-year-old Mary to Stafford, then age fifty-one, for one dollar. In essence, they were a gift. It may have been that Marguerite simply wanted to do another good deed for Stafford. More likely, she was facing bankruptcy and looking out for Zabette's welfare. By presenting her to Stafford, she was trying to protect the slave woman from the possibility of being sold to a harsh master.

At Stafford Place, Zabette had separate living quarters—a comfortable tabby cottage next to her master's big house. Georgia law forbade female slaves to live under the same roof with an adult white male. Nevertheless, she stayed many a night with her master. Their five other children were testimony to that.

Zabette never really loved Stafford, it was said, but she knew where her bread was buttered. She was making the best of a world that kept her in bondage.

Stafford obviously felt some affection for her. No doubt, he had great love for their children, taking a strong fatherly pride in them despite their being born of a slave. He desired the best for them. But he faced some daunting choices in that regard: he could admit he was their father and raise them as his children; he could declare them slaves and then grant them freedom without ever admitting he fathered them; or he could hold them in bondage.

He was stuck squarely between a rock and a brick wall. Under Georgia law, he could not keep slave girls over age fourteen or boys over age ten under his roof. Acknowledging they were his progeny would make him a social pariah among his white neighbors. The heady power and influence he had built up would come crashing down. Even if he were willing to bear the social stigma, it might not have done much good— under Georgia law, children born of a female slave were slaves themselves. Simply freeing them would have created a legal morass. The state legislature had curbed a master's right to grant freedom to his slaves, such responsibility thenceforth resting mostly with the legislature. The lawmaking body also was making it increasingly difficult for masters to grant freedom to their slaves in wills. On the eve of the Civil War, it struck down that privilege entirely. In any case, the position of free black people in the South before the Civil War was in many respects inferior to that of slaves. If they behaved, most slaves at least enjoyed the master's protection and some assurance of subsistence, medical care, and support in old age. But free blacks had to scrap for themselves in an environment where laws and white domination restricted their every move.

To protect his children from such a future, Stafford hatched a daring plan. He would secret them out of Georgia and send them to New England, where they could live without fear of enslavement. In violation of Georgia law, he never had registered them as slaves. He faced dire consequences if found out.

In his efforts, he had the help of his trusted boyhood friend Belton Copp, the son of the Connecticut family with whom he had boarded while in school in Groton. Belton's father, Daniel Copp, had arranged Stafford's schooling. Belton had followed his father to Georgia and become a lawyer, a ship owner, and a state legislator.

In an arrangement worked out between him and Stafford, the first three children—daughter Mary and sons Robert and Armand—were taken to Groton and freedom. Most of their journey was in Copp's ship. For Copp, it was a perilous trip because taking unregistered slaves out of state—in effect, helping them escape—was a serious breach of the law. If he were caught, Georgia's slavery enforcers would be unmerciful. They could confiscate his boat and make him pay a heavy fine and spend time in jail.

In Groton, he and Stafford's other friends became guardians and foster parents of the children. Mary was enrolled in the prestigious Bacon Academy of Colchester, Connecticut. The two boys went to a small agricultural school.

By 1852, Stafford and Zabette produced two other daughters, Ellen and Adelaide Clarice. They also were sent to Connecticut. At first, they stayed with Copp's family and other friends. But a year after their arrival, Stafford built an imposing home for all of the children.

Once they were ensconced in Groton, there was no turning back. A plethora of antiblack statutes and runaway-slave laws made dangerous any attempt to return to Georgia. Stafford would have faced criminal charges if found out.

Zabette was a different matter. She was a registered slave. The Fugitive Slave Law of 1850, ironically, made it easy for registered slaves to travel with their masters to nonslave states and live there temporarily with their master's blessing. On a visit to Groton in 1853, Zabette gave birth to Stafford's sixth child, Medora.

Stafford went to Connecticut a couple of times a year to visit the children, but he stayed across the river in a New London hotel. Decked out in elegant broadcloth and linen, sporting gold-rimmed spectacles and a watch on a gold chain, the Georgia slaveholder moved in a lordly strut about Groton. He spread money liberally, often paying double for services if they were rendered promptly and efficiently. For that, the hotel staff looked forward to his coming. But he never let on that he was the father of the well-behaved children he visited in Groton. Most people thought he was a rich uncle or other relative from Georgia.

His zest for wealth continued in New England. In time, he came to own several Connecticut properties, including a farm, office buildings, and the hotel where he stayed during the visits. He also invested heavily in Northern banks, railroads, and other ventures. Belton Copp helped manage his business affairs up north. Copp also set up trust funds for the children, arranged their schooling, and saw to their household needs.

Amazingly, the children, especially the daughters, thrived in New England, where they passed as whites even though their skin was soft brown and their hair jet black. Their physical traits suggested perhaps Indian or Mediterranean ancestry. They lived in a higher social stratum, in fact, than most Groton citizens. Their fashionable education included instruction in French, Italian, music, and painting. "They gave musicales and amateur theatricals, inviting guests from New London and New York," one historic account said. "Portraits show them as attractive young women, dressed in the high fashion of the day."

It was never let on that Zabette was their mother. During her visits, she was regarded as the children's live-in nurse. She was there when the Civil War erupted, and remained for its duration.

At the time Stafford was settling his children in Connecticut, he owned 350 slaves on Cumberland. Another 150 belonged to other island planters, making a grand total of about 500 slaves there ten years before the Civil War.

Then came the great conflict. Harried and frightened, most of the white families fled Cumberland early in 1862, when Union soldiers overran it. Phineas Nightingale deserted Dungeness for Savannah. But Stafford stubbornly refused to leave, which was a mistake.

Union forces rounded up all the slaves on the island and sent them to nearby Amelia Island, Florida. Some of the former slaves then were armed by the Union commander on Amelia. To Stafford's great chagrin, they were granted passes to return to Cumberland.

On the sultry morning of September 1, 1862, Stafford dispatched an urgent message to the commander of the USS *Alabama*, anchored in Cumberland Sound, complaining that his former servants had come back with guns and were holed up in his private residence. He said they were riotous, had killed his cattle, and were threatening the same for him.

The *Alabama's* commander ordered the vessel to steam up the Brickhill River as far as it could go, at which point he dispatched an armed party to Stafford's house. They found the elderly white man scared out of his wits. He had reason to be frightened. His former slaves were lounging in his house, watching his every move, and doing as they pleased with his property. In the former slave quarters, they had an arsenal of guns, pistols, and ammunition.

Stafford pointed out nine of the men he considered the most dangerous. Union sailors rounded them up, hauled them off, and locked them in the steamer's brig. Stafford wanted permanent protection, but the Union officer could not guarantee it. Stafford felt he had suffered enough by that point. "For God's sake, send a boat and hands to take me to a place where I can be made comfortable," he said in a message to the officer. The officer complied. His unusual willingness to help a white Southern planter might have been because of rumors that Stafford provided supplies to the Union army.

————————

After the war, the military government created a forty-mile-wide belt called the "Sherman Reserve." It stretched from Charleston to Jacksonville, Cumberland Island included. The land within the reserve was seized by military decree. Its purpose: to redistribute the old plantation lands to qualified freedmen.

Former plantation owners and Confederate sympathizers, though, were eligible to get their land back under certain conditions. One was that they take an oath to the United States. By the end of 1867, Stafford's property, which still included the vast majority of Cumberland, was restored, and he was living on the island again.

He might have been contented except for one thing: there was a piece of property he desired but never got—Dungeness. Phineas Nightingale was obsessed with holding on to his ancestral home and its gardens even though the Union troops had ruined them. Despite his heavy debts, including repaying a huge loan from Stafford, he stood steadfast.

Stafford persisted. "I am anxious to know what you mean to do relative to the notes I hold of you," he wrote Nightingale in 1868. "You mentioned to me when I last saw you, you wished to sell Dungeness. The place has been occupied by Negroes and headquarters for others, both black and white, coming over from Fernandina, stealing my cattle, hogs and nearly everything else they can lay their hands on, even my dogs. I think it would be best for me to purchase it, and put some clever man there in charge, to keep them off. The house can never be repaired again and will cost considerable to remove the old walls and rubbish off the grounds and out of the way."

Nightingale turned him down flat. He still was mortified that the son of a former overseer had the audacity even to offer a price for the

Greenes' old home. Stafford's constant reminders of his IOUs were even more galling.

Nightingale died in 1871. Before his death, he had received a loan from Savannah businessman Edmund Molyneux and had pledged Dungeness as security. When Nightingale died, Dungeness became the property of Molyneux's estate as a result of a $51,250 claim brought against Nightingale's heirs.

Another former slave returned to Cumberland shortly after the war's end: Zabette.

She had stayed in Connecticut as long as she could, but she never felt comfortable there. She never fit in. Her children were on a higher social stratum than she. Her speech, mannerisms, darker color, and lack of education set her off from them and their friends. The truth is that they were embarrassed over her. Zabette pined for Cumberland, her sanctuary. Her earliest ties were with the barrier islands of coastal Georgia. Cumberland was her true home, not New England.

Whether her daughters were sad at her leaving or whether she was sad that she was departing from them has not been recorded. Her youngest daughter, Medora, was only twelve.

Perhaps in coming back to Cumberland, Zabette thought that Stafford still might be fond of her and that they could resume their relationship. But she was in for a stark awakening. During her absence, he had taken up with another woman of color, Catherine Williams, and fathered two daughters by her. In despair, Zabette retreated once again to the little tabby cottage next to the big house, where she was listed in the 1870 census as a housekeeper.

As for Stafford's other former slaves who came back to Cumberland, a long-told story says he ran them off because he was embittered and vengeful following his frightening experience at their hands during the war. In a diabolical act, he supposedly torched their cabins to make sure they would not return again. Some of them congregated in one of Cumberland's old cotton fields, where they erected makeshift huts and lived as squatters. Others abandoned the island altogether to live on the mainland.

Zabette's daughters, on the other hand, did remarkably well. Mary, the eldest, married lawyer and mortgage broker Frederick Palmer, who became a carpetbagger Republican in South Carolina's Reconstruction legislature. When that marriage failed, she wed a Yale-educated doctor. Ellen, the second daughter, also remarried after a divorce. Both of her husbands were prominent artists. Medora, the youngest, married a naval captain prominent in New York political circles. The fourth sister, Addie, outdid them all. She became a countess. Having moved to Paris, she met and married a nobleman, Count Charles Cybulski, who was a member of the Russian diplomatic corps residing there. They married in Notre Dame. "She sent wedding cards to her friends in Groton and New London . . . adorned with the coronet, and bearing the words in Italian: 'Countess Cybulski, Paris,' " the *New York Sun* said on October 31, 1888. "She is described as tall, lithe, and graceful with olive-tinted skin and lustrous eyes."

Her sons did not fare as well. The firstborn, Robert, was retarded and died at age thirty. The second, Armand, died at age twenty-one of consumption. At the time, he was a Union army soldier.

A *New York Times* correspondent who visited Stafford in 1866 said the former slave owner's only companions were "an aged Negress, a decanter of choice brandy, the *Journal of Commerce* and thirty-four dogs."

Stafford died eleven years later, at age eighty-seven, of old age. He was buried beside his mother and sister in their tabby-walled cemetery. A daguerreotype taken before his death shows him sitting stiffly in a formal chair, his high cheekbones and sour face looking as if he had just sucked a lemon. He had a shock of white hair and a white, scraggly beard. He was viewed by neighbors and acquaintances as a sick, eccentric old man who drank heavily.

His estimated worth was $1 million, a fantastic sum at that time. He never acknowledged that he had children. Even so, his property in Connecticut, his Northern bank and railroad stocks, his bonds, and his other assets went to his surviving daughters. His real estate on Cumberland passed mostly to his sisters' children, who immediately started looking for buyers.

But he had made no provision for Zabette. She had to give up her cottage. She moved to the squatters' field on Cumberland's north end to live in a dirt-floored hut. She survived long enough to see the Carnegies buy up the Stafford tracts and build their fabulous mansions on the south end. She outlasted Stafford by ten years and died in obscurity.

No one knows where she is buried. Because of her common-law status with Stafford, and because she was the mother of six of his children, she may have been entitled to half his estate when he died. But she never tried to get any of it.

———•——

Some historians say Robert Stafford has gotten a bad rap.

Mary Bullard feels that Stafford actually might have been benign. The 1866 *New York Times* article said Stafford "opposed the [Civil War] from the start, and had been uniformly kind to federal soldiers." Certainly, the extraordinary arrangements he made for his children showed a tender side, although a twisted code of honor.

"I think he was a caustic person, an abrupt person," Bullard says. "But I cannot any longer think of him as a cruel person."

As for the former slaves who threatened Stafford during the Civil War and then were locked up in the brig, Bullard says they were freed at Stafford's request and allowed to work as part of the ship's crew.

John Ehrenhard, the Park Service archaeologist, believes Stafford was falsely blamed for a nefarious deed—the burning of the slave cabins to drive away the freedmen. "I just don't think he did that," Ehrenhard says. "We never had an indication that he burned them down. We couldn't find any evidence of any charred material that would suggest a fire. The nails weren't burned. They were rusty, but there was no evidence they were burned."

Ehrenhard suggests that Stafford might have torn down the cabins and recycled the timber for other structures.

Whatever fate befell the slave quarters, evidence that they were once there remains today in the form of twenty-three brick chimneys. Some are rubble, but most are still standing, though they teeter under their patina of green moss and resurrection ferns. The Park Service has propped up many of them to keep them from toppling. It would one day like visitors to the national seashore to see the eerie chimneys as part of an interpretative exhibit on Cumberland's African-American history.

"This is one of the best-excavated sites in the world," says David Brewer, a short, rotund National Park Service archaeologist, as he strolls among the chimneys on a sweltering day in June 1999. The sharp, prickly sand spurs that abound in the area attach themselves by the scores to his pants legs, socks, and shoelaces.

The site is mostly undisturbed, Brewer notes, because the Carnegie family, which bought most of Stafford's property in the 1880s, left it alone. "You just don't find a site like this anymore," he says, swatting at the gnats circling about him.

The scientists' main goal was preserving the chimneys, but they had to dig first to check the land surrounding the structures. They found evidence that Stafford segregated his slaves by marital status and gender, married couples living in one part of the village, single men in another, and single women in still another. The arrangement of two of the chimneys—about twenty-five feet apart and facing each other—suggested that they were attached to a community structure, possibly a plantation infirmary.

The neatly scraped, precisely mapped digs, shaded by the ever-present live oaks, also revealed that the slave quarters were segregated by job skills, black overseers living in different areas from laborers and craftsmen. Many gun flints were found, indicating that the slaves had weapons to hunt for food on the island. In addition, the dozens of military uniform buttons unearthed suggested that the slaves wore surplus uniforms as clothing. Other items found included pipe stems, hand-painted marbles, bottles, ornate pottery shards, an 1819 half dollar, fishing weights, a metal lice comb, a broach, and an earring—all indications that the slaves had a social life.

Brewer and the other researchers say they also can tell much about life in the village by what they didn't find.

"We found no manacles or anything else for restraining slaves," says John Cornelison, Jr., another Park Service archaeologist. "We generally believe that Stafford treated his slaves pretty good, as good as you can treat somebody you are holding against their will."

For right now, "the Chimneys," as the area is known, is off-limits to park visitors. It is surrounded by a private tract owned by a Carnegie descendant, Lucy Coleman Carnegie Sprague Foster, Whit Foster's mother. She blames the Sierra Club, which has battled with her and other residents over Cumberland's future, for putting out rumors about Stafford and the slave-cabin chimneys.

"I've always thought that one of the most wicked things are the tongues of outsiders, like the Sierra Club," she says. "They probably put this rumor out, but I'm not sure that Stafford burned out his slaves. I've always thought that was so nasty. If you look at the lintels, they're not burned. Mr. Ehrenhard proved that was not true. There was no charcoal or anything. The wood just fell in. So I'm glad that's straightened out because everybody likes to make Stafford the mean plantation overlord."

———

Robert Stafford, despite his wealth, never came close to being as famous as a man who died penniless on Cumberland and was buried there—Light Horse Harry Lee.

In March 1912, the Virginia General Assembly appropriated the money to dig up what was left of General Lee in the tiny cemetery at Dungeness and haul the remains to Virginia for burial next to his son, Robert E. Lee, at Washington and Lee University.

A committee of Virginia's distinguished citizens arrived on a sweltering day in May 1913 to perform the somber chore. Madison Drummond, a black man who lived on the mainland across from Cumberland, helped exhume the bones. He was twenty-nine years old at the time.

"When I went over to the island," Drummond recalled in a memoir, "there was an old colored man there who had been a slave boy. His name was Primus Mitchell. He said he was there the day they buried the general by a small sprig of an oak tree. He pointed out the spot where he was buried. We dug down five feet before we reached the slab, which marked the grave from head to foot. We dug and dug before we reached the casket.

"My shovel struck something that had been buried with him—stirrups, something that looked like a bit from a horse's mouth, a sword and a pistol. The officials took all of these things to clean up and keep. The general's coffin was made of boards about four inches thick. They told me to pick up the ball of moss there, and when I fetched it out I discovered it was the general's hair. He still had all his teeth, and they were perfect. His bones were white, like they were bleached. When we measured the bones, they showed him above five-feet-five."

They were removed to a new casket draped in an American flag. It was borne by an honor guard back to Virginia. Upon reaching Lexington, it was escorted to the Washington and Lee chapel by faculty and students and the entire cadet corps of the Virginia Military Institute.

On Cumberland, the original gravestone that marked the general's grave was left in place at the insistence of the island's new owner, Lucy Coleman Carnegie, a powerfully strong woman.

CHAPTER FIVE

Steel and...

THE CIVIL WAR laid waste to Cumberland's plantations. The years following the great upheaval were a time of desolation and ruin. The planters returning to their former homes found little of the order and serenity they had known before the war. Houses were rotted, farm buildings were demolished, and fields were weed-choked. Most of the furniture was either stolen or destroyed.

When he visited his father's grave on Cumberland in 1870, Robert E. Lee noted that only a four-story skeleton of Caty Greene Miller's once-glorious Dungeness still stood. The old cotton fields, once studies in orderliness and symmetry, were seas of thistles and cockleburs, sad pictures to behold. The fields never again would attain the lushness they had before the big fight.

The war did more for the nation than abolish slavery. The demands of battle hastened the transformation of the North from a region of farmers and small manufacturers to a highly industrialized area ripe for making great fortunes. The stage was set for the Gilded Age, an era of relentless capitalism when industry moguls—the robber barons—controlled America's industrial might through powerful monopolies. Wealth was celebrated as never before. The unimaginably rich tried to outdo each other in ostentatious displays of conspicuous consumption, erecting great mansions in which they threw stupendous parties. In New York during that time, Mrs. Stuyvesant Fish threw a dinner party to honor her dog, which arrived sporting a fifteen-thousand-dollar diamond collar.

Away from their chugging railroads, coal mines, and smoky factories, the rich and mighty built private resorts and three-story "vacation cottages" in the mountains and along the seashore. They snatched up the South's old plantations for hunting preserves. Georgia's barrier islands, with their haunting beauty, subtropical climate, hushed seclusion, and cheap land, especially lured the millionaires.

In 1886, a group of one hundred industrialists and financiers—J. P. Morgan, Pierre Lorillard, William Vanderbilt, Joseph Pulitzer, Richard Crane, Frank Goodyear, William Rockefeller, and others—bought all of Jekyll Island for $125,000. They then formed the most exclusive organization ever known—the Jekyll Island Club. All told, the members represented one-sixth of the world's wealth. On their island, they built gingerbread cottages of fifteen to twenty-five rooms, tennis courts, swimming pools, a rambling Victorian clubhouse with turrets and manicured lawns, and a Gothic-style chapel with gargoyles copied from Notre Dame.

Club members and guests came to the island between Christmas and Easter for fifty-six years. During that time, no uninvited person ever set foot there. By the start of World War II, the golden sojourns had ended. By that time, the millionaires' descendants had lost interest in the island. Their fortunes were petering out, and many of them were worried about their safety because of German submarines lurking offshore. At any rate, the club disbanded and the descendants sold the island to the state of Georgia in 1947.

Other millionaires chose other Georgia islands—St. Catherine's, Ossabaw, Sapelo—for winter getaways. Howard Coffin, founder of Detroit's Hudson Motor Company and chairman of the company that became

United Airlines, bought Sapelo Island, located north of Jekyll, in 1911. He later developed the former Retreat Plantation on St. Simons into a championship golf course. On exclusive Sea Island, immediately north of St. Simons, he and cousin Albert W. Jones built the famed Cloister hotel as a winter resort for the rich and famous.

Pittsburgh steel magnate Thomas Morrison Carnegie, brother of the more famous Andrew Carnegie, and his wife, Lucy Coleman Carnegie, chose Cumberland. Some say that the Carnegies were snubbed by Jekyll Island's old-money crowd, and that Lucy Carnegie was determined to outshine them on Cumberland. Others say the Carnegies desired an island of their own, not wanting to share even an acre with other millionaires.

Lucy had heard of Cumberland when she was a girl in boarding school in Fernandina, Florida, a few miles from the island's southern tip. Years later, when she was the mother of nine children, she took genuine notice

Thomas Morrison Carnegie
Courtesy of the National Park Service

of the island. Riveting her attention was a *Lippincott's Magazine* article in 1880. In flowery detail, it hyped Cumberland's languorous beauty and marveled over the ruins of Dungeness. "It is one of the joys of the earth to walk through the Grand Avenue of Dungeness at sunset," wrote Frederick Albion Ober. "The delicious climate of this island, several degrees warmer than that of the mainland in the same latitude, enabled the proprietors of this insular Paradise to grow nearly all the fruits of the torrid zone."

Lucy suggested to Tom, who was thinking of retiring, that Cumberland would be a good place to raise their children. They visited Dungeness in 1881. Captivated, they vowed to buy it. "It's so delightfully away from the city," Lucy said.

At that time, Dungeness's owner was crusty ex-Confederate general William George MacKay Davis, a first cousin of Confederate president Jefferson Davis. He had bought the plantation from Phineas Nightingale's creditors. He intended to reestablish the olive groves Louisa Shaw had planted decades earlier. By using methods employed in Italy and France for growing olives and squeezing out their oil, he aimed to prove that olive growing could be just as profitable as orange growing in Georgia.

He built a small bungalow near Dungeness and lived there. He freely let visitors come to Cumberland to see the noble ruins of Caty Greene Miller's old mansion. Steamboats made scheduled trips from Fernandina and Brunswick to let passengers gape at the remains. The operators of a hotel on the island's north end hauled guests in horse-drawn carriages to get a look. Dungeness's beautiful gardens especially attracted Northerners.

Davis intended to build a resort at Dungeness. His son, Bernard, moved to the island to help him. Then, one day, the younger Davis's breechloader accidentally went off while he was stalking some birds, mortally wounding his five-year-old son beside him.

"My darling, did Papa shoot you?" asked the father as he held his dying son.

"Yes, Papa," the child answered feebly, and then died.

A few months later, the grief-stricken father committed suicide. A distraught General Davis abandoned his plans for a resort and an olive-growing operation and looked for someone to buy Dungeness.

At first, he was picky. As far as he was concerned, Tom Carnegie's pile of money was no good on Cumberland. Still aggrieved by the South's defeat, he swore never to sell his property to a "damn Yankee."

But after Tom's entreating and cajoling, and at the intervention of intermediaries, Davis finally accepted an offer in 1882. Tom paid $35,000 for 4,000 acres comprising the Dungeness estate, including the remains of Caty Greene's mansion, stables, gardens, orange orchards, and olive groves.

Lucy Coleman Carnegie as a young woman
Courtesy of the National Park Service

Tom then made Dungeness a present to Lucy, who promptly persuaded him to buy another 8,240 acres from Robert Stafford's two nephews for $40,000. "We will not have to worry about encroachers," she said.

She and Tom lost little time in transforming Dungeness to their liking. Money, of course, was no concern. In what they said was an agonizing decision, they razed the ruins of Caty's old Dungeness. Tom had considered restoring the mansion but quickly abandoned the notion.

The cornerstone of the second great mansion to stand on the spot was laid in a formal ceremony in 1884. Several of Tom and Lucy's upper-crust Pittsburgh friends came down for the occasion. "I, too, shall call my new home Dungeness," Lucy announced.

Soon afterward, she and Tom notified the hotel on Cumberland's north end and all other excursionists that visitors no longer could come to Dungeness without an invitation. For that, mainlanders labeled the Carnegies "elitists."

An enthusiastic Tom and Lucy set about restoring the lawns, gardens, and walks from the Caty Miller era. Hundreds of orange, olive, plum, apricot, pear, and lemon trees still bore fruit. They set out more. They planted rare bulbs, shrubs, and trees collected from remote rain forests, steppes, and swamps all over the world. They retained Grand Avenue and cut other roads through the dense forest. The roads were surfaced with pearly white oyster shells from the salt marsh and the ancient Indian middens. Wherever they could, they kept what was historically and esthetically significant, though they didn't hesitate to get rid of what didn't fit their plans.

The new Dungeness, built in the Queen Anne style, was a three-story structure with a granite face. It was completed in 1885 at a cost of more than $4.5 million in today's dollars. Newspapers of the day called it grandiose and said it combined the solid strength of a Scottish castle with the subtropical flavor of a Louisiana planter's house.

To the south, it faced a tidal creek and a salt marsh. To the north, it looked out on Grand Avenue stretching to the island's other end.

Dungeness in the 1890s, before Lucy Carnegie expanded it
Courtesy of the National Park Service

Early Carnegie family photographs show broad verandas half-hidden in creeping plants and tropical flowers. The main roof, the dormer windows, and the pyramid-shaped top of the tower were covered with Vermont slate. Ornamental iron crests crowned the roof.

It had twelve bedrooms on the second floor and in the attic and a hundred-foot-tall tower with soft settees. From the tower, guests had panoramic views of the beach, the maritime forest, and the salt marsh stretching to the Georgia mainland. Lucy's children said the real purpose of the tower was to enable them to find her when she took off by herself—as she was wont to do—and failed to show up when she was due. She was prone to falling asleep in the flat-bottomed johnboat she rowed in the creek behind Dungeness.

The high ceilings, doors, and wainscoting were of polished Georgia pine. Olive wood from centuries-old groves in Europe became parquet floors and paneling. The floor in the vestibule was made of blocks of blue-colored Bordillio marble with an inlaid border of black marble. The bathroom basins were of Carrera marble, said to be the finest marble in the world. On every level, sunlight was filtered through stained glass with designs of flowers and tropical birds, made by Gibson & Sons of New York. There was a music gallery with a ceiling twenty-six feet high, a gun room, a library, a reading room, a huge dining room, and an octagonal great hall that measured twenty-five feet by fifty feet and had an awesome sixteen-foot-high fireplace and an oak mantel. Carved in the mantel was a Carnegie motto: "The Hearth our Altar; its Flame our Sacred Fire." Dungeness's builder told the Carnegies that the legend was too long for the mantel, whereupon Tom's brother Andrew—who had a keen interest in his younger brother's new abode—said that if that was the case, then to make the fireplace bigger or else pull the house down and build it bigger. "But at your peril, don't cut a letter out of that motto," Andrew warned.

The demand supposedly reflected the brothers' belief in the Victorian values of home, hearth, and family. Building beautiful homes would encourage domestic virtues, they felt.

To fill the shelves of the paneled library, Lucy ordered leather-bound books, including numerous first editions, by the box load.

The new Dungeness was a stupendous start to the Carnegies' reign on Cumberland. Tom and Lucy intended it to be a winter getaway for their family. But Tom had little time to enjoy it. A year after the mansion was finished, he was dead at age forty-three of pneumonia at his home in Pittsburgh. He thus suffered the same fate that had befallen a previous Dungeness inhabitant, Phineas Miller, nearly a century earlier.

Tom's death in 1886 propelled his dauntless widow to the role of indisputable matriarch, or empress, of Cumberland. Lucy Carnegie would bend the island to her rule. With a single-minded determination and a huge fortune at her command, she would run the island like a feudal barony.

The Carnegies' rise from abject poverty to unimaginable wealth and power is one of the most remarkable stories in America.

Andrew and Thomas Carnegie were born in a little tile-roofed cottage on Moodie Street in Dunfermline, Scotland, Andrew in 1835 and Thomas in 1843. A sister, Ann, died in childhood. Will Carnegie, the boys' gentle father, was a master handloom weaver in Dunfermline, an ancient town across the Firth of Forth Bridge from Edinburgh. For centuries, Dunfermline had enjoyed a reputation for producing the finest damask linen in Great Britain. Its highly skilled weavers were considered the aristocrats of craftsmen. Will Carnegie's beautiful damasks were in great demand.

Linen, made from flax, was rivaled at that time only by wool. Then

Andrew Carnegie (left) and brother Tom shortly before
they emigrated from Scotland to the United States
Courtesy of the National Park Service

Eli Whitney's invention of the cotton gin made cotton cheap. It quickly became a low-cost alternative to linen and wool. With the development of water-powered and steam-powered looms, factories employing women and children as cheap labor began turning out thousands of yards of inexpensive cotton cloth. The days of Dunfermline's handloom weavers were numbered. By the year of Andrew's birth, the town's once-booming linen industry was nearing collapse. Britain already had a hundred thousand power looms kept humming by a plethora of low-cost cotton.

With demand for his product plummeting, a dejected Will Carnegie moved his family to a smaller home shortly after Tom's birth. The boys' strong-willed mother, Margaret, opened a little shop in the house to sell food. In the evenings, she sewed thick leather shoes on consignment. But it was not enough. A nagging fear came over her that the family would be

Margaret Carnegie, the mother of Andrew and Thomas
Courtesy of the National Park Service

tossed into the streets. The boys were highly conscious of their mother's anxiety.

The final thud came in 1847. A large, steam-powered weaving factory opened in Dunfermline, throwing the handloom weavers out of work for good. Making a grim situation bleaker was the potato blight.

Will Carnegie possibly could have competed with scores of other desperate men for a factory job, but he was probably blacklisted because of his role in a failed political uprising a few years earlier. Defeated, jobless, and utterly broke, he wondered if he and his family would survive another year. Neighbors in similar straits were sending their children to bed supperless. The luckiest of the former weavers got jobs at a shilling a day building a new railroad. Others hired out as underground coal miners under squalid conditions that blackened their lungs and propelled them to an early grave.

Will was a gentle, artistic man who was fond of reading. He was not molded for the harsh life he faced. It was his wife, Margaret—frugal, aggressive, hard-toiling, determined to go to the top—who vowed to fight. Emotionally, she was much stronger than Will. During the hard winter of 1847-48, she determined that her family must emigrate to America, the land of opportunity. A brother and two sisters already had left eight years earlier. Kitty and Anna Morrison had married and settled in Allegheny City, Pennsylvania, now part of Pittsburgh. Brother William Morrison had achieved a degree of prosperity on an Ohio farm. Come to the land of opportunity, they advised their sister. "This country's far better for the working class than the old one," Kitty wrote.

Anything would be better than what her family had in Dunfermline, Margaret surmised.

The Carnegies auctioned all their belongings—including Will's one remaining handloom—only to find they were fifty dollars short of the amount needed to take them to America. They had absorbed a considerable hit on the handloom, which was no longer of much value. At the last minute, Margaret borrowed the sum from a cousin. Aboard the *Wiscasset*, an old whaling vessel built in Maine and square-rigged for merchant service, young Andrew and Thomas Carnegie wept as their homeland faded from view.

A month later, they sailed into New York Harbor. They then made their way by canal boat to Pittsburgh, the soot-laden city that would become synonymous with the Carnegie name and the family's smoke-belching steel mills.

———————

By now, Margaret was the dominant influence in her sons' lives. She instilled in them that only hard and earnest work would accomplish what was worthwhile. One must trust God, do one's utmost to understand and appreciate people, grasp every opportunity, and work unflaggingly, she advised. She wrung a promise from Andy—that he would not marry while she still lived.

Andy and Tom religiously followed their mother's advice.

Andy loved Tom. When Tom was six, Andy told him about his dream—that someday the two of them would go into business together, and that there would be an imposing Carnegie Brothers sign on their company. They would be rich and live in fine mansions and ride in chauffeur-driven carriages. Andy, though, was not sure what their business would be.

Unlike Andy, Tom was quiet and reserved, discreet in manners, not as impetuous and ambitious.

Andy's rise in business was meteoric, and he made sure Tom was in on every deal. Once he had some money under his belt, he moved Tom and his mother out of Pittsburgh into a Victorian house in Homewood, a Pittsburgh suburb.

Shortly before the Civil War ended, Andy invested in the Columbia Oil Company to get in on an oil boom north of Pittsburgh. William C. Coleman, a neighbor in Homewood and an iron manufacturer Andy immensely respected, had helped found the company. He persuaded Andy to get in on the deal. Andy, in turn, brought in Tom. They made a pile of money, but Andy tired of the business's chaotic state and sold out.

That oil money plus some other investments put the Carnegies on the verge of wealth. It proved the springboard to their great fortune in steel.

———————

One of Tom's boyhood friends from Pittsburgh's Slabtown area was Henry Phipps. Phipps and Thomas Miller, a boyhood friend of Andy's, had joined Anthony and Andrew Kloman to form the Pittsburgh firm of Kloman & Phipps. The company's Iron City Forge on Twenty-ninth Street was producing the finest railroad-car axles on the market. The partners sold Tom Carnegie an interest in their firm.

After a time, there was bitter dissension between Andrew Kloman and Miller over the company's direction. The quarrel escalated into a control struggle. To settle it, Miller asked his friend Andy Carnegie to step in as mediator. Andy negotiated a controversial settlement. In the process, he made Tom a full partner in the company, even putting up Tom's share of the money. At the same time, the other partners ejected Miller through a buy-out clause inserted into the agreement. The turn of events made Miller furious, and he joined Andy to start a rival firm, Cyclops Iron, to drive Kloman & Phipps out of business. Andy made Tom a partner in Cyclops, too.

Andy, however, had no intention of destroying his brother's other firm; his goal was a merger of the two. This he accomplished in 1865 with the creation of the Union Iron Mills Company.

This was the way the Carnegies first went into the iron business.

———————

As early as 1864, Tom Carnegie was cutting eyes toward his neighbor and business partner William Coleman's dark-haired, brown-eyed daughter, Lucy. She was lithe, trim, and short, no more than five feet tall.

That was a good thing, because the Carnegie brothers, not being much taller themselves, were self-conscious about their stature. Lucy was spunky and domineering but at the same time possessed of an infectious good humor. Her pluckiness probably came from her stern but adoring father.

After attending boarding school in Fernandina, she and a younger sister were sent to Linden Hall Seminary at Lititz, Pennsylvania. An old Moravian school with high academic standards, Linden Hall was among the first institutions of higher education in the United States aimed at young women. Lucy, age seventeen, remained there for one year.

Back in Pittsburgh, she had throngs of beaus, including Tom and Andy. Mindful of his promise not to marry before his mother died, Andy did not figure as a serious suitor. Tom did, and it was he who caught Lucy's eye. They married in June 1866 in Pittsburgh. She was twenty, he twenty-three. The wedding had been postponed for several months until Andy could return from an extended trip to Europe.

After honeymooning in Europe, Tom and Lucy returned to Pittsburgh, and Tom plunged back into the busy daily life of a mill manager.

Andy then made a momentous decision. He gave the new bride and groom his house in Homewood, and he and his mother moved to New York, where they took up residence in the St. Nicholas Hotel, one of the luxurious apartment-hotels that were still novelties in Manhattan in the 1860s.

Andy's move was not intended simply to give Tom and his bride their own dwelling. He moved to New York because he saw that if Union Iron Mills was to become the biggest iron maker in the United States, as he intended it should be, then it must get more orders. The best place to obtain orders was New York City. He was thirty-two at the time. By 1867, he came to dominate Union Iron, buying out partner Thomas Miller and consolidating his holdings.

With the company's operations now running smoothly in Tom Carnegie's hands, Andy turned to bond brokering. As with nearly everything else he touched, he made another fortune. Within four years, he placed $30 million worth of American securities in England and on the continent.

Now came the turning point that would take the Carnegie brothers down a treacherous path that few people ever negotiate—the road to unimaginable wealth and power. It was Tom Carnegie who steered them in the right direction.

Andy had a few blind spots. One was a stout opposition to the new process of making steel from pig iron in ten minutes. The process, invented almost simultaneously by William Kelly of Ohio and Henry Bessemer of England, had taken the latter's name.

Tom Carnegie and father-in-law William Coleman had seen a Bessemer converter at work in Johnstown, Pennsylvania, and another in Cleveland. They urged adoption of the Bessemer process. Andy demurred—which in essence meant no. The new process conflicted with his theory that pioneering is unprofitable. So Tom and his father-in-law went ahead without him. They took an option to buy 110 acres twelve miles up the Monongahela River in Braddock, where General Edward Braddock had been defeated by the French and Indians more than a century earlier. They then tried to interest several well-to-do Pittsburghers in forming a partnership to erect a new plant to make steel by the Bessemer process.

Meanwhile, Andy was traveling in Europe on a bond-selling spree for a new railroad that was to run to Davenport, Iowa. While there, he happened to see for himself how easily, cheaply, and quickly the British were making steel rails using the Bessemer process. It was his epiphany. What he saw in Europe convinced him that the American railroad system had to switch to steel rails as soon as possible.

He rushed back to Pittsburgh, where he told Tom and William Coleman that he now wanted in on their undertaking. He anted up $250,000 of the $700,000 needed to build the new plant. Coleman dropped in another $100,000. Henry Phipps and Andrew Kloman, Tom and Andy's old Union Iron partners, kicked in $50,000 each, and other investors contributed smaller amounts. The new company was called Carnegie,

McCandless & Company. Probably to entice the Pennsylvania Railroad into purchasing its rails, the company's mill was named the Edgar Thomson Steel Works for the railroad's president, who was one of the small investors.

Construction was put on hold temporarily in 1873 when a nationwide financial panic caused thousands of businesses to go belly up. In a hasty reorganization, Carnegie, McCandless & Company became the Edgar Thomson Steel Company. The plant-building project was saved mainly because of the liquid capital William Coleman had at his command. His cash also helped pull Union Iron Mills through the financial upheaval. Andy manipulated the financial scare to freeze the Kloman brothers out of Union Mills, which gave him control of that company.

The Edgar Thomson plant opened in 1875 and was an immediate success. It became the largest and most modern steel mill of its time, devoted mostly to making Bessemer steel rails. Andy made sure that Tom was the new firm's board chairman.

After the 1873 panic dissipated, America's appetite for steel was gluttonous. Concentrating on steel production, Andy and Tom began acquiring other firms. In 1881, they combined Union Mills, the Edgar Thompson firm, their furnaces, and other interests into Carnegie Brothers, Ltd. Andy's dream of a business run by him and his brother had come true.

In all of their acquisitions, the Carnegies adhered to their formula for success—developing efficient business methods, cultivating close alliances with railroads, and employing able lieutenants.

Henry Clay Frick, whose company produced the high-quality coke vital to steelmaking, would become the Carnegies' ablest lieutenant. He was known as the "King of Coke." His firm produced about four-fifths of the coke in Pennsylvania. Tom was greatly impressed with Frick's business acumen and urged Andy to buy into the coke monopoly. Andy was permitted to buy a modest amount of H. C. Frick Coke Company stock. By 1883, the Carnegies controlled a majority of the stock. Tom became a director of the firm.

Obviously, Frick was a young man headed for the big time. The Carnegies proposed he ally himself with them and become general manager of all the Carnegie properties. He would be given, they promised, a considerable share of stock. Frick—cool, taciturn, at times given to ruthlessness—accepted. The relationship would be a stormy one.

Frick engineered a huge expansion of the Carnegies' business by buying out competing companies and acquiring large holdings in railroad securities and Lake Superior iron-ore lands. In 1892, he played the key role in assembling and consolidating all of the Carnegie holdings into the Carnegie Steel Company.

———•———

Neither Tom nor his mother, however, would be around to witness the pinnacle of the Carnegies' success.

On a Friday in October 1886, Tom complained of a cold and left his downtown Pittsburgh office early, telling the clerks he was unwell. The cold developed into pneumonia, and he died several days later in the family residence in Homewood. He left behind his widow, Lucy, and their nine children, ranging in age from nineteen to four: William "Bill" Coleman Carnegie, born in 1867; Frank Morrison Carnegie, born in 1868; Andrew Carnegie II, born in 1870; Margaret "Retta" Carnegie, born in 1872; Thomas Morrison "Morris" Carnegie, Jr., born in 1874; George Lauder Carnegie, born in 1876; Florence Nightingale "Floss" Carnegie, born in 1879; Coleman "Coley" Carnegie, born in 1880; and Nancy Trovillo Carnegie, born in 1881. Except for Retta, who was at boarding school, all the children were at their father's side when he died.

Historians say it was really alcoholism that killed Tom. Many believe that his heavy drinking was an escape from the overzealous demands of his older brother. Tom had become wealthy in his own right, thanks to his numerous lucrative investments in steel, coke, oil, and gas. But his star never shot as high as his big brother's. An able manager, he spent most of his life in Andy's shadow, helping manage the mills and other businesses

Andy acquired with a power-mongering zeal matched by few people.

Joseph Frazier Wall, Andrew Carnegie's biographer, said Andy felt Tom wasn't aggressive enough. "Andrew was always jealous of Tom even though Tom was the younger brother, always felt that the mother loved Tom more than she loved him," Wall said. "And when Herbert Spencer, the famous English philosopher, came and preferred the company of Tom to Andrew, this was a severe blow to Andrew's pride intellectually as well as personally."

Not present at Tom's deathbed or final rites were his mother and Andy. They themselves were gravely ill, Margaret with pneumonia and Andy with typhoid. Margaret died a month after Tom at age seventy-six. Andy grieved for Tom, but he was devastated by his mother's passing. He was so sick himself that he was not told of her death until a week after she was buried.

He then went down to Cumberland and spent two months at Dungeness to recuperate from his illness and mourn his brother and mother. Carnegie family members said he wanted to marry Lucy after Tom died, but that she would not listen to him. She was still petite, dark, pretty, and amazingly young-looking, considering that the eldest of her nine children was twenty years old.

Unshackled from the oath to his mother, Andy looked around for other suitable brides. He chose Louise Whitfield of New York, whom he had known for years. They were married in April 1887. He was fifty-five, she twenty-eight. Perhaps it was a good thing Andy's mother had passed away. Louise once confided to a friend that she thought Margaret Carnegie the most unpleasant woman she ever knew.

Andrew and Louise had a daughter, whom they named Margaret, after his mother.

The story has been told many times of how Andy Carnegie—with Henry Frick's assistance—continued amassing wealth and power. By 1900, the Carnegie Steel Company was churning out a quarter of all the steel in the United States—more than the output of the entire steel industry of Great Britain. The company controlled iron mines, coke ovens, ore ships, and railroads.

It was in these circumstances that the U.S. Steel Corporation, led by financier J. P. Morgan, was formed to buy out the company. Andy, now sixty-five, sold Carnegie Steel for $480 million and retired from business. His entire fortune came to about $500 million, making him—a mite of a man in size-five shoes—one of the three richest men in the world.

He took to living a large part of each year in Scotland in his great estate, Skibo Castle on Dormoch Firth. Scottish bishops and lords had reigned there for more than seven hundred years. Now, the once-penniless lad from Dunfermline was the ruler of Skibo.

In January 1901, he began giving most of his great fortune away. The benefaction for which he was best known was libraries. In all, he built twenty-eight hundred Carnegie libraries, spending a total of $60 million. Of all his gifts, libraries were closest to his heart.

Lucy, his widowed sister-in-law, got an estimated $40 million and other considerations in the Carnegie Steel sale, for she inherited Tom's share of the fortune. The great wealth enabled her and her nine children to live on Cumberland Island in full baronial splendor.

No sooner was Tom buried in Pittsburgh than Lucy, then forty, began snatching up every scrap of land that came up for sale on Cumberland. She wanted total control, even to the point of buying back from her children the land bequeathed to them by their father. By 1908, she had clear title to the entire island—more than sixteen thousand acres—except for about two thousand acres at the north end at the place called High Point. The handful of white families living there refused to sell to her.

Lucy quickly put her stamp on Cumberland, naming natural features for her children and friends. A freshwater slough became Lake Retta, for daughter Margaret. The largest slough was named Lake Whitney, for Harry Whitney, a big-game hunter and explorer, the close friend of one of her sons.

She loved her children dearly. For the rest of her life, she sought to make them—and later her grandchildren—contented so they would stay close to her bosom.

At first, family members viewed Cumberland as a winter retreat. Soon, they began to call it home. Lucy gave up her estate in Pittsburgh to settle on Cumberland, although she continued to take her family up north to escape the island's hot, humid summers. For a few summers, she rented a rambling house in Greenwich, Connecticut, so her boys could play golf at the exclusive Greenwich Country Club. Later, she bought rustic but comfortable North Point Camp on picturesque Raquette Lake in the Adirondacks in upstate New York.

But Cumberland was the permanent address. Near Dungeness, Lucy had workers carve a clearing out of the woods for the family's cemetery. Tom's remains were disinterred from the Pittsburgh grave and laid to rest in Cumberland's dark soil.

With her children growing older, Lucy had a gnawing urge to expand Dungeness, though it was only five years since she and Tom had built the grand and imposing original. She added considerably to its dimensions, giving it a more formal design. Undoubtedly, the additions reflected her eclectic tastes. Ultimately, Dungeness contained fifty-nine rooms and was a vastly larger and more elaborate structure than what she and Tom started with. It metamorphosed from a Queen Anne mansion with simple lines to an immense structure more in the ostentatious style of the Italian Renaissance. Now, Lucy had a mansion to suit her boundless ego.

Outside, on the extensive grounds, the grand scheme continued. Surrounding the big house were spacious lawns and gardens of strong formal lines and symmetry and of great variety and color. A big, saucer-shaped fountain in the center of the wide south lawn was the focal point of the floral display. From the splashing fountain, brick-and-stone walkways led

Lucy Carnegie inspects the expansion of Dungeness at the turn of the twentieth century. Standing in front of the horse is her estate manager, William Page.
Courtesy of the National Park Service

to smaller gardens enclosed by clipped hedges. Arches in the hedges framed gorgeous views. One arch gave access to the formal garden with its maze-like box hedges and topiary shrubs. Another led into the fragrant rose garden, where varieties from around the world flourished. Holding forth over the sweet roses was an imposing marble statue of the Greek god Mercury blowing his horn.

A wide walkway led directly from the fountain to a broad flight of concrete-and-marble steps, which descended twelve feet to a terra-cotta terrace where spread the extensive kitchen garden and orchards reclaimed from the salt marsh. A cornucopia of fruits and vegetables thrived in the lower garden, in large part because of the rich black muck dug from the marsh and heaved onto the gardens—the same formula Robert Stafford had followed. A huge cellar preserved harvested vegetables until they were needed at the table. At the far edge of the lower garden, next to the marsh, a lawn bordered by a low hedge was graced by a large sundial and a quaint waterwheel. An elaborate network of clay pipes drained the entire garden.

The fundamental garden plan was remarkably unchanged from Caty Greene Miller's plan for the original Dungeness garden.

To lure her children outdoors and to provide a good time for her many guests when they were not partying, dancing, or feasting indoors, Lucy ordered other changes. An old cotton field become a skeet-shooting range. Old roads were turned into horse-riding trails. Beach houses and yellow-painted gazebos with white gingerbread trim were erected along the dunes. New roads paved with white oyster shells were cut to make it easier for hunters to go after ducks and deer. Some of the roads led to rustic "duck houses" next to the freshwater ponds. Duck hunters spent the night in the cabins so they could be out on the bird-filled sloughs by daybreak.

Lucy's pride and joy, by far, was the pool house, erected a few hundred feet from Dungeness and linked to it by a broad stone walkway. Of all the pleasure structures she ordered built on Cumberland, the cedar-shingled pool house was the most elaborate. Built in 1900 in the Queen Anne style, it was the indoor recreation retreat for the Carnegies. It was 150 feet long and completely enclosed a heated, white-tiled swimming pool 75 feet long and 25 feet wide. A series of six parallel rings hung from the ceiling over the pool. A springboard could be used to propel a daring person to the first ring. The person then could swing from one ring to the next like an acrobat, and so cross the pool. A marble floor surrounded the pool. Nearby were steam rooms, baths, a squash court, a gymnasium with exercise equipment, a barbershop, a billiard room, and a huge, 24-by-46-foot recreation room for dances. On each side of the recreation room was a huge stone fireplace. Upstairs were four large bedrooms used by visiting bachelors. The south wing was a luxury apartment for Lucy's unmarried son, Frank. Flanking the pool house were two castle-like turrets. In one was a gun room, where upright wooden racks held firearms and deep-drawered cupboards held ammunition. It seemed like an arsenal to awed visitors. In the other turret was the well-equipped office of a Carnegie-employed doctor, who kept regular office hours.

When her children married, Lucy made an extraordinary offer: she would build each one a mansion of his or her own on the island.

Four of them took her up on it, and Lucy spared no expense to erect the most bodacious manors for them. Three of the palatial abodes took the names of some of the island's old plantations—Plum Orchard, Greyfield, Stafford. The fourth was simply called "the Cottage."

Each child was responsible for running his or her mansion and paying servants' wages, but Lucy instructed her lawyers to make sure each house stayed legally bound to her estate. In essence, the mansions could not be expanded or sold without her say-so. Lucy loved her children, but she feared that one day they would sell their mansions and the surrounding land to outsiders.

Lucy Carnegie with her nine children on the steps of Dungeness, circa 1901
Courtesy of the National Park Service

The operation of so many big houses and outbuildings on a relatively isolated island demanded that it be mostly self-sustaining. The Carnegies, of course, did not suffer any lack because of the remoteness. Far from it. Cumberland was run and maintained far better than most American towns at the time.

Dungeness was the town hall, the pulse of the domain.

Scores of gnat-swatting workers hammered, sawed, nailed, and laid stone to erect every conceivable facility for self-sufficiency and convenience at Dungeness and the other mansions. More than forty outbuildings were built at Dungeness alone, on acreage given over to cotton fields and orchards in Caty Greene Miller's time.

No matter what its function, each structure was carefully designed and planned. Some were architectural gems in themselves.

The Dungeness stable, a massive, sprawling affair, had stalls for sixty horses, all in the south wing. There were saddle horses for the adults and

The south side of Dungeness in the early 1900s, after its expansion
Courtesy of the National Park Service

The Dungeness complex. The pool house is the turreted building to the left.
Courtesy of the National Park Service

fat little ponies for the children. Upstairs over the horses was the area where hay and straw were stored. The rest of the second floor was devoted to rooms for grooms. Horse-drawn carriages and buggies of all types were lined up in the north wing. Later, the electric cars in which Carnegie children, grandchildren, and guests flitted about the island were parked there and their batteries recharged overnight.

Across the dirt-and-shell road from the stables, the powerhouse's two huge, coal-fired dynamos generated electricity and ran the ice-making machines. The manager and three engineers lived over the immaculately maintained powerhouse, whose floor always was polished to a mirror-like sheen. In the icehouse, huge containers were filled with water, and ammonia was used to freeze it into two-hundred-pound ice blocks. An ice wagon daily delivered the blocks to the individual mansions.

There were chicken houses and a house for the man in charge of the chickens. There was a house for the head dairyman. Twice a day, forty cows were milked by hand in the spacious dairy, after which their creamy milk was pasteurized, bottled, and delivered to each mansion. It was no surprise that Lucy's cows were some of the best milk producers in the nation. Her head cattleman traveled around the country selecting top pedigreed animals to build up the herd.

The Dungeness bakery, wafting mouth-watering aromas, produced daily bread for the families.

The laundry building provided clean clothes and bed linens.

The woodworking shop was powered by a big, one-cylinder gas engine. "The engine used to go *pop-pop-pop-pop-pop*," George Davis, a Carnegie family friend, said. "You could hear it all over the island when it was running."

As many as three hundred employees of various skills labored daily to keep the Carnegies happy and the island shipshape. At the Dungeness mansion alone, a retinue of cooks, kitchen maids, chambermaids, waitresses, parlor maids, laundresses, butlers, and cellar men were at the beck and call of Lucy and her guests.

Lucy's ornate mahogany desk had six mother-of-pearl buttons she could push for the housekeeper, the pantry maid, the back-hall servant, the cellar man, the butler, and others. It was called a "partner

Lucy Carnegie at her desk in Dungeness in the early 1900s.
Courtesy of the
National Park Service

desk" because her personal nurse and secretary, Miss Laughran, sat across from her to take daily instructions.

Around the mansion, a slew of workers kept the roads and gardens in showcase condition at all times. A mower pulled by mules, driven by a worker hunkered down on the rattling machine, trimmed the lawns. During dry spells, he hitched the mules to a big tank wagon and sprinkled water on the roads to settle the choking dust.

A herdsman kept track of the four hundred white-faced Hereford cattle that provided steaks and roasts as needed.

In the greenhouses and attached potting sheds, gardeners experimented with every type of vegetable and plant, pretty much in the style of Caty and Phineas Miller. Gourmet mushrooms were grown in a special windowless structure.

Carriage makers—and later auto mechanics—strove to keep the Carnegie vehicles shiny and in good repair, no small feat given the salty winds and hot sun. When the family started driving electric cars, the jet-black machines were lined up in military precision in front of Dungeness every morning, charged up and ready to go.

Most of the unskilled work—road maintenance, stable cleaning, brush clearing, buggy driving, lawn mowing, grave digging—was done by black people, some of whom were descendants of Robert Stafford's former slaves. One worker was wrinkled old Primus Mitchell, born a slave on Cumberland. He was the one who claimed to have witnessed the burial of Light Horse Harry Lee. The Carnegies were intrigued by his stories of slavery days.

The family paid wages common to that period—a dollar a day for whites and fifty cents for blacks. The discrepancy may have been because whites held supervisory and skilled jobs.

Two-story dormitories, dining halls, and recreation rooms were built to house and feed the workers, black workers using one set of buildings and whites another. In the dorms, the men slept in double-decker iron beds. The wooden dormitories bore a remarkable resemblance to army barracks built during World Wars I and II.

Front view of the stables, which later became the carriage house, at Dungeness. It was one of more than 40 outbuildings constructed by Lucy Carnegie.
Courtesy of the National Park Service

White workers employed by the Carnegies on Cumberland Island in the early 1900s
Courtesy of the National Park Service

In the evenings, the workers played cards in the dorms or sat and chatted on the porches or on benches under the trees. The black workers sang the mournful hymns and songs of their ancestors. Their stirring music caused the Carnegies and their guests in the great mansions to pause and listen.

Fundamental to life on any island is a boat. Lucy Carnegie, of course,

The Carnegies' African-American workers playing a game of craps on Cumberland Island in the early 1900s
Courtesy of the National Park Service

would never settle for a mere vessel. Her first in a succession of boats was a 75-foot steam yacht, the *Missoe*. It plowed the choppy waters between Fernandina and Cumberland daily, carrying supplies and people to the island. A crew of seventeen operated her. In 1894, Lucy bought an even more elaborate vessel, the 119-foot *Dungeness*. With the Carnegies and their guests aboard, the big yacht cruised the Bahamas and the East Coast.

In command of the fleet was Captain William Yates, a red-mustachioed English Cockney. A lodge for him, his wife, and their three children was built near the Dungeness dock. In his spiffy navy-blue uniform, he tromped under the spreading oaks to Dungeness each evening with a little notepad, in which he jotted the errands the family wanted him to run and the items—shoelaces, candy, cigars, buttons, bows—they wanted picked up in Fernandina. He spent a few minutes bringing the family up to date on news picked up in Fernandina that day, then set the tide clock on Dungeness's front porch. The next morning, he collected outgoing mail deposited in a three-legged bronze container in Dungeness's entry hall. At midmorning, he made the run to Fernandina. On the return leg, he sorted the mail into the various mailbags for the mansions.

The commissary at Dungeness received the goods, groceries, and mail

Some of the Carnegies enjoy a day on board Lucy Carnegie's yacht, Dungeness.
Courtesy of the National Park Service

from the incoming boat. Those items were stored in wooden bins marked for each house, then delivered by a creaky horse-drawn wagon driven by an ever-grinning servant called Bubbles, who also was in charge of the dog kennels. A yapping brown spaniel named Rex adored him and rode with him on the wagon. Plum Orchard, the mansion most distant from Dungeness, got its mail and supplies about five-thirty in the afternoon.

If a family had an urgent need for something, it dispatched a chauffeur to pick it up at the commissary.

———

To help run her fiefdom, Lucy hired her sons' former tutor, William Page, as manager in 1891. A quiet, affable Harvard graduate, Page was put in charge of Lucy's entire estate, including all the mansions. In rising from

The Carnegies and their guests in front of Dungeness in 1900
Courtesy of the National Park Service

tutor to manager, he followed the path taken nearly a century earlier by Phineas Miller.

An old tabby house built by Caty Greene Miller next to the original Dungeness was converted from the Carnegie boys' school room into his office. The hands came there for their pay.

In effect, Page became the island's chief personnel officer, harbor master, farm superintendent, commissary agent, banker, surveyor, cartographer, and bookkeeper. In plantation days, he would have been regarded as the overseer. It was also his duty to help the Carnegies and their friends go riding, hunting, shooting, and fishing. To that end, he maintained a game preserve.

He dressed in formal clothes and sauntered over to Dungeness nearly every evening to dine with Lucy and her guests. In 1903, in a great show of affection, she built him a two-story house next to Dungeness. Called "the Grange," it was an imposing structure in its own right. Two years later, he married Elinor Bickford, the society reporter for the *Chicago Tribune*, and they set up housekeeping in the Grange.

Lucy's sons didn't always like his decisions, especially some of his hunting rules and his handling of their mother's accounts. Some said he spent a lot of Lucy's money and gave little accounting for it.

Lucy was never good with money, which annoyed brother-in-law Andy to no end. But while the money lasted, Lucy remained one of the most formidable women of her time.

The wedding of Florence "Floss" Nightingale Carnegie and Frederick Perkins on the south terrace of Dungeness on April 9, 1901. A local newspaper called the wedding one of the "most important social events" that ever occurred in that region.
Courtesy of the National Park Service

CHAPTER SIX

THE SOCIAL LIFE on secluded Cumberland was legendary in Lucy Carnegie's time. Her estate reaped national notoriety when a lilting waltz entitled "Dungeness," composed by J. T. Wamelink, was performed at the Cleveland Opera House in the early 1900s.

Lucy had a yen for throwing lavish dinners and fancy parties for important people. Celebrities in the world of business, finance, politics, science, and arts and letters came to Cumberland in the fall and winter to entertain or be entertained by the Carnegies. Dungeness, of course, set the tone for the island's social swirl during "the season."

Weddings especially were celebrated with great pomp. Lucy spared no money for them. When her seventh child, the lovely blond-haired, brown-eyed Floss, married Frederick Perkins of New York on Dungeness's south steps in April 1901, a local newspaper called the wedding "one of the most important social events that ever occurred in this section." Champagne fountains flowed. Tables sagged with caviar and gourmet pâtés shipped in from New York. The bride had a dozen debutante bridesmaids. They, the groomsmen, and guests from Pittsburgh, New York, Boston, and other points north arrived continuously over three days. In addition to using her own yacht, Lucy chartered a vessel and decked it out in bright flowers and green palms to shuttle them to the island.

Her taste for rubbing elbows with people in high places paved the way in 1884 for her to become the first female member of the New York Yacht Club—an astonishing achievement for a woman of her day. Her acceptance was not unanimous. The club's notes speak of a hot debate among members over admitting a woman. Some saw her membership as tantamount to supporting women's rights. The New York Herald Tribune followed the arguments in its lively society pages.

Lucy was delighted with her membership. Brother-in-law Andy called her "Commodore." She wore her spiffy club hat, kept in place by a diamond-studded hatpin, about the island and even to some social functions. Like other "flag members," she was awarded her own pennant to fly from her boat's stern. Her children called the pennant—a flag with a yellow background sporting a rampant eagle—the "family buzzard."

In large part, she had her yacht, Dungeness, to thank for her membership. She got around far and wide on the big boat. An entry in its leatherbound logbook on September 11, 1894, said it had sailed more than 3,550 miles since departing Bar Harbor, Maine, on June 12. Along the way, it had stopped at Newport and Block Island for the Astor Cup regatta. Then it had continued to Florida, where Lucy and her guests fished for tarpon. A scribbled entry noted that Lucy, "after fighting a shark for half an hour, lost hook and line. Also lost three tarpon."

———————

To Lucy's children and grandchildren growing up on Cumberland or

Lucy Carnegie, her nine children, their spouses and some of her grandchildren on Cumberland's front porch, circa 1901. (l-r) Florence Carnegie, Bill and Gertrude Carnegie, George Carnegie, Frank Carnegie, Lucy Carnegie, Oliver and Retta Ricketson (holding Lucy), Andrew Carnegie II, Oliver Ricketson Jr., (on swings) Nancy Carnegie, Bertha Carnegie, Margaret Carnegie, Virginia Carnegie, Thomas Morrison Carnegie, Jr., Coleman Carnegie
Courtesy of the National Park Service

spending much of the year there, life was filled with hunting, fishing, skeet shooting, riding, sailing, racing on the beach, picnics, gala dinner parties, poker games, formal dances, tennis, golf, frolicking in the indoor pools, and sipping mint juleps on the veranda. They took midnight sailing trips to other Georgia islands. Clad in elegant dress, they sipped champagne and danced the night away at Gatsbyesque lawn parties. Their picnics were only slightly less formal than the dinners. Outdoor tables were covered with white tablecloths and set with silver. Servants toted down hot food from the mansions' big kitchens.

Tournaments of whist, bridge, and chess were held among the mansions. Dungeness's immaculate west lawn was the venue for "field days," when the Carnegies and their guests raced bicycles, played baseball games,

The Carnegies, their cousins and in-laws at an Easter egg hunt on Cumberland's beach circa 1930s. (l-r) Carter Carnegie, Retta Wright, Phineas Sprague, Lucy Sprague, Cynthia Perkins, Nancy Rockefeller, Andrew Rockefeller, Lucy Ferguson, Bob Ferguson, Pebble Rockefeller, James Rockefeller, Andrew Carnegie II. (l to r, middle row) *Bobby Ferguson, Peggy Perkins, Curtis Perkins* (behind), *Martha Graves, Nancy Carnegie Johnston, Lucy Sprague, Bertha Carnegie, Bill Carnegie, Fred Perkins Sr., Rasty Wright, Nan Rockefeller, Shaw Sprague.* (l to r, back row) *Marius Johnston, Mory Johnston.*
Courtesy of the National Park Service

held croquet tournaments, and raced on horseback to pick off a ring hanging from a post. The noisy events, most of them organized by Lucy, were quite competitive and lasted for hours.

On late-spring nights, the family took guests down to the beach to see the loggerheads coming ashore to lay eggs. Some of the men hopped on the creatures' backs and rode them on their return into the surf.

The center of indoor frivolity was the magnificent pool house. Young Carnegie swains and friends in ankle-length bathing suits grandstanded on the high diving board or swung across the pool on the parallel rings, to the admiring glances of young heiresses. Sometimes, one of the Carnegie kids secretly greased the second ring, then bet an unsuspecting guest he couldn't make it across the pool. The mischievous Carnegies squealed with glee as their victim struggled to hold on to the greased ring before tumbling into the water below.

In the building's great front room, flanked by the two big fireplaces and walls mounted with moose heads and other trophies of the hunt, were billiard tables, dartboards, and card tables. Servants cleared them away to make room for the lively dances.

In the smoke-filled bachelor quarters, cocky young heirs with silk collars and loosened cravats vied for stakes in the thousands of dollars in endless poker sessions. So intent on winning were they that servants were instructed to shield them from the least diversion.

"They liked to drink," recalled Polly Stein Carnegie, the wife of one of Lucy's grandsons. "They were careful not to annoy their mother with the sort of serious drinking that went on in the pool house."

In the fall, Lucy and her children and their spouses drove cars or rode horses up to the old Rayfield Plantation, twelve miles north of Dungeness, to

The indoor pool at Dungeness was 75' by 25', was lined with white tile, and contained sulfur from an artesian well. The parallel rings were used to swing across the pool.
Courtesy of the National Park Service

camp and hunt for a week. They slept in tents and ate food cooked in a barbecue pit. Their idea of roughing it was to have their ever-present retainers set up the camp, build the fires, cook, straighten up the tents, haul in water, and perform the other campsite chores.

They baited wild turkeys or shot them from cars, practices that now would land hunters in jail or saddle them with a heavy fine. They used dogs to drive white-tailed deer from cover. Sometimes, hunters sat on shaky platforms in trees and shined lights into animals' face to blind them and render them easy marks.

Sometimes, the quarry was not wild game, but rather poachers. It was great sport to try tracking down trespassing hunters, although Carnegie stalkers rarely succeeded in nabbing one.

"In those days, Mama Carnegie was more male than female," one of her great-granddaughters said. "She liked to go hunting and fishing and be outdoors with the men. She didn't like anything to do with housework."

Sometimes, she rowed a flat-bottomed boat into the tidal creek behind Dungeness and fished much of the day. Occasionally, she took off into the woods alone with a rifle. She might order her chef to cook what she caught or shot, even if it was only a squirrel.

She and the children and friends fished for black bass in Lake Whitney, surf-cast along the beach, clammed south of the jetties on the island's extreme southern tip, and crabbed off a dock. Quite often, they pulled a long, bulky seine net through the ocean surf and harvested a variety of sea creatures.

———•·•———

When they were young, Lucy's sons had a hard time staying in their exclusive boarding school, Germantown Academy in Pennsylvania. They yearned for the freedom of their island. She may have been partly at fault for their longing. "She would write us how the fish were biting, how the deer and turkey were running over the place," son Andrew Carnegie II recalled. "And sometimes, we'd leave school and just go home."

Lucy admitted her guilt: "I would write [the boys] that I had shot a big buck in Rayfield or a duck in the sloughs, and it was too much for them. They would just appear back on the island."

Nevertheless, back on Cumberland, the mainland beckoned to island boys feeling their sap rise. From time to time, Lucy's sons and grandsons, in relief of hormonal urges, took the boat to Fernandina, boarded her private rail car, and ventured to hedonistic spots in Jacksonville. After a night of carousing, they would return to Fernandina—reeling and singing and a little worse for wear—and board the boat back to the island. "A lot of them discovered there was more to life than just fishing and hunting and living on Cumberland," a great-grandson said.

A few times, they didn't get back to the boat, ending up in the local slammer for the night. Lucy's daughter Floss got so worried about her son Curtis's landing in the Fernandina hoosegow that she paid to have it remodeled. "Aunt Floss got very upset about her poor boy having to spend overnight in jail," a nephew recalled.

Later in life, Curtis, described by his Carnegie cousins as a spoiled brat, opted not to leave the island at all when he wanted to get drunk. On occasion, he had his servant take him down the road and set up a card table in the woods. He sat at the table while his retainer poured cocktails. Screened by the bushes, he would drink himself into oblivion beneath the spreading oaks. He died in his early thirties, his legacy one of heavy imbibing.

In the island's spacious mansions, such scandalous stories were whispered from one generation to another. One tale, though, was repeated with great pride before crackling fires in the big fireplaces—that of the family's rise from pauperism to riches.

Retta Ferguson McDowell, a great-granddaughter of Lucy's, said she heard the stories on her mother's knee. "With the Industrial Revolution coming at about 1840, our family, along with many other families, grew very hungry, particularly the ones who were doing weaving in their little cottages. That put them out of business.

"Somebody could get a fine damask scarf a whole lot cheaper. And so my great-great-grandfather William, in Scotland, was persuaded by his strong little wife [to come to America].

"There's a picture of her, and, boy, is she a little meatball, . . . very able and determined, and you see where Andrew got it.

"The mother, Margaret, borrowed fifty dollars, which was a lot of money in those days, from a cousin to book passage to Pittsburgh, where there were other cousins to receive them. The mother was the stronger, I gather.

"They get to New York—I don't know how it was handled then. In those days, was there an Ellis Island? I'm not sure. They went on a canal boat—and the speed of a canal boat is the speed of a horse walking— across the Allegheny Mountains, into Pittsburgh, all the way by canal.

"They lived probably on the north side, all of them in one room, as I understand, and great-great-grandfather tried to ply his trade, and it just didn't work. He tried to sell the linens he brought over with him, and probably could not sell them. This was a frontier country at that point, and who had the kind of money and who had the house to take beautiful dinner linens? Probably nobody. So he became very discouraged, and he died quite early on.

"So Andrew, in order to help his mother, just went out and got a job delivering anything. And Thomas, I guess, was at home. The mother cobbled shoes. Her father had taught her. This was no different from any other family. They had to work hard, and they did it just to keep it all together.

"So you can picture Andrew at twelve, taking any job he could get, delivering messages, telegraph messages. Anything he could do became business.

"It's a fascinating story, I think. . . .

"The story is that Andrew goes along and Thomas is not only his brother but his best buddy and [works] with people on the home front while [Andrew] travels."

―――•·•――

In the tradition of Caty Greene Miller, Lucy Carnegie came to be celebrated as the gracious host of Dungeness.

If you visited in, say, 1910, when the mansion was in its glory, you boarded the Carnegie boat in Fernandina and got off at the Dungeness dock. The captain's signal of an incoming guest was two whistle toots. One toot meant mail only. A servant or perhaps a family member drove you to the mansion along shell-flecked Coleman Avenue, bordered by live oaks and fragrant magnolias. On the final approach to the mansion, four-foot-high terraces with manicured lawns, palmetto trees, sago palms, and exquisitely trimmed shrubs beautified the way. You went past two pillars spanned by black ironwork before you finally stepped onto the large circular driveway in front of the imposing house.

You walked past a stone seat and a mounting block for horse riders and climbed the wide flight of steps to the north veranda with its green wicker furniture and big wooden swing. Passing through the heavy golden-oak doors with black-iron hinges and door handles, you entered the house and stepped into a square hall. The three-legged brass container there was for the outgoing mail. If you continued straight ahead, you walked into the card room, where the guest book was kept and a table with pigeon-holes held mail and newspapers for individual Carnegies and guests. If you turned left and went through the archway, you came into the great hall with its magnificent fireplace and the Carnegie motto chiseled in the mantel. A long, wide bench with a leather cushion was in front of the fireplace. Near it was a large sofa upholstered in red tapestry, where Lucy took her naps. You dared not sit there. At one end of the great hall, underneath the staircase, was a toilet room for men, racks for their guns, and a wall-mounted telephone that connected only to the other mansions.

Lucy Coleman Carnegie, 1912
Courtesy of the National Park Service

At breakfast, you dined English-style in a small dining room that was part of the original Dungeness. You selected your food from polished silver containers on a sideboard, the food warmed by Sterno-fueled brass heaters.

At five in the afternoon, you were served tea from a cart in front of the great hall's fireplace.

Before-dinner cocktails were served in the same chamber. If you were a gentleman, you had to wear a tuxedo, if a lady, full evening dress. When a servant rang the big Chinese gong for dinner, Lucy might grab you by the arm—if you were the latest male guest—and say, "Hi, bub, will you take me in to dinner?"

You dined in the formal dining room at an enormous round table. Lucy, often wearing a tiara, an egret feather, a flower, or a bow in her well-coiffed hair, presided over the repast from her black leather chair with a high back. Her tailor-made gown was of the most stylish cut. She loved fancy attire and kept more than fifty pairs of shoes in her closet. She sat facing the dining room's east end, where a large portrait of her with a bright red cape over her shoulder stood sentry on the wall.

Dinner was formal—white tablecloths, candelabras, sparkling crystal. The china might be a set of gleaming white dishes trimmed in fourteen-karat gold, or one with hand-painted flowers. The silver bore the Carnegie name. The glasses were emblazoned with gold scrolls. On the superbly set table were dishes from the island—vegetables, chicken, eggs, milk, cream, venison, turkey, bread, oysters, fish. The gourmet stuff was brought in from New York by the Clyde line. Garnishing the table were bright floral arrangements of roses, violets, magnolia blossoms, daisies, peonies, carnations, lilies, and, at Christmas, holly with red berries, red poinsettias, and mistletoe, all from Dungeness's gardens and woods. On

The ivy-covered pergola stretching between Dungeness and the Cottage, circa 1901
Courtesy of the National Park Service

George Washington's birthday, you found a small hatchet made of olive wood at your place. No fewer than three liveried servants waited on you and fellow guests.

Lucy liked people of importance at her table. Seated next to you might be Max Fleishman of Fleishman's Yeast Company; Booker T. Washington, the black educator; the governor of Georgia (though not when Booker T. was there); or Andrew Carnegie, the old robber baron himself. Seldom were there fewer than twelve dinner guests. The kitchen always prepared several extra dinners for last-minute invitees.

After dinner, you might adjourn to the library, stocked with hundreds of slick, leather-bound volumes, many of them first editions. On a summer evening, you might ascend the stairs to the tower, relax on a settee, and gaze at the sun setting over the salt marsh. Or you might take an evening stroll in the garden or mix with the other guests in the great hall for after-dinner libations or a game of charades. Quite possibly, there was a dance at the pool house, where you might find a partner for a waltz.

———————

Brother-in-law Andy Carnegie, wife Louise, and daughter Margaret came to Georgia in their plush private railroad car and over to Cumberland via Lucy's yacht to visit three weeks each year. Andy and Louise felt that the Georgia sunshine was good for Margaret's frail health, though Louise was not totally enamored of Cumberland. Being a serious and reserved person, she found Lucy and her big family a bit too much.

To welcome Uncle Andy, Lucy's grandchildren, dressed in kilts, followed the butler carrying the haggis on a large silver tray into the dining room. Her children persuaded her to stop short of ordering bagpipes for the occasions.

In the evenings, in Dungeness's spacious parlors or on its wide front porch, she and Andy would argue almost any topic, shouting boisterously at each other. At the end, though, they usually found themselves laughing uproariously at each other's sallies.

The Carnegies relax on the front porch of Dungeness, circa 1901 (l to r) Lucy Carnegie, Bertha Carnegie, William Page, Andrew Carnegie II, Nancy Carnegie
Courtesy of the National Park Service

They talked about old Pittsburgh friends, argued over places they had been to or owned—or wished they owned—and laughed at family jokes. Sometimes, the frugal Andy annoyed Lucy when he wagged his finger and chided her about the enormous sums she spent running Cumberland. "You should be paying more attention to your finances, Lucy," he said.

<hr />

There were people who believed that Lucy had rooked them out of a rightful share of Cumberland. Her lawyers more than once had to defend her title to the island.

On a chilly day in January 1907, a lanky United States deputy marshal from Savannah served a subpoena notifying her that two women—Cornelia Stafford Williams and Nancy "Nanette" Stafford Gassmann—had filed a lawsuit against her. They claimed they were the offspring of Robert

Carnegie children put on a skit for their great-uncle Andrew Carnegie, seated to the right, *during one of his visits to Cumberland Island.*

Stafford and a slave named Catherine. They said they were the rightful heirs to seventy-seven hundred acres that once had belonged to Stafford and were now in Lucy's name.

Lucy and her lawyers had known for years—and local newspapers had occasionally reported—that certain alleged Stafford heirs were moving to recover portions of his former property on Cumberland. Some of them had combed through courthouse records in Camden County, trying to find evidence for their claims.

Lucy and her cadre of managers reportedly were quite shaken by the sisters' lawsuit, which demanded compensation for the land they claimed was rightfully theirs. In 1908, however, a judge dismissed the suit. It never reached the courtroom. Stafford's daughters, Lucy's lawyers said, didn't deserve a dime.

But for her own children, Lucy spared no fancy.

CHAPTER SEVEN

THOMAS MORRISON "MORRIS" CARNEGIE, JR., Lucy's fourth-born, was the first recipient of her munificent offer of a mansion for each child. For him and his wife, Virginia Beggs Carnegie of Pittsburgh, Lucy in 1899 built a twenty-nine-room house at the end of Dungeness's west lawn. They called it, simply, the Cottage.

Featuring broad upper and lower porches on three sides supported by Doric columns on the first floor and Ionic columns on the second, the white-painted mansion resembled old plantation houses along the lower Mississippi River. Most of its windows actually were French doors. A beautiful, curvy duck pond shaded by oaks and tall Chinese bamboo was in back of the house. An artesian spring filled the pond. Stretching two hundred feet between the Cottage and Lucy's estate office in the old tabby house was a twelve-foot-wide pergola. A low brick wall bordered it on each side. Its wooden frame was supported by round columns and was covered

Thomas Morrison "Morris" Carnegie, Jr., was called "Johnny Palmseed"
by family members because he rode about the island strewing palm seeds.
Courtesy of the National Park Service

with thick English ivy—a cool, shady tunnel for promenading Carnegie women.

Morris, studious, pipe smoking, given to daydreaming, was a budding botanist. In a steamy greenhouse attached to the Cottage, he doted on delicate cattleya orchids, banana plants, and other tropical flora. A spiral staircase ran from the greenhouse to his separate bedroom and library. Family members said the setup helped him avoid Virginia when he sipped too much bourbon, which was often.

But what really was unusual was his penchant for seeding the island with tropical plants. He would get on his horse and scatter the seeds from a sack as he rode. His family took to calling him "Johnny Palmseed." When they spied a palm looking out of place, they blamed it on him. They surmised that his odd habits were from when he and a brother were cleaning their .22 rifles and Morris's accidentally went off, the bullet grazing his head.

He was one of Lucy's favorite children. Both were avid readers. She ordered the Cottage designed so that his bedroom window faced hers in Dungeness. When she awakened in the morning and raised the shade, he knew she was ready for him to come over. They would read either in her library or her bedroom until nearly noon.

Despite his family's wealth, Morris was a liberal intrigued by Karl Marx's writing—another oddity chalked up to his close encounter with the bullet. A family story went that, when in New York, Morris would buy the socialist tabloid *Daily Worker* and carefully stick it inside his folded

The Cottage, which Lucy Carnegie built for her son Thomas Jr. and his wife, Virginia, circa 1901. The house burned in the 1940s.
Courtesy of the National Park Service

New York Times. Then he'd stroll into the Racquet and Tennis Club, a bastion of corporate conservatism, surreptitiously scan the tabloid, leave it on a table, and walk away. Other club members who came across it dared not touch it, fearful of communist plots and worker uprisings. Not even the waiters and houseboys wanted to pick it up.

Morris also was one of his uncle Andrew Carnegie's favorites. Family lore says Morris helped persuade him to establish the philanthropic foundation that gave away his hundreds of millions of dollars. When Andrew forked over a pot of money to build the World Court at The Hague in the Netherlands, Morris helped him select the site for the beautiful Palace of Peace there.

———————

For her firstborn, William "Bill" Coleman Carnegie, and his wife, Gertrude Ely of Cleveland, Lucy didn't build a new mansion—not initially, at least. The newlyweds chose the old home of Robert Stafford, five miles north of Dungeness. It was the frame house Stafford had built for his mother and sister in the 1820s, where Zabette lay in his four-poster bed and conceived his children. Lucy had bought the mansion, like just about everything else on the island.

Bill was named for his grandfather on his mother's side, following a Scottish custom of naming the first son after the wife's father. A tad over five feet tall, he was the jokester of Lucy's children, given to the sporting life. "Uncle Bill, Uncle Bill, never worked and never will," Carnegie children would say, laughing. His clear blue eyes sparkled as if he were always up to something. When visiting New York, he went to the opera with his mother in a sleek carriage but sat up front with the coachman and smoked a fat cigar.

He liked fast horses and fast cars. He drove hellbent in his sporty electric down Cumberland's narrow lanes. Fearing that sooner or later he would end up in a gruesome crash on the stretch of Grand Avenue where it made a sharp turn, Lucy ordered the division of the road there into what the family called the "Pant's Leg." The two lanes were separated by trees and bushes, each becoming one-way.

Bill was a heavy wagerer who stacked the odds whenever he could. In his twenties, he taught himself an amazing feat—to leap flat-footed into a whiskey barrel and back out again. He practiced to where he was perfect. Then he set up his suckers. At New York's old Explorer Club, he bet unsuspecting members he could vault into a whiskey barrel. When the wager shot up to five thousand dollars, bemused servants brought up from the basement an empty barrel still giving off a bourbon aroma. It was placed before the cocky Bill, who neatly sprung into it. Once inside, he bet them double or nothing he could leap back out. He walked away with ten thousand dollars.

That's a story handed down by generations of Carnegies. Another tale is that Bill never wore the same shirt twice.

He and comely Gertrude remodeled and lavishly furnished Stafford House, Lucy footing the bills. The furniture alone cost hundreds of thousands of dollars.

Stafford House, which Lucy Carnegie built for her son Bill and his wife Gertrude after the originial Stafford House burned
Courtesy of the National Park Service

An avid golfer, Bill had old cotton fields next to Stafford cleared and graded for a nine-hole course, which, when finished, had a clubhouse and a well-stocked bar. Rounding out his private country club were tennis courts and an indoor swimming pool.

A brawny twenty-three-year-old named Thomas Hutchinson from the famed golfing area of St. Andrews in Scotland came over to lay out the course. But before he could finish, he was thrown from a spooked horse and landed headfirst on a pine stump. He died the next morning and was buried in the cemetery at Stafford, surely becoming the first golf pro buried in America. His brother Jock then sailed over, finished the course, and stayed to teach the family the finer points of the game. He married a Carnegie employee and became a champion golfer in the United States and Europe.

The Cumberland course was famous among East Coast socialites for its short hole of sixty yards, described by one player as "so beset with hazards that a three was welcome and a four was not unusual." Family members often golfed in their Carnegie tartans. When they wanted to play, they rang an old plantation bell atop a tall pole, and two sprightly caddies called Nervous and Pervous came running.

Lucy and brother-in-law Andy played often when he was on the island. He got great satisfaction golfing with her, for she was an opponent he usually could defeat. "I beat Lucy today, really broke my record, and now I can say I can do something credible," he boasted.

On a fall day in 1900, Gertrude and some lady friends were sipping tea on Stafford's front porch and Bill and his friends were teeing off at the ninth hole when flames erupted inside the house. The women screamed, and the men came running. Despite the smoke and flames, several of them dashed inside to save what they could. Embroidered pillows and fine china were tossed from windows. A grunting man toted out a huge bronze statue of a fellow in a tall hat strumming a banjo. Gertrude scooted upstairs to retrieve a gold, bejeweled rat she usually wore to keep her pompadour in place. Not much else was saved, and no one ever knew the cause of the blaze that burned the dwelling to the ground.

To take its place, Lucy had another mansion—a carefully designed, two-story Mediterranean-style structure—built on the same spot. This time, an exquisite garden with a small lake also was laid out. Egrets by the score took to coming in the late evening to roost in the palmettos and oaks around the lake, a daily spectacle that awed visitors.

Then, in 1906, Gertrude died, probably from diphtheria. Bill was nearly hysterical.

He had her buried in Stafford's backyard garden so he could gaze at her grave from his now very lonesome mansion. Lucy tried to comfort him, but he would not be consoled. "Oh, Mother, you can lose a mother or a sister, but losing a wife is so hard to bear," he moaned. After the

Gertrude Ely Carnegie, wife of Bill Carnegie
Courtesy of the National Park Service

funeral throng departed, his anguish was unbearable. That night, he and Stafford's cattle manager, Henry Miller, took spades and shovels and exhumed her cold body. Bill snipped off a long braid of her blond hair before they reburied her. He carried the braid with him for the rest of his life. When his mother learned of the ghoulish act, she shuddered. Years later, Gertrude's remains were removed to the Carnegie cemetery and laid to rest next to Bill's.

Bill never fully got over her death. He left Cumberland and moved to a Pittsburgh suburb, where he took to liquor to blunt his grief. His suffering and heavy drinking were great worries to his mother.

He then married his nurse Betty, a big-boned woman who had a reputation for looseness. He wanted to move back to Georgia and be near his family again, but his kinfolk thought his marriage scandalous and would have nothing to do with him or his new bride. That Bill would marry beneath his station, and a floozy to boot, was a stain on the entire family. An outraged Lucy amended her will to cut Bill and any forthcoming children out of an inheritance, except for a limited trust fund.

Banished from Cumberland, Bill and Betty lived on a boat moored to a St. Marys dock across from Cumberland. Bill would sit in a deck chair, sip his bourbon, and gaze longingly at Cumberland in the distance.

Then their marriage fell apart. Betty went a little batty. She tried to stab Bill with scissors and douse him with boiling water. To the family's relief, she ran off with an Armenian sailor. Everywhere she went, she denounced the Carnegies. Finally, she hanged herself.

Bill built a small house on the St. Marys waterfront. The townsfolk saw a lot of him. "When he was down there, I'll tell you this: he had women down there," said Elsie McDowell, whose father worked on Cumberland for the Carnegies for forty-seven years. "They were young girls. The young boys around there liked him, too. He housed some of them. Everybody in town liked him. His mother apparently didn't leave him penniless 'cause he had a chauffeur.

"The girls who hung out at Mr. Bill's didn't run around in our bunch.

Greyfield, built for Lucy's daughter Margaret and her husband Oliver
Courtesy of the National Park Service

They weren't from around here. I think they were from up north."

———————

Greyfield, a graceful, three-story mansion two miles north of Dungeness, was built in 1901 for Lucy's daughter Retta and her husband, Oliver Garrison Ricketson. Oliver was a man of refined taste; Greyfield's design was his inspiration. He wanted it built along the lines of a large, late-eighteenth-century coastal plantation house raised on a high basement. Its design, in fact, was patterned after the old Stafford House, with three stories, wide porches, and an attic.

Sixty-four years later, in 1965, Lucy Carnegie's namesake, the redoubtable Lucy Ferguson, who would become Cumberland's most memorable matriarch, turned the grand house into the exclusive Greyfield Inn.

———————

Grand as they were, though, neither Greyfield, Stafford, nor the Cottage could match the magnificent residence called Plum Orchard, built

Plum Orchard, built for Lucy's son George and his wife Margaret
Courtesy of the National Park Service

on a bend in the Brickhill River nine miles north of Dungeness.

Lucy constructed Plum Orchard for her son George Lauder Carnegie and his wife, Margaret. Margaret told George she wanted a house to outdo anything that might be built for his siblings. She also wanted it far away from Dungeness, to avoid Lucy's meddling.

Margaret was used to big houses. Her father was railroad magnate William Thaw. Her marriage to George "unites a great deal of wealth," a Pittsburgh newspaper reported. Tall and fair next to the diminutive George, Margaret was the sister of the notorious Harry Thaw, who in 1906 shot and killed famed turn-of-the-century architect Stanford White because of his torrid love affair with Thaw's wife. Harry was judged to be suffering from dementia when he shot White and was let out of jail early. He visited Plum Orchard, where George's nieces and nephews did their best not to stare at him as he fidgeted like a nervous hen. "All I remember were his wild eyes," one of George's nieces said.

Margaret regretted being childless, which was why she often had her nieces and nephews up for lunch or tea or to spend the night. At Easter, she gave frolicking egg hunts and served the children ice cream shaped like a hen and eggs, nestled in spun-sugar nests.

George contracted muscular dystrophy sometime after 1914. He never walked again. Fortunately, an Otis elevator operated by an underground hydraulic system already had been installed in Plum Orchard. When it was in use, the water could be heard swishing through the pipes like a commode refilling after flushing.

George's mobility may have been impaired, but one of his great pleasures was his polished-mahogany powerboat with a handsome deck. He kept it moored to Plum Orchard's dock.

Their childlessness notwithstanding, Margaret and George decided they needed more room. They added two wings to Plum Orchard in 1906, just a few months before Gertrude died at Stafford. The west wing housed a large gun room that was supposed to be a gathering place for the Carnegies but was seldom used. The east wing held a squash court and a

Margaret Thaw Carnegie,
wife of George Lauder Carnegie
Courtesy of the National Park Service

twelve-foot-deep swimming pool surrounded by a black iron railing. The water in the pool was always cold, even in summer, owing to the deep artesian well that fed it. Steps along the pool's inside wall led to the bottom. A favorite children's game was to see who could walk to the bottom and back up to the surface without having to come up for air.

Margaret employed a French theme throughout the house. The rooms sported intricately carved French furniture and centuries-old tapestries. The wine cellar was stocked with heady, top-vintage French wines.

Outside, the columned mansion was painted often, so it always was a gleaming white. Like Dungeness, Plum Orchard had numerous outbuildings—servant dormitories, chicken houses, a laundry room, barns, a greenhouse, and a water tower, all grouped in back of the mansion to resemble a European farm. Near the big dairy barn, a low brick wall protected the grave of Peter Bernardey, Plum Orchard's first owner.

Margaret and George transformed the grounds into a garden paradise of manicured lawns, geometric formal gardens, and herbaceous borders where riots of red, yellow, blue, and white flowers—irises, peonies, lupines, primulas, salvias, geraniums, day lilies, dahlias, daisies, impatiens, begonias—bloomed profusely. Royal palms and other exotic species were set out in front of the mansion. A big kitchen garden produced vegetables, oranges, grapefruit, pears, apples, and other fruits.

To get to the gardens from the back of the mansion, one had to cross a bridge of split red-cedar rails that arched over an hourglass-shaped pond. Its inky black water reflected the moss-draped oaks, azaleas, and bamboo stands crowding around it. In the water were pink and white water lilies, goldfish, swans, and a couple of alligators, which caused edgy nerves among those crossing the pond for the first time.

Margaret and George raised terrapins, prized for the rich soup made from them. "Terrapin soup was a delicacy," explained Retta McDowell, one of George's grand-nieces. "The terrapin pen went right down into the marsh so that the salt water could come into the pen. It was a large pen, and there was land where the turtles could lay eggs."

The Carnegie daughters—(l to r) Margaret "Retta," Florence "Floss," and Nancy
Courtesy of the National Park Service

Plum Orchard's cedar-shingled carriage house and stable complex was one of the most distinctive of its kind on the East Coast. The stable, an architectural prize, held fifteen large stalls and a huge room for carriages, buggies, and carts. The stable hands slept upstairs. On either side were paddocks where the horses were turned out.

George died in 1921, five years after Lucy. Following a decent mourning period, his still good-looking widow, Margaret, went to Europe, where she courted and married a smoothly charming French peer, the Count de Perigny. To the great horror of the Carnegies on Cumberland, the count came to Plum Orchard a few months after the wedding and "cleaned out the wine cellar and took everything but the bricks," as one Carnegie put it. Nearly all the furniture, the bric-a-brac, the crystal chandeliers, and the gold bath fixtures—even George's guns, trophies, and first-edition books— were toted from the house and shipped to New York for auctioning. The count even suggested ripping up the mansion's oak parquet floors and selling them. It was then that the appalled Carnegies advised that he get himself back to France.

He and Margaret later settled in Kenya, where they died and were buried.

———•—•———

Lucy's other children—Nancy, Frank, Coleman, Floss, and Andrew II—elected not to have their own mansions on Cumberland.

Coleman, or "Coley," as he was fondly called, was Lucy's bachelor son. He lived off and on in a third-floor bedroom at Dungeness when he was not hunting and fishing somewhere in North America's wilds. He died in 1911 at age thirty after catching pneumonia during a fishing trip to Glens Falls, New York. It broke Lucy's heart. For the rest of her life, she carried a great void for her youngest son.

Frank, her second-born child, lived in the bachelor pad in Dungeness's pool house. An avid hunter, golfer, tennis player, horseman, and sailor, he piloted his schooner, *Sonsy*, along the coast in the summer when he was not at the family's North Point Camp in the Adirondacks. His pool-house quarters included a bedroom, a bathroom, and a large living room with a billiard table and a well-stocked bar.

His bright and high-strung sister Floss and her husband, Frederick Perkins, lived at first in Pittsburgh and then at the Plaza Hotel in New York City. Occasionally, they came with their three children for short stays on Cumberland. When Cumberland's manager, William Page, died, Floss and her family took over his house, the Grange, next to Dungeness.

Andrew II, Lucy's third-born son, actually wanted a house of his own, but Lucy said she dearly needed his help and forbade him to leave Dungeness. A nervous, uptight fellow, he was the mainstay of her nine children. He was a light drinker, an unusual trait among her offspring.

He, his wife, Bertha, and their two daughters lived in three cramped rooms on Dungeness's first floor. Bertha, who was from Cincinnati and whose father had come over from Ireland, supervised housekeeping and

Andrew Carnegie II
Courtesy of the National Park Service

other arrangements for the demanding Lucy. She planned parties and balls and smoothed out trouble spots when they arose in the big house.

Her duties included losing at bridge. When Uncle Andy Carnegie visited Dungeness, he loved to play the game but could not stand getting beat. Lucy cajoled Bertha into playing with him and losing. "But don't ever let on that you're following my instructions, else he will have a fit," she told Bertha.

Lucy originally intended that Bertha be Frank's bride. She met Bertha and her mother, Nancy Sherlock, while summering at a hotel in Crescent, Pennsylvania. Lucy took a great liking to the slender, full-bosomed Bertha and envisioned the young woman making a good mate for Frank. She invited the Sherlocks to Cumberland. Then Bertha ran into Andrew II during a Dungeness party and forgot about Frank.

Bertha and Andrew had little privacy at Dungeness. They had to cope with demanding guests and to please Lucy.

Nearly every evening, their two young daughters, Nancy and Lucy, named for her grandmother, went to Mama Carnegie's room, where they watched her dress for dinner. As the maid fixed her long, graying hair, Lucy would ask her granddaughters, "What dress shall I wear tonight?" Giggling and squealing, the delighted girls would go through her chest and huge closet and triumphantly suggest an elegant frock. Unbeknownst to them, their grandmother's maid already had selected the evening wear. Lucy would say, "Oh, I'm too fat to get into that. Shall I try this?" And the maid would hand her the dress already chosen for the night.

As they sat there, the little girls sometimes gazed at the photo in a small silver frame next to the fresh bouquet of flowers on Lucy's dressing table. The beautiful woman in the black-and-white picture was Gertrude, their uncle Bill's dead wife. Lucy told them what a lovely daughter-in-law Gertrude had been. But she never mentioned a word about Uncle Bill's second wife.

Bill, though, was not the subject of the juiciest scandal to jolt Cumberland. That dubious honor belonged to Lucy's youngest child, Nancy Trovillo Carnegie. It fueled gossip mills in New York and Pittsburgh for years.

Nancy ran off at age twenty-two with James Hever, the sexy, Irish-born, red-haired young hunk in charge of Dungeness's stables, who was teaching her how to ride. She may have been pregnant. Lucy's other children had at times spied their sibling casting eyes at Hever and rubbing more than elbows with him when he gave her riding lessons. They warned their mother of potential danger. Lucy replied that none of her children would do anything wrong.

She therefore was horrified when Nancy eloped with Hever in May 1904. She was visiting her daughter Retta at Greyfield when she learned the news from Frank, who was at Dungeness when he heard about it. He sped posthaste to Greyfield and bounded up the steps two at a time, not even taking time to say hello to his little niece, Retta's daughter, sitting on the steps.

"He got grandmother and mother and they went into the sitting room," said the niece, Lucy Ricketson Ferguson, in her unpublished memoirs. "I went to the peephole and listened. Mother suspected that was what I was doing, so she opened the door and I fell in. So she and grandmother and Uncle Frank went upstairs to talk in mother's bathroom. They didn't want me to hear, but I followed them and listened through the bathroom peephole.

"I heard Uncle Frank say, 'I'd rather see my sister dead than married to that man.' It shocked me badly, his wishing his sister dead."

When Lucy caught up with the renegade couple, she dispatched them to England, where their first child, Margaret, was born.

Then what Lucy feared most happened: the newspapers got hold of the story. "Miss Nancy Carnegie Married to Her Mother's Former Coachman," screamed a front-page headline in the *Pittsburgh Times* on April 19, 1905. The subhead read, "Secret Had Been Kept from All but the Near Relatives." Lucy, through son-in-law Frederick Perkins, denied that she was against the couple. The sensational story said that an Irish priest married them in New York. Nancy, an Episcopalian, had waived her religious scruples for her husband, the newspaper reported. "You have my positive assurance that the family was informed beforehand that the marriage was to take place," Perkins told the reporter. "There never was any objection, from what I have heard. The family was scattered about and so didn't attend the wedding. Mrs. Carnegie had a throat infection and makes it a point to keep away from New York weather at this season because it doesn't agree with her. Her uncle, Mr. Andrew Carnegie, was abroad at the time. The wedding was not made public because we wanted the couple to be as unembarrassed on their honeymoon as possible."

Uncle Andy made the best of it. He gave the couple twenty thousand dollars to get them started. When asked for comment, he said, "I would rather that Nancy married a poor honest man than a worthless duke."

Whereupon the duke of Manchester in England took personal affront, thinking that Andy, with whom he had a running spat, was directing the comment toward him. "I suspect it's cheaper to endow coachmen than libraries," he quipped.

Nancy and Hever's three other children were born after the family moved to Long Island, New York. A heavy drinker, Hever sometimes treated Nancy like a punching bag. When she no longer could stand it, she bundled up the children and retreated to Cumberland. She was a "sad, pathetic person" when she came back, a family member said.

Then Hever developed cancer. When no nurse would care for him, Nancy went back up north to fill that role. He was moved to Lucy's apartment in the Life Building in New York, where he lingered in considerable pain before he died.

The Carnegies later learned that he had fathered four children by another woman, who had died before he married Nancy. One child was James Hever, Jr., buried at Arlington National Cemetery. Nancy, a supersensitive woman—"You couldn't tell an off-color story around her, she was so proper," said a cousin—sent money to help her late husband's offspring by the other woman.

But even before Hever died, Nancy had become enamored of another man she met on Cumberland—Marius Johnston, a young doctor from an old-line Kentucky family. At Lucy's request, he had come to the island to tend the scrapes and ills of her big family and her employees. He worked out of the office at the Dungeness pool house.

Marius fell in love with Nancy. At six feet, he was a foot taller than she. Once, upon catching Nancy and Marius holding hands under a blanket, one of Lucy's grandchildren promptly tattled to her family. Hever was not dead yet. Lucy, smelling another scandal in the making, encouraged Marius to go to Africa on a safari. By the time he returned, Hever was dead. He and Nancy married in 1912.

The marriage propelled Nancy back into the good graces of Carnegie family members, who were thrilled with Marius. She and Marius had a child of their own. They also changed the last names of her children by Hever to Johnston. They took to calling Marius "Daddy." Later, the children's offspring called him "Pawdaddy." They and their cousins for a long time were kept in the dark about Hever. Some were adults when they learned the truth.

"The elopement was the scandal of the year back then," said Lucy Foster, great-granddaughter of Lucy Carnegie. "But we never knew a word about it growing up. Nancy must have loved him, because she stuck with him even though he was an alcoholic."

But they all loved Marius. He was not a handsome man. A terrible scar ran down the left side of his face, the legacy of a childhood hunting accident in Kentucky. He had been climbing over a fence with a rifle when it went off and took away nearly half his face. His lip was pulled back, and the scar radiated from the center of his cheek. At first, it shocked you. Family members warned strangers of it before they met Marius. But his bright smile, lively blue eyes, sparkling wit, and gentleness won over the Carnegies and everyone else who knew him.

Marius was whopping lucky in one sense. When he was coming back from the African safari, his route took him through England, where he was supposed to board a ship on her maiden voyage to New York. He had a bad case of the flu and was unable to get out of bed. He missed the boat.

Its name: the *Titanic*.

For a long time, he kept his *Titanic* ticket in a safe spot, just to look at it and be thankful he never used it.

———•◦•———

In the closing months of 1915, Lucy came down with a head cold and an upper respiratory infection. She had grown very stout and was self-conscious and unhappy about it. Her once-dark hair had turned a snowy white. Much of the luster had faded from her dark eyes. She begged her grandchildren not to remember her as a fat old woman.

Worried that she was unable to shake her illness, some of her children took her to Johns Hopkins in Baltimore for treatment. When she seemed to get a little better, she checked out and went to a Carnegie estate in Waverly, Massachusetts, to recuperate. Waverly was chosen because her doctor lived nearby and son Andrew II and daughter Retta had summer homes in the area.

But instead of getting better, Lucy took a turn for the worse. On a sleeting January 16, 1916, at age sixty-nine, she died in her sleep. Pneumonia was listed as the cause of death.

Louise Carnegie, the wife of brother-in-law Andy, said in a letter to Robert Franks, Andy's former business secretary, "The whole family revolved around Lucy, and life can never be quite the same to any of us. Mr. Carnegie bore the news better than I expected. I tried to break it very gently, and his quiet acceptance of it was very pathetic. He does not say much, but he is not brooding over it."

Lucy had said she wanted to die on her beloved Cumberland. That was not to be, but she had her next-best wish—to be buried there. Her body was interred next to Tom's in the family cemetery. To her immediate left was the grave of her baby son Coley, whose remains also had been reburied there. A short distance away was the new grave of daughter-in-law Gertrude. The great Cumberland matriarch left five sons, three daughters, and fourteen grandchildren as heirs to her vast estate.

One of her grandsons said, "She was a strong-willed lady. When you look at Cumberland and see what she accomplished, she had to be strong willed."

———————

Even then, Lucy controlled Cumberland. Before she died, she had created a complicated trust whose basic purpose was to maintain her sixteen-thousand-acre island estate as a home for her children and grandchildren. Under the trust, none of the lands or mansions could be sold while any of her children was alive. Her fiefdom would dissolve only after all her children were deceased. Her sons Andrew II and Morris and daughter Retta became the estate's first trustees.

Under a second trust, the money to manage the island would come from the rent of the Carnegie family's office building in Pittsburgh.

Lucy's will became the island's Magna Carta. "Every decision about the island was based on that will, which said, 'You can't do this, you can't do that,' " a grandchild said.

But while Lucy's will still called the shots on Cumberland, she no longer held sway over her large brood. While alive, she had been the binding force among her children and grandchildren. For a short while, the unity she hoped to retain persisted. For a time, the life of great leisure she had set on Cumberland—financed by Tom's fortune—continued among her offspring.

Then the family's cohesiveness began weakening. It would take some other strong women to prevent what Lucy feared most—the development of her beautiful island into a place containing thousands of homes, hotels, stores, amusement parks, and God knew what else.

CHAPTER EIGHT

CUMBERLAND'S CHARM BEGAN to wane among Lucy's children and grandchildren.

First, some of them were drawn to the glitz and the big-money possibilities in New York and other cities. Then the Great Depression put a crimp in what was left of the Carnegie fortune, although the family came through the financial upheaval better than many of their wealthy acquaintances. In large part, Lucy's ironclad will protected the family's assets.

But facing a depleted fortune and the advent of heftier income taxes, many of the heirs found themselves in a pinch to maintain the opulence Lucy had introduced them to. Saddled with a trust that left them little latitude in making money from the island, they retrenched. They let go many of their household servants and estate workers and cut corners wherever they could.

Ironically, the first to feel the pinch was Dungeness, once the heart of Cumberland's high society. Andrew II and Bertha, who were married on the mansion's ample steps, tried to maintain the home after Lucy's death but found it too much. In 1925, they vacated the cavernous house and took over the more manageable Stafford mansion, which a grieving Bill Carnegie had given up years earlier.

Dungeness's stained-glass windows and hand-carved doors were boarded up. Most of its furnishings and bric-a-brac were divided by drawn lots among family members, who hauled their prizes to their own homes. Dust covers were draped over furniture pieces no one wanted immediately.

The ice house, the power plant, and other operations that had once served the entire island were shut down because of high operating costs. The bakery was closed. The family began importing ice from the mainland. Each mansion was equipped with its own power system run by gasoline or diesel fuel.

The big boats had to go, too. Shuddering at the cost of keeping up a yacht like those favored by Lucy, her offspring bought a much smaller launch, the *Dream*, to take them to and from the island. When it gave out, they replaced it with a remodeled shrimp trawler equipped with a powerful diesel engine. In deference to Lucy's old yacht, it was named the *Dungeness*.

Abandoning the mother mansion was hard for the family. Some wept. Dungeness had been Cumberland's nerve center, the seat of Lucy Carnegie's wealth and power. The shocking sight of boards nailed over its windows was a stark reminder that the Carnegies' heyday was history.

———◦◦◦———

Stafford was quickly cleaned up and made livable according to Bertha Carnegie's exacting standards. The moldy old pool house was wiped down and reopened for the family's pleasure.

With Andrew, Bertha, and their two daughters now ensconced in their new home, Cumberland's command center shifted to Stafford. Andrew and his family began spending most of the year there. The girls were tutored in the little house behind the mansion where Zabette, Robert Stafford's slave mistress, once lived.

Stafford sprang back to life. Workers began tending a huge kitchen garden. Now, the island's other households sent their servants to Stafford instead of Dungeness for fresh fruit and vegetables, or had the produce delivered by the old ice wagon. Stafford's barnyard again became a clopping, squealing, clucking place after years of idleness. In the fall, a small grinding mill, powered by a bored horse walking in a circle, squeezed sweet juice from sugarcane grown on the island; boiling the juice produced a dark, sticky syrup. At hog-killing time in the winter, freshly killed porkers were dunked into a big vat of boiling water to loosen their hair for easy removal before butchering. Iver Miller, Stafford's head gardener, supplied the Carnegies with venison and wild turkeys. When the family desired turtle eggs in the summer, he excavated them from nests on the beach. Turtle eggs made a rich cake. Some Carnegies liked them better than hen eggs.

Bertha and Andrew tried to maintain the social zeal they had known under Lucy. Life at Stafford—at dinner, at least—was no less formal than it had been at Dungeness. The family and guests were called to meals by a butler in a crisp white jacket and satiny black pants ringing a chime. Dinner was a structured occurrence at the long table, Andrew at one end and Bertha at the other. Andrew always wore a necktie and Bertha a long gown.

Andrew, a champion golfer, often played the nine-hole course next to Stafford. Even then, he wore a tie. In the afternoons, he tore about the island in a blue, two-seat Oldsmobile with a rumble seat. He seldom slowed down for anything. "You see Mr. Andrew coming, you better get off the road and in the bushes," Lester Morris, a Carnegie laborer in the 1930s, said. "If you didn't, he called our boss and say, 'Hey, check them damn boys there. I come up yesterday, and they don't want to give me the road.' "

Andrew liked to tell his wealthy friends in elite clubs up north about his Cumberland encounters. Once, when he was strolling the beach, a small plane landed on the hard-packed sand, and the pilot climbed out.

Andrew thought he looked vaguely familiar. Walking up to Andrew, the lanky fellow introduced himself as Charles Lindbergh. The famed aviator later became close friends with Andrew's oldest daughter, Nancy, and her husband, J. Stillman Rockefeller, Sr., the National City Bank of New York chairman and an emissary for Franklin D. Roosevelt.

In later years, Stafford's old inhabitant, Uncle Bill, was invited back on the island. With Lucy long dead, his relatives had eased off their estrangement of him. He began visiting his old home, sitting on Stafford's porch, and talking to the family, always puffing a cigarette, a shriveled little man who still had his twinkling eyes.

He died in 1944 of jaw cancer. A dentist gave him radium treatments for it, but they left his mouth terribly burned. About the only relief was holding beer in his mouth.

After he died, his sister Floss and niece Lucy Ferguson had a test of wills over who would get his elaborate Queen Anne dining-room chairs. One winter, the chairs were hauled back and forth on the express wagon between Greyfield, Ferguson's home, and the Grange, Floss's home. The feistier Ferguson ultimately got most of them.

Bertha and Andrew were in Boston in March 1943 to have a doctor fix Bertha's arthritic knee. They both caught terrible colds and then came down with pneumonia. Bertha died. Andrew loved her deeply and never was the same afterward. He died of cancer in 1947 at age seventy-seven.

Upon his death, the Peoples Bank in Pittsburgh became the trustee of Lucy Carnegie's estate.

Next to the shuttered Dungeness, Morris and wife Virginia still lived in the Cottage most of the year. They spent the summer in their other home, in Southampton on Long Island. Virginia, who had great musical ability, once said she preferred civilized Southampton over Cumberland. But as she and Morris grew older, they began staying on Cumberland year-round.

After his mother's death, Morris became a penny pincher, refusing to invest in modern conveniences. Even though washing machines could be had, his servants still washed clothes and bed linens by hand, scrubbing them on a washboard in an outbuilding near the mansion. A coal-burning stove heated the water and the irons. It took a whole week to do the laundry, which cost Morris much more money than a washing machine would have. But that economic fact seemed to escape him.

His two sons, Thomas Morrison Carnegie III and Carter Carnegie, did not get along. About the only thing they had in common was a thirst for liquor, their relatives said. Once, when Carter was drunk at a New York City hotel, he punched his left fist through the glass panel of a re-volving door. He cut some ligaments and thenceforth had limited use of his hand.

To shore up his sagging income, he once tried setting up a tung-oil farm on Cumberland—after securing the trustees' permission—and at a leased plantation near Monticello, Florida. He aimed to produce barrels of lucrative tung oil, used in paint and other products. But the market went bust, and he abandoned the project. Tung trees now grow wild on Cumberland, crowding out native vegetation.

Carter's constant drinking didn't help his business ventures, his fam-ily said.

He was being treated for alcoholism in a New York hospital when his father hired a nurse named Polly Stein—a divorcee who had a one-year-old son—to tend him. Even when he was nasty drunk, she stuck close to him. She finally married him. She wanted him to adopt her little boy, Henry, whom she had by her first husband, the owner of a New York fur store. Henry didn't want to be adopted, but according to the law, he had to be twenty-one before he had a say in the matter.

Carter brought Polly to the Cottage, where they spent most of each year with his parents. "I first came to Cumberland late at night," Polly said. "We came to the big dock. I could see just a few lights on, and I could make out the Cottage through the trees. I knew nothing at all. The next morning, I woke up and didn't believe my eyes. I saw such sheer beauty. I was facing Dungeness, and in between, there was a beautifully mowed lawn, like an English garden. And there were these beautiful palm trees."

Perhaps Cumberland's strong-woman magic worked on her, because she quickly took an upper hand at the Cottage. "My mother-in-law had never been in its kitchen," Polly said. "I went in there, and I came out and told my husband, 'I love you, but I'm not eating out of that place. I want it clean.' "

Virginia allowed Polly to take over the kitchen and the mansion's fifteen-member staff. Polly in turn instituted European cooking for the family. Virginia, though, was not happy with her son's marriage to a divorcee with a young child. Morris, on the other hand, loved his new daughter-in-law.

"I'd say to him, 'What do you want for breakfast?' And he'd say, 'I feel like a trout.' So I'd get down to the big dock, and I'd get four or five trout," Polly recalled. "If he wanted a sheepshead or a flounder, I'd go down to the big dock and cast a net, and bring up sheepshead, a flounder, maybe a mullet. We got our own shrimp, small shrimp. We got our own oysters. We got crabs. We drove a little pickup truck down to the dock and could fill it up with crabs in twenty minutes. And if Mr. Carnegie wanted clam fritters, we'd go to the jetties at low tide and get a couple of bushels of clams. And if you wanted fresh pork, you just set the trap, and the next day, you had a two-hundred-pounder. We would smoke about two thousand pounds of pork a year."

The rest of the Carnegies felt that Polly was taking Morris for a ride. He died at the Cottage in 1944, a victim of diabetes and liquor. Virginia moved up north and never came back to Cumberland.

Carter, who had long battled the twin demons of depression and alcoholism, shot himself to death in Palm Beach in August 1957.

Polly died in 1986 in Jacksonville. Her ashes were buried in the Carnegie family cemetery with Morris, Virginia, and Carter.

But long before Carter and Polly died, the Cottage burned down.

Morris's other son, Tom III, was blamed for it. During the winter of 1949-50, five years after Morris died, he came to stay at the Cottage for a few days. Some say he was smoking in bed when he accidentally set the house afire. Others say he built a fire in the fireplace with fatwood and that while he was asleep, the sparks lit a nearby stack of paintings wrapped in paper and muslin.

It's a wonder he wasn't burned up, his family said.

Whatever the reason for the blaze, the house burned to the ground. The caretaker, a black man named Rogers Alberty, saved most of the good china, but fifty fine paintings and ten thousand books—many of them first editions—went up in flames.

With the insurance money, the trustees built a smaller brick house for Tom and Carter near where the Cottage had stood.

Tom, who had played football and baseball at Harvard, was offered a tryout with a major-league baseball team. He didn't make it. When the Carnegie wealth was petering out in the 1930s, he turned his hand to the restaurant business. He built some tourist cabins, a restaurant, and a lounge along U.S. 17 in Kingsland on the Georgia mainland. Long before I-95 was constructed, the two-lane U.S. 17 was the main artery between New York and Florida. Tom named his complex Tomochichi, after the Indian chief who had roamed Cumberland with Colonel James Oglethorpe. Much of Dungeness's remaining furniture, including Lucy's formal dining-room set and the big chair she had sat in at dinner, was moved to the restaurant and cabins.

Tom sold liquor in the lounge, an illegal practice in a dry Georgia. Local authorities conveniently turned their backs on it. Some of them came in with other locals on Saturday nights to dance to the jukebox or the occasional live band. One steady patron was Uncle Bill, who showed up with his entourage to drink and dance the night away.

To further entice tourists, Tom built what he called a zoo next to the cabins. In cages made from chicken wire, wooden slats, and cinder blocks were alligators, rattlesnakes, boa constrictors, and other crawly creatures. The alligators were wrestled from ponds on Cumberland. A black bear and a bald eagle also snared on the island became zoo denizens.

Tom brought in good cooks to run the restaurant kitchen. It became a well-known eatery for Florida-bound tourists. As at other white-owned Southern restaurants of that era, blacks had to order food through a window at the building's side. They were forbidden inside as customers. They could cook the food, though. Most of Tom's cooks were black.

His first marriage was to Dorothy Duncan; their child was Thomas Morrison Carnegie IV, born in 1926. The second marriage was to Blanche Strebeigh; their child was Andrew Carnegie III. They were the half-brothers who would sell their shares of Cumberland to developer Charles Fraser in the late 1960s, triggering near panic in the family. It would take some very strong women to kick Fraser out and persuade Congress to make Cumberland a national seashore. Tom's third marriage also ended in divorce. His heavy drinking was the major factor in his faltering health, business, and pocketbook. He died in St. Augustine in 1954.

———·—·———

Meanwhile, Plum Orchard was reoccupied. The trustees tapped Nancy and Marius Johnston over other family members to take control of the mansion, mostly because the couple had five children and Marius had an independent income. They had to refurnish it, partly with pieces from Dungeness, because the French count had removed nearly everything that wasn't nailed down.

The Johnstons never lived in Plum Orchard full-time, staying there only between Christmas and Easter. Their permanent address was Lexington, Kentucky, where they lived at Marius's family estate, Montrose. The Johnston children went to summer school in Kentucky to make up for school days they lost while on the island.

Marius raised thoroughbreds at Montrose and kept a thoroughbred mare as his personal mount. He once owned the famous racehorse Saracen. Unfortunately, he sold the horse as a yearling, not realizing what the young steed would become.

But Nancy longed for Cumberland. She told family and friends that she gained a certain strength on the island. Given her green thumb, she spent much of her time there in Plum Orchard's lush flower gardens. Her bright delphiniums and hollyhocks won prizes at garden shows, and her calla lilies were amazing.

Marius was known for going down to Cumberland's beach with a loaded rifle when the children were in the surf. He would sit on the car hood, rifle ready in case a shark attacked one of the kids frolicking in the water. His Captain Ahab-like disdain came from his own encounter with a hammerhead, which had chomped a hunk of flesh from his right leg and left a bad scar. "He and Grandmother were surf-casting in the water, and the shark came up and bit him in three places on his leg," granddaughter Nancy Talbott recalled. "Grandmother put a tourniquet on him, and somehow they got into a car and down to Dungeness to get help."

He was a great storyteller. At Plum Orchard, the children would gather around the relaxed Marius, who regaled them with glowing tales of his African safaris and his Arctic expedition. He kept a medical bag in a little downstairs bathroom. When a child got a splinter in a finger or scraped a knee, he treated the simple wound with great ceremony and dried up the tears. He often led the children about the island on expeditions for what he said were "museum pieces." Soon, the spacious shelves in one of Plum Orchard's passageways became the Johnston family's "museum," loaded with arrowheads, shells, bones, skulls, old bottles, and other jetsam found on the island.

The clan at Stafford liked to get together with the Johnstons at Plum Orchard. The chemistry was good between them.

"We would go up to Plum Orchard before supper for cocktail hour," recalled Pebble Rockefeller, Bertha and Andrew II's grandson. "All the grownups—uncles, aunts, cousins—would be there. It was a wonderful smell there of guns and oil, mint and leather from furniture. And then the Kentucky heritage would come out; bourbon was always there in the evening. Aunt Nancy was always fun to see sitting over there in the corner, smoking a cigarette."

Old age had caught up with Nancy. "She was a little teeny-weeny woman," a niece recalled. "She had these mean dachshunds that terrified us. And you know how you get to look like your dog when you get older? Well, she had whiskers and . . . she looked very doggy."

The gathering place was the library to the left of Plum's great front hall. Clad in tweed coats, khaki hunting pants, and plaid wool shirts, the adults, relaxed in an atmosphere of monied grace, chatted about daily adventures on Cumberland and other island goings-on.

With its long corridors, its many rooms, and its nooks and crannies for hiding, Plum Orchard also was ideal for a favorite game, "Watch on the Threshold." The lights were turned off, and children and adults crept about in the dark, trying to take the other team captive or make off with its guarded talisman.

Parties, dances, and predawn duck hunts also continued on Cumberland, though not on as grand a scale as when Lucy was alive. Sometimes, the clans, whooping and hollering, held "rodeos" to break in wild horses. Marius managed those affairs. Some of the broken horses were mated with his thoroughbred stallion brought down from Kentucky to improve the wild herd's genetics. Other times, mounted on their steeds and imagining themselves on the old Chisholm Trail, Carnegie cousins, aunts, and uncles spent all day rounding up the cows and driving them to a cattle dip just north of Stafford. It was great sport and hard work herding the skittish cows. Bellowing and kicking, they were forced through a twenty-five-foot-long trough, where they were coated with a pesticide to ward off ticks, screw worms, and other parasites.

On the south end, the forlorn Dungeness mansion had become a wonderfully mysterious place for young Carnegies to prowl. "It went on and on, with lots of nice dark corners to explore," Pebble Rockefeller remembered. "We'd go up to the tower and look down over the marsh. You could imagine Mama Carnegie and that story about her, when she always had a little boy up there watching for her when she went out in her boat, so she wouldn't fall asleep and drift away down the channel."

Carnegie children loved to take visitors through Dungeness at night. "You had to close the doors behind you, and then you had to find your way up to the tower in the dark," one of them recalled.

The old pool house, also closed, was heaven for kids. "It was my favorite place on the island," Pebble Rockefeller said. "On rainy days, all of us cousins would go down there and swing on those great rings over the water and have the most marvelous time."

It was the place where they played their biggest practical jokes. "At night, when there were no lights, we would go in with flashlights and flash on the rings," a Carnegie remembered. "Somebody that was on the inside crowd, who had been there before, would swing across to show how it should be done. We had the flashlights on so they could see the next ring. Then you let somebody who was new try it, and a lot of people were so cocky they wouldn't bother to wear a bathing suit, just do it in their street clothes. And then we would turn the flashlight off when they got to the middle."

———————

The great turning point for Cumberland and the whole Georgia coast was World War II. The government viewed the sparsely populated islands as exceptionally vulnerable to German infiltrators, who could land on the beaches from U-boats and steal inland.

The military set up radio stations and outposts on Cumberland and every other island of significance. The main missions of the troops deployed on them were to maintain constant vigilance for submarines, to scan the skies for enemy aircraft, and to patrol the beaches by foot and horseback to collar—and shoot, if necessary—enemy agents who might sneak ashore.

Most of the Carnegies left Cumberland for the war's duration. An army encampment called Lucy's Village was set up near Dungeness. The mansion's tower proved perfect for sky scanning. Some old servant quarters became barracks. The patrol's horses were quartered in the old stables. The pool house with its big swimming pool and gym full of exercise equipment was an ideal recreation hall for the troops. At the old laundry house, aging washing machines were cranked up to turn out clean uniforms and fresh sheets.

The enemy never made an overt threat against Cumberland. Its heat, rattlesnakes, and alligators were greater dangers. Troops from places like Kansas and Nebraska were not used to the sixteen-foot gators they encountered in the ponds and alongside the sandy roads, where the hissing reptiles stood their ground against approaching Jeeps and trucks.

When the war ended, the military quickly left Cumberland. Within a year, few traces that it was ever there could be found. But something else was gone. Before the war, enough money had come in from Lucy Carnegie's trust fund to keep the mansions, outbuildings, and grounds in decent repair. But postwar inflation and higher labor costs made running the island as Lucy intended it should be run a daunting financial challenge.

Everything had gone up. Servants were hard to come by. Men and women once paid a dollar a day on Cumberland had gotten used to heftier wages earned building army bases, airfields, Liberty ships, and tanks on the mainland.

The Carnegies cut more corners, but there were few left to cut. With little money coming in to maintain them, docks rotted, roads became impassable, and buildings caved in from neglect. The magnificent gardens and lawns surrounding Dungeness went to seed. The big fountain stopped flowing. Walkways cracked and crumbled. The hedges once clipped so precisely became shapeless blobs. Greenhouses once lush with tropical flora collapsed. And the once-glorious Dungeness became pitiful.

"A caretaker sometime in 1950 let us into the mansion," said Shirley Ann Ward, who was visiting her Carnegie-employed sister at the time. "One thing that really impressed me was going through the library and seeing the beautiful red wallpaper there. But I saw the books of Lucy Carnegie lying around on the floor and different places. They were lying like they were just intentionally put into disarray, like someone had been through the house and was just throwing things to the side. And I thought, 'What a waste.' "

One family member ripped out the prized olive-wood parquet floor and paneling and used it to build a boat that he sailed to the South Pacific. The marble washstands, the statuary, and the fireplace mantels—including the one with the engraved quotation Andrew Carnegie had demanded—were taken. The Chinese gong that had summoned Lucy's guests to dinner was toted to Greyfield. In several rooms, rainwater got in and the floors buckled and rotted, making it dangerous for anyone who trod on them.

Lucy's daughter Floss entertained a fleeting notion of restoring the old place but realized quickly that the cost of living in it and maintaining it would be beyond the means of any surviving Carnegie.

Dungeness's final hour came quickly, dramatically, unexpectedly. A few hours after sunset on June 24, 1959, some island workers spotted the great house on fire. It had suddenly blazed up on the third floor. Fed by tinder-dry heart of pine, old wallpaper, and rotting curtains, the fire roared through the fifty-nine-room manor. The bright orange glow could be seen as far as Brunswick, forty miles away.

A Carnegie descendant, Joe Graves, Jr., his fiancée, and some Kentucky friends were spending a few days at Plum Orchard at the time. "We were entertaining the manager of the island, Hugh Schloss, and his wife," Graves said. "They were up for drinks before supper, and one of the hands came up in a great rush and said, 'The house is on fire.'

"We rushed down there. We had no water supply and no firefighting

Ruins of the Carnegies' Dungeness, which burned at the hand of an arsonist in 1959
Courtesy of the National Park Service

equipment. We couldn't put the fire out, but we worked hard to prevent it from spreading because when the sparks would land in the trees, they would catch on fire. If we couldn't put the fire out, we cut down the tree."

The fire burned furiously all night. By morning, a hot, glowing shell of the structure was all that stood. Only the wind blowing from the south saved the tabby house and the Dungeness records stored in it.

The prevailing theory is that a disgruntled poacher, shot by a Dungeness caretaker a few weeks earlier, sneaked back to the island and set the blaze. The same culprit also was blamed for scuttling the *Dungeness*.

For the most part, the heirs' sojourns at Stafford, Plum Orchard, and the Grange became shorter and shorter, dwindling to only a few days or a few weeks of the year, rather than months.

One exception was Morrie Johnston, one of Nancy Carnegie's children by James Hever. During the 1950s, he spent months on end alone at

Plum Orchard trying to recapture the love and freedom he had known as a child on Cumberland. In the library, he kept a big vase of his mother's white calla lilies, which still blossomed in profusion on the grounds.

Bright and good looking, Morrie had married a Lexington girl from a prominent family. They had a son and two daughters. But Morrie wrestled with the demon alcohol. The more he drank, the more belligerent he got. He ended up divorced and alienated from his family.

Some men from the mainland occasionally brought him a case of whiskey. He in turn called them his "guests." Sometimes, they cooked steaks and fish in the big fireplace in Plum's entry hall. What most of those men really wanted, though, was to hunt on the island, a privilege granted to guests of family members.

Morrie sat in the house and sipped his liquor. He was nocturnal. He played the violin, walking about the big house in the darkness for hours fiddling "Some Enchanted Evening." He slept most of the day.

"He was always calling me up to Plum Orchard for something," said Howard "Smitty" Smith, a mechanic and handyman. "One day, I met him upstairs, and he offered me a drink, and I sat there and drank with him. Then he said, 'Go in there and get Joe,' this big old dog. He wanted me to walk Joe through every room in Plum Orchard and then get him to the back door and kick him out. Morrie thought that if I walked Joe through all the rooms, the fleas would jump on the dog, and when I got him to the back door, all the fleas would be gone from Plum. But it didn't work.

"Morrie had a motorcycle, a big old Harley-Davidson. He wanted me to put it back in running order. So I showed him how to ride it, and he took off on it. The next thing I knew, he sent word to come pick it up; he never wanted to see it again. He had tried to crank it. I told him, 'When you crank it, put all your weight on it, and make sure it goes through or it will kick you.' Well, it kicked him, and his heel hit the guard and knocked out a chunk of flesh. His motorcycle days were over then.

"And he was always wanting me to shoot that gator in the pond behind Plum Orchard. You know, I could walk up to that gator without my gun, and he'd just look at me. But when I went there with the gun, he would dive. I reckon that gator had been shot at before, and I never did get him."

Morrie spent his last years on the French Riviera. When his liver gave out after years of alcohol abuse, he was cremated and his ashes buried in Cumberland's Carnegie cemetery.

———————

Some twenty gawky-eyed people saunter across the flat, weed-eaten lawn toward the front door of the still-handsome Plum Orchard. Browsing on some stringy grass near the front steps is a brown, bony mare, seemingly oblivious to the squinting people snapping her picture. This must be a prime grazing spot, because horse droppings are everywhere.

The visitors paid an extra sixteen dollars apiece at the Cumberland Island National Seashore visitor center in St. Marys for the tour, held the first Sunday of each month. The ferryboat brought them up the Brickhill River and let them off at Plum Orchard's dock.

Park ranger Charlotte Friese, wearing a green-and-gray uniform and a Smokey Bear hat, unlocks the weighty front door. It groans and scrapes as she pushes it open. The visitors step into the grand entrance hall, whose walls are hung with faded linen wallpaper. There are huge, light brown stains in the coffered ceiling and the wall near the door—water damage.

The guests' eyes are drawn quickly to the humongous fireplace set in the beautiful arched alcove, or inglenook, as Europeans call it. It is graced with dark walnut paneling in which intricate designs are carved. Cozy benches flank each side. With a fireplace like this, one would long for a cold winter night. "It's wonderful to have the inglenook here for you to see when you walk in," Friese says. "It immediately makes order out of so large a house." Carnegies snuggled up in the cozy inglenook—a refreshingly cool spot in the summer and a warm niche in the winter when a fire was roaring, she says.

The floors are parquet. On the walls are intricate sconces and other

The inglenook fireplace in Plum Orchard's entrance hall
Courtesy of the National Park Service

fine detailing—the work of artisans who would command a fortune for their craftsmanship if they were working today. There is something fascinating, riveting, about these remnants of a leisure class whose only duty was to bask in life's pleasures.

The visitors go left out of the entry hall into the twenty-by-eighteen-foot library. "This was the main gathering place for the Johnstons when they lived here," Friese notes. Before and after dinner, they sprawled on comfortable chairs and sofas to chat, read, play chess, sip cocktails, and play charades. The wallpaper has a lily pattern, which reminded the family of the water lilies at Lake Whitney a few miles away. In the room's center, sitting on a mahogany table that is the only piece remaining from Margaret and George's day, is a magnificent, pink Victorian dollhouse. Its Lilliputian organdy curtains are stiff with age, but its tiny French doors still open. It once belonged to Nancy Johnston. Amy Carter, the former president's daughter, was so enraptured by it when she visited Plum as a little girl that she wanted to take it home with her.

The procession continues down a long gallery in the west wing, added in 1906, to a huge room with a marble-faced fireplace, oak paneling, and beam ceiling.

"We are in the drawing room, also known as the gun room or the music room," says Friese. In the glory days, the room's cabinets were crammed with shotguns, polo mallets, fencing swords, and other sporting paraphernalia. The walls were hung with trophies of the hunt. Floor-to-ceiling bookcases stood at both ends. The musty room is empty now except for an out-of-tune baby-grand Steinway with stained yellow keys and a table holding a cloudy amber-glass Tiffany lamp that belonged to Lucy Carnegie at Dungeness. Friese sidesteps a question about the lamp's value. A stout, fiftyish woman whispers that the Park Service probably doesn't want it known.

On the other side of the great entrance hall is an elegant dining room, where a long, polished table is set with formal place settings, as if dinner guests in evening attire are expected any minute. "Dinners at Plum Orchard were formal affairs, with two butlers dressed in green livery attending," Friese says. On the east wall hang original oil portraits of Thomas and Andrew Carnegie, whose fortunes made possible all of this sumptuousness. Someone asks if Andrew was ever here. "Yes," Friese replies. "He came for several weeks at a time. Before he was married, he spent two months on Cumberland recuperating from typhoid fever. It was right after his mother died."

The formal stairway winds above the fireplace and behind a large cornice supported by two Ionic columns. Upstairs in the master suite, Lucy Carnegie's imposing sleigh bed, brought over from Dungeness, stands on a parquet floor. The commodious bathrooms have enormous showerheads and soap dishes with exquisite detail. Steam-heated racks that once warmed towels still stand in the his-and-hers dressing rooms. Off the bedrooms, the linen closets with rich walnut cabinetry are as large as today's average kitchen. In some rooms, the plaster has fallen in large chunks.

Back downstairs, the wing extending to the house's rear contains what were once the servants' dining room, the family's breakfast area, and the kitchen, whose monstrous stoves are now rusted out. Next to it, the pantry has drawers marked "Breakfast Mats" and "Luncheon Napkins," suggesting a high level of household organization.

The group comes into the east wing, leading off the piazza. Here is the twelve-foot-deep indoor swimming pool—now cracked, peeling, and drier than a bone—along with the squash court and the dressing rooms. Friese cautions the visitors to stay away from the pool's edge because there is no railing. Carnegie children, she says, often complained that the pool's water smelled of sulfur and was icy even on hot summer days.

She asks if there are any questions. The stout woman has an opinion. "It seems to me that this is a waste," she says. "Here's this beautiful home not even lived in, while there are so many people who don't have a home."

The tour is over. Friese wraps up: "Lucy Carnegie wanted to keep her children near her, so she built this and other mansions for them on Cumberland. This gives you some idea of the Carnegie wealth."

———————

But for all her wealth, there was one part of Cumberland that Lucy never got—the island's north end. She wanted that, too, but the people living there refused to sell to her.

CHAPTER NINE

CUMBERLAND'S NORTH END, generally known as High Point, comprises the 10 percent of the island Lucy Carnegie never owned. A handful of white families who together controlled about fifteen hundred acres there refused to sell to her. Their yeoman farmer ancestors had purchased the land from Phineas Nightingale, who had been trying to keep it out of Robert Stafford's hands. Some of them boasted forebears who served in Colonel James Oglethorpe's regiment. They thought Lucy pushy, overbearing, and a Yankee to boot. They loved the island, too, and had no intention of letting go their share of it.

The north end also was where many of Robert Stafford's ex-slaves and their descendants came to live after the Civil War, in shanties with roofs of thatched palmetto fronds. Several of them later would move up to more substantial housing—rustic cabins in the little village known as the Settlement.

In the 1890s, when Lucy still was trying to snatch full control of Cumberland, the Settlement was at its zenith, if it really ever had one. Most of its inhabitants worked for the sawmill at High Point or for the sprawling resort that had opened in 1875 on the north end. The remaining residents worked either for the Carnegies at their various mansions or for the smaller white families—the Clubbs, the Millers, the Bunkleys, the Burbanks—who owned most of the north end. Some of those families together owned the resort.

The breezy spa drew scores of middle-class vacationers and conventioneers from around Georgia during the spring and summer. Methodists, Baptists, and professional groups like the State Dental Society held conventions there.

A rumbling horse-drawn trolley on steel rails met guests arriving by steamboat at the two-hundred-foot-long High Point Wharf and hauled them to the hotel complex. The central structure was the rambling Cumberland Island Hotel, which stood just off Christmas Creek and had a Moorish white gingerbread facade.

Guests opted for a room in the hotel or for one of several stand-alone cottages. Many stayed two or three weeks, often bringing their black maids—status symbols of a sort—to look after the children. They took the trolley to the beach, where they built sand castles, reclined on blankets, and frolicked in the surf in baggy bathing suits that covered most of their bodies. If they spied an egg-laying loggerhead on the beach at night, they took great delight in riding her like a horse back into the surf. Digging up the eggs was just as much fun. Guests were showed how to poke sharp sticks deep into the sand to find a nest. Drawing forth a punctured egg meant there was a hidden cache.

Guests also had opportunities for sailing, rowing, motoring, and fishing. There were bowling alleys, a shooting gallery, a livery stable with fine saddle horses, and an orchestra. Interested parties could arrange horse-drawn carriage excursions to Cumberland's south end to see the prestigious Dungeness mansion when the Carnegies were away. The all-day, thirty-six-mile round trip was made one way on Grand Avenue and the other way on the beach, depending on the tides. At low tide, the beach was as wide and smooth as a paved road. The hotel packed a lunch for the sightseers to munch along the way. Fresh water to drink gushed up from free-flowing wells along the road.

The Settlement had its beginnings in the late 1880s, when Mason Burbank, one of the hotel's owners, acquired five acres at High Point near Half Moon Bluff, named for the steep, red-clay banks along a concave curve of land overlooking the salt marsh around Christmas Creek. He divided the wooded tract into fifty lots, each measuring fifty feet by a hundred feet. Ten-foot-wide roads were cut through the nascent village. The lots were then sold to black workers. By setting the lots aside for employees, the hotel owners simply were trying to provide themselves some assurance of having loyal, long-term laborers. The pride of ownership might keep them from drifting over to the mainland.

Most of the workers were only one generation removed from slavery. Two of them, Primus Mitchell and his wife, Amanda, actually were born slaves on Robert Stafford's plantation. Their seven daughters and the daughters' husbands populated the Settlement with their own children.

Amanda was a strange woman. She was born in 1830, long before there were thoughts of a civil war. By all accounts, she was a good mother and a sweet grandmother, but she also was a voodoo practitioner—what island people called a "cunjuh woman." She could conjure up spells to make people well or to make them sick.

Occasionally, she came to the hotel kitchen for a snack. Perhaps because of her witch-doctor reputation, she was treated with great deference. But one day when she showed up, the pompous cook ordered her out. He was new on the job. Unused to such ill treatment, she started mumbling something and shuffling toward him. He grabbed a pothook in each hand and began swishing them at her. Fellow hotel workers, black and white, pressed up against the wall in fright, thinking the cook would be struck dead. Instead, he shouted, "Get out of here, old woman! I ain't scared of the devil, much less you." Amanda retreated. She turned and slowly walked out of the kitchen and back to her cabin a mile away. The workers were impressed. They laughed, for they no longer were afraid of the old hag called "Witch Mandy." Her prestige took a nosedive. But within a year, the cook was dead of tuberculosis. Once again, Amanda enjoyed great respect, for the island people thought she was the cause.

She died in 1902, eight years before Primus, who was still piddling around for the Carnegies when he passed on at nearly a hundred years of age. They were buried in the little High Point Cemetery, located at the end of a winding path down from the First African Baptist Church.

Carved out of a grove of gnarled oaks in the thick forest, the cemetery today holds the bones of both blacks and whites who lived on the north end. Blacks' graves are segregated from whites', but wild hogs root around both alike. Rusting wrought-iron fences enclose the whites' graves; a low brick wall surrounds the blacks'. To get the bricks, some of the Settlement's residents knocked down the chimneys of old slave cabins.

The gravestones are a who's who of the Settlement's original occupants. The most poignant reads,

> Uncle Primus Mitchell and wife Amanda
> Born slaves at Stafford
> Faithful field hands on Cumberland Island until death

Nancy Carnegie Rockefeller, daughter of Andrew Carnegie II, erected the marker, now chipped and lichen covered.

The Settlement's population began dwindling after Lucy Carnegie's death in 1916, when her children and grandchildren slashed the size of the island's work force. Several Carnegie employees living at the Settlement lost their jobs. More jobs were lost when the old sawmill on the north end closed. But the biggest blow fell in 1920, when the resort shut

(Left)
*Primus Mitchell supposedly witnessed
the burial of Lighthorse Harry Lee on
Cumberland Island when he was a
young boy. After emancipation,
Primus worked for the Carnegies.*
Courtesy of the National Park Service

(Below)
*Headstone on the graves of Primus and
Amanda Mitchell in High Point
Cemetery. The marker was placed there
by the Carnegies.*
Courtesy of the National Park Service

UNCLE PRIMUS MITCHELL
AND WIFE AMANDA
BORN SLAVES AT STAFFORD
FAITHFUL FIELD HANDS ON
UMBERLAND ISLAND UNTIL DEATH

down, most of its former patrons opting for the more accessible spas on St. Simons Island and the new resorts springing up in Florida.

A quickly organized group of rich Georgians who called themselves the Cumberland Island Club bought the hotel property. One member was Howard Candler, Sr., of Atlanta, the former Coca-Cola chairman whose father, Asa Griggs Candler, had introduced Coke to the world. Despite its members' wealth, the club soon ran into financial straits. Members bickered over the cost of fixing up and maintaining the old hotel complex. The club dissolved in 1930. Howard Candler and his son, Howard Jr., then bought the property and more than a thousand acres surrounding it, which was just about all of High Point. The old hotel complex became a private retreat for the Candlers. They built a couple of summer homes—though not as ostentatious as the Carnegie mansions—along with an airplane landing strip, a hangar, barns, and other structures. They named their estate High Point.

A few of the Settlement's unemployed residents found work with the Candlers. They and others still working for the Carnegies kept the little village alive. In 1937, the future was still bright enough for them to construct a new First African Baptist Church from salvaged lumber. It replaced a crude log structure they had worshiped in since 1893, when the church was founded. The tiny new sanctuary would be where John F. Kennedy, Jr., married Carolyn Bessette fifty-nine years later.

———————

Beulah Alberty was the Settlement's unofficial mayor. Had she been born white, she may have vied with Lucy Carnegie for power on Cumberland. As it was, she was one of the strongest woman ever on the island.

She was plump and gray-haired and smoked a pipe. She was fond of going to a beautician in Fernandina when she had the time and could afford it. She made gut-burning moonshine in the back of her bungalow in the middle of the Settlement. In the living room, she ran day-long poker games.

But in no way was she a bad person, her close-knit network of neighbors, family, and friends emphasized. Her purpose in life was noble—to see that her niece Peggy, the daughter of her dead sister Viola, got a good education, so that one day she could help school the black children of the South. To that aim, Beulah scraped up dollars wherever she could.

She and Viola were born in the Settlement. Their mother was Renda Mitchell Alberty, one of Primus and Amanda Mitchell's seven daughters. Their father was William Alberty, one of three brothers who lived on the north end. William's brother Rogers Alberty kept up the rose garden at Dungeness for Lucy Carnegie. Later, he worked at the Cottage; it was he who tried to save the prized books, paintings, and china when it burned down. William cut timber and labored at the sawmills that sprang up occasionally on Cumberland. In between those jobs, he worked with Renda at the hotel. Renda also did laundry for the north end's white families, picking up clothes and bed linens at the beginning of the week and returning them clean and fresh-smelling at week's end.

But even on isolated Cumberland, the Albertys did not escape racial discord. In August 1911, Ed Fader, son of a ship pilot living on the north end, got into an argument with William Alberty. The true cause has been forgotten, but it may have been over Fader's operating a liquor still on a tiny uninhabited island near Cumberland. Some say he suspected William of telling local authorities about it. Whatever the reason, part of the Albertys' cabin was dynamited. William and daughter Beulah were injured. There seemed little doubt that Fader was the perpetrator, but he claimed he had spent the night digging clams on the other side of Cumberland. Hearing about the explosion, his wife, unaware of his possible involvement, gathered food and medical supplies to help the Albertys. But when she went to their cabin, an angry Renda met her at the door with a hatchet and ordered her away.

A couple of days later, Fader, armed with a shotgun, drove his buggy to the Albertys' home. William, holding a loaded rifle, stood in his doorway. Renda was at an open window with another gun. Fader fired first. Buckshot and flying splinters hit both William and Renda, slightly injuring them. They fired back, hitting the buggy. Fader whipped his horse and sped away.

A preliminary hearing was held in superior court, but the grand jury declined to indict Fader. Nothing else was done. In Georgia in 1911, it was difficult for an all-white jury to convict a white man of shooting at blacks.

After that, the families managed to steer clear of one another.

———•—•———

Beulah attended the Selden Institute in Brunswick, a private school for blacks run by Episcopal missionaries from the North. She got a half-decent education—far better than what the vast majority of Southern black women of her era received.

Viola died in 1938, leaving behind Peggy, her only child. Beulah swore that the bright youngster would have a good upbringing and schooling and would help lead black children of the South out of oppression and ignorance.

To get the money for Peggy's education, Beulah taught in a country school in Camden County. But the pay was lousy and the work unsteady. The school often closed when it ran out of funds or when students' parents demanded the kids help plant or harvest crops, cut timber, butcher hogs, or do anything else needed on the farm.

Beulah found more regular work with the Carnegies on Cumberland, cooking for the help at Dungeness and cleaning and cooking in the other mansions. Living at the Settlement and having no car, she sometimes had to walk all the way to the south end if she couldn't hitch a ride. When she got enough money to buy a car, she needed gas to run it. Cumberland's families learned not to leave gas cans in unlocked places or to leave fuel in their cars when they departed the island, for Beulah had a knack for siphoning.

The wages from the Carnegies still fell short of what Beulah needed for Peggy's schooling, so she turned to other moneymaking schemes. She trapped furry gray raccoons, tacked up the hides on barns and other structures to cure, then sold the hides. She raised a few head of cattle and lots of grunting hogs. If she found an unmarked pig in the woods, it soon sported her mark, even though its mother might have someone else's brand. In addition to concocting whiskey at her jerry-built still, she made sweet wines from elderberries, wild muscadines, and other fruits growing on the island. Saturday afternoons, at the end of their work week, the black workers from "down below"—as they called the south end—trooped up to Beulah's house, a pretty place surrounded by red, white, and lavender azaleas and winter-blooming pink camellias. There, they could drop a nickel into the slot of her beat-up jukebox, gamble a little at poker, or buy a tangy barbecued pork dinner for seventy-five cents. When they headed back to their south-end quarters, they toted a week's supply of her homemade hooch with them.

"Peggy was well educated, and nobody worried much about some of the ways Beulah got the money," said the late Mary Miller, the north end's unofficial historian. "It was for a good cause."

———————

One of Beulah's old classmates at the Selden Institute was a light-skinned black man named Bobby Rischarde. She ran into him one day on the mainland. She had not seen him in years. He told Beulah that he and his wife, Della, were retiring and were planning to buy a small house—an unusual one shaped like a ship—in Fernandina. Beulah said that was nice but suggested they also buy a retreat on Cumberland. They could live there, she said, and when they had to go to the mainland, they could stay at their Fernandina place. Bobby liked the idea.

Beulah had just the place in mind. Her elderly uncle Rogers Alberty had moved to the mainland and sold her his house—a small, red-painted frame structure—in the Settlement. Unbeknownst to Bobby and Della, she had paid only seventy dollars for it. She sold it to the Rischardes for seven hundred, the profit going toward Peggy's education. Bobby and Della moved into what they called their "red barn," only two hundred feet from the First African Baptist Church.

They brought a dab of continental flair to the Settlement. Bobby was a porter for Air France, which paid him well and allowed him to travel all over the world. He was a man of impeccable dress and manners. Popeyed, his head shaved bald, he had a Mr. Magoo likeness. In his work, he met the famous and the infamous, from Duke Ellington to Lucky Luciano. He talked knowingly of the Astors and the Vanderbilts and other acquaintances.

He grew up in Brunswick on the Georgia coast. His forebears, he said, were a New Orleans slave owner named Rischarde and an attractive slave girl who bore the master's twelve children. Bobby's tender grand-mother raised him, supported by the earnings of his flamboyant aunt, who

Bobby Rischarde's cabin in the Settlement
Courtesy of the National Park Service

ran a whorehouse for Brunswick's white gentry. Bobby remembered her as resembling Diana Ross. She had a feisty temper and wore rustling silks purchased from fine department stores in New York. She made money enough to send him to Atlanta Baptist College (now Morehouse College) in Atlanta, where he knew W. E. B. Du Bois, the influential author and educator who helped lay the foundation for the civil-rights movement decades later. Bobby also shined white men's boots at the famed Herndon Barber Shop on Atlanta's Peachtree Street. Herndon's, which catered exclusively to whites, was one of the biggest and fanciest barbershops in the United States, with twenty-five chairs on a marble floor. Atlanta's power structure and elite congregated there. You could get a shave, a shower, and a massage—and, of course, a great haircut.

Bobby served in World War I, after which, like many men of color in the South, he headed north to the promised land, where black people made better wages and faced fewer hassles. Ending up in New York, he worked at several jobs before becoming an Air France porter.

Living in his same apartment house in Harlem was a poised, strikingly beautiful black woman named Adele, whom everyone called Della. She had earned a master's degree in speech therapy from New York University and taught mentally retarded children at Bellevue Hospital. One of her private students was the son of a Gimbel's Department Store executive. He left her a goodly sum of money. She painted, wrote poetry, and was a gifted musician, her favorite instrument being the harp. She and Bobby married and began traveling together. In some of their favorite places, they made investments—a "windmill house" in the countryside near Lisbon, Portugal, and a tract in the Adirondacks in upstate New York.

But in retirement, Cumberland became their favorite place. Bobby spent much of his time fixing up the frame house, wandering the woods, and throwing a cast net in Christmas Creek. Della said she wanted something more substantial than the little red house, so Bobby built a small brick home for her near the cemetery at High Point. There, she slept, played her harp, painted, and penned her poems.

"I would go up to the Settlement and sit for hours and watch her paint in her studio there," Gogo Ferguson said. "She was a mentor. There was such an amazing elegance about that woman. She was so soft-spoken and so elegant and always had that tiara—a shark's-tooth tiara—on her head for any formal occasion."

Bobby and Della brought a refinement never before approached in the Settlement. Their taste for good food, good wine, good music, and good company was matched only by their wealthy white neighbors. Visitors to Bobby's little place found a certain grace and charm. Pots and pans hung neatly in the tiny kitchen. Shelves held aromatic herbs. A well-stocked bar held fine cocktail glasses and good whiskey. A silver coffee urn with white china cups and saucers sat tidily on a little chrome table. The shell of a loggerhead turtle lay by the fireplace. The long table on which Bobby and Della took their meals was beneath a window that caught the full splendor of Cumberland's sunsets. On a wall hung two of Bobby's most cherished documents—Della's master's degree and the deed to his Cumberland property.

Outside, in a makeshift garage, he parked his 1949 Jeep; the oldest Jeep on the island, it had a roof made of red boards. On a drying rack, he cured the fish he and Della caught in Christmas Creek. Nearby was a scuppernong grape arbor—a hand-lettered sign called it "the Carousel"—from whose fruit he made a wine he kept in Coca-Cola bottles, in deference to his north-end neighbors, the Candlers. He stored the wine in a pungently sweet wine cellar dubbed "the Conchshell." In front of his house, he had a collection of what he called his "statuettes"—stumps and driftwood picked up during his walks about the island. The gnarls, cracks, and protuberances in the wood reminded him of certain people, he said.

A gourmet cook, he loved to entertain. In his early seventies, with seemingly no haste or fuss, he could whip up a scrumptious impromptu meal when guests suddenly called. Or he could spend hours carefully preparing an elegant seven-course dinner, served with great ceremony by candlelight under the spreading oaks. The guests might include college educators from up north, his friend and neighbor Sam Candler, some of the Carnegies, conservationists from Atlanta, or even the Candlers' handyman, Jesse Bailey, still muddy from a day in the creeks and marshes.

At his dinners, hors d'oeuvres were set out on a little outdoor table. Wedges of Camembert and black caviar were served on toast with a slice of lemon. Guests drank Cutty Sark from frosted glasses. Bobby would lift his polished silver mug in a toast to Cumberland. "Such a wonderful place," he would say. Dinner was served continental-style, a crisp green salad first, then perhaps a pot roast stuffed with potatoes, broccoli, and a side dish of pork, over which he poured a rich sauce concocted from his homemade beer.

In the fall, he had "low country boils." He built a fire under a big black kettle and half filled it with water. When it was boiling, he tossed in chopped-up lemons, Old Bay seasoning, and about as much Tabasco sauce as the tongue could stand. Then he dumped in sweet Vidalia onions and small red potatoes. When the taters began to soften, he added chunks of pork sausage and whole ears of corn. When the water boiled again, he pitched in several pounds of peeled shrimp, the main ingredient. When the shrimp turned bright pink after a few minutes, he dipped out the concoction and spread it on a table for everyone.

After dinner, barefoot and stretched out in a lounge chair, relaxed in shorts and a loose-fitting shirt, he would tell stories about his childhood in Brunswick, about his aunt and her bawdyhouse, and about his global travels. He might talk about the futility of war or the discrimination he had endured as a child in Brunswick and as a young man in Atlanta. He would discuss the arts, theater, and music, especially that of Duke Ellington and Count Basie, and express his philosophy of work: "Eight months a year is enough for any man."

The talk, though, inevitably came back to Cumberland. He would speak of man's need for beauty and solitude. He was quite certain he had lived a thousand years ago on the island. He said heaven was not somewhere else, but rather right here on earth. "We're living in heaven this minute, right here on Cumberland," he would say. He condemned those who wanted to develop the island, "to rape and despoil it."

He said he believed in a superior being, in God, but had never been persuaded to join an organized religious group. That did not stop him, though, from helping his fellow Settlement dwellers take care of the First African Baptist Church. He and the others painted it each year. "I feel I'm doing something for God when I take care of the church, and that makes me feel good," he said.

Somewhere along the line, one of the Candlers introduced him to Jimmy Carter. Carter fell under Bobby's charm and became an occasional guest at his soirees under the oaks. When Carter was elected president, Bobby and Della received engraved invitations to the inaugural. They spent the night in the White House's Lincoln Bedroom. Bobby said later that he and Della did not go to the inaugural parties because they didn't have clothes for the affairs.

Della died unexpectedly while in Fernandina. She was buried in the cemetery at High Point, near the graves of Primus and Amanda Mitchell. Someone played a stirring harp piece at her funeral.

Bobby couldn't quite cope with her death. He went to pieces, friends said. The zest for living seeped out of him. He gave his windmill house in Portugal to the man who looked after it. The property in upstate New York was given to another family. He sold his land and house at the Settlement to the Park Service for the new national seashore. Then he developed cancer. For a while, he was in the veterans' hospital in Lake City, Florida. Realizing he wasn't going to recover, he gave away his last property, the ship house in Fernandina, to the man who built it. He spent his last days in a nursing home in Jacksonville. Since he'd given away everything, there was no money for funeral expenses.

But the many friends he had made along the way raised the money for his burial. A boat was arranged to bring his body to the Dungeness dock. From there, a truck would transport the casket to the cemetery. As it backed onto the dock to receive the pall, its whole back end sunk through some rotten wood and dangled just above the water. A big tractor had to be brought in to pull it out. Then, impeded by low-hanging live-oak branches, the wheezing truck made a slow trip to the north end. Some of the limbs had to be cut by whining chain saws to get Bobby's casket to the cemetery.

The thirty-minute graveside ceremony was simple and dignified. People spoke of their love and respect for Bobby. Then he was buried next to his beloved Della. There was no music. He had once said he wanted his funeral celebrated with a cocktail party and three pieces of music— "Clair de Lune," Rubinstein's Melody in F, and Duke Ellington's "Prelude to a Kiss." Instead, coffee and doughnuts were served at Greyfield Inn.

"Here's to you, Jessie, you old black bastard," Bobby would say in a toast to his friend Jessie Bailey. For Bobby, it was an endearment. If Jessie was offended, he never once let on.

Jessie was not of the Settlement, but he might as well have been, since he hung out there more often than not. He mostly drank, fished, and did chores for the Candlers, but in the process, he became one of Cumberland's most famous residents. Stories were written about him in magazines and newspapers. He, too, was friends with Jimmy Carter, although he was not invited to the White House. Carter got a kick out of Jessie's calling him Jimmy when he was governor and, later, president. Jessie took Carter fishing in Christmas Creek and tried to teach him how to throw a cast net. Once, when someone told Jessie that Carter was running for the nation's highest office, he said, "Jimmy run for president? He'll win. He know how to talk to people. But I can show him something about throwing that net."

Jessie was strong but not big. He spoke gruffly and abruptly yet was gentle as the dew. He spoke in the lilting Gullah dialect of the Georgia sea islands, a patois nearly incomprehensible to outsiders. He always wore a dirty, paint-spattered hat and a stubble of white whiskers. A lit Camel was stuck most of the time between his lips. The whites of his eyes seemed always bloodshot, probably because he drank too much. But no matter how much liquor he sipped, he was always coherent.

Born in 1916 on Sapelo, north of Cumberland, he was a member of the well-known Bailey family of that island. His cousin by marriage was Cornelia Walker Bailey, long the matriarch of Sapelo's tiny African-American village, Hog Hammock, a collection of small wooden bungalows, a church, and a store. She claimed to be a descendant of Bilali, an African chieftain before he was captured, chained aboard a slave ship, and dispatched to Georgia.

Growing up on Sapelo, Jessie helped raise his sister's son and bragged that he was an expert diaper changer. He watched his back because he believed in the hags, ha'nts, and other evil spirits of the voodoo world.

Jessie was discovered by Oley Olsen, who in 1934 went to work on Sapelo for playboy tobacco heir R. J. Reynolds, Jr., who owned most of the island. The son of Norwegian immigrants, Oley sold his interest in a boatyard on Sea Island to work for Reynolds. Jessie was about eighteen then, and Oley hired him to help out. It was a turning point in Jessie's life. He had fallen in love with a Hog Hammock girl and she with him. But their families said they were too young and forbade them to wed.

Oley's wife did not like living on Sapelo because she said there was too much partying. So the family returned to the mainland. Oley and his son opened a small boatyard on St. Simons. Oley also occasionally picked up cash hauling people and supplies back and forth to the neighboring islands. Some trips were for the Candlers at High Point on Cumberland. They had known Oley when he ran his boatyard on Sea Island, where they used to dock their boat. Lacking an estate manager in 1936, they offered the job to him. He accepted and also became their boat captain.

Aching over the sweetheart he was forbidden to marry, Jessie followed Oley off Sapelo. He slept in a shack at Olsen's boatyard, sort of as a night security man. He briefly tried other employers, but he was greatly annoyed that they deducted for Social Security and income tax. He came back to Oley, saying, "Captain, if you just leave my pay alone, I'll go back to work for you." And he did.

A strong bond developed between them. Jessie became Oley's side-kick, helping him at High Point and the boatyard and working as a mate. Jessie could drive the boats, including the Candlers' yacht, just as well as Oley. But he had one major fault—a yen for strong drink. Many times, Oley had to bail him out of jail on the mainland, where his public drunkenness occasionally earned him a night in the lockup. Jessie was not a rowdy or mean drunk; folks just didn't want a drunken black man reeling down the streets.

Oley took to leaving him on Cumberland, mainly to keep him out of the poky. And somewhere along the line, Jessie was added to the Candlers' payroll. The spell of Cumberland came over him. Christmas Creek became his great love. In short order, he was familiar with all of its twisting tributaries. He knew where the best spots were for fish, shrimp, clams, oysters, and crabs. He kept the Candlers and other north-end residents in fresh seafood. "I ain't clean them, though," he told them. "I catch them. You clean them."

Wearing a ragged denim jacket, an old hat, and khaki pants stuffed into boots—what he called his "marsh clothes"—he was poetry in motion on Christmas Creek. When the murky waters were ebbing out to sea, when the creek teemed most with life—that was his time. Standing in the prow of a weathered bateau, he would fling his handmade cast net into a tidal pool. Weighted with lead sinkers, it would smack the water with a *swish* and sink quickly. Then Jessie would pull it into the boat. In it would be glistening creek shrimp, flopping mullet, white-bellied sea trout, and a blue crab or two. Jessie would dump the catch into the bottom of the bateau. He did this many times until he deduced he had enough to feed himself and whoever else was destined to share his catch that day.

If he wanted oysters, he poled the bateau to an oyster bed and jabbed at the mollusks with a stout stick to loosen them, like someone stoking flames in a fireplace. He dropped the ones he liked in the bottom of the boat. Sometimes, he stepped onto the muddy bank, his boots sinking into the muck, to get the more delectable medium-sized oysters.

To get the black clams that abounded in the creek bottom, he rolled his sleeves up to his elbows and knelt in the boat, facing the prow. Like a blind man communicating by touch, he plunged his arm over the side and felt around in the soft mud for the succulent creatures. He talked to them. "Come to me now, baby," he would say softly. He called them Eunice, Sadie, and other feminine names. He pulled them into the boat by twos. He used the same procedure for getting conchs with their white spiral shells and rubbery, muscular feet.

The feasts he sometimes made from Christmas Creek's bounty rivaled Bobby Rischarde's soirees. Beneath spreading live oaks near the old hotel at High Point, he hosed down the clams and oysters to get the mud off. Then, using a pitchfork, he heaved them onto a sheet of corrugated tin over an open fire. He draped croker sacks soaked in salt water over the mollusks to ensure plenty of steam. Thus covered, they roasted about twenty minutes. He then pitched the red-hot clams and oysters onto a big wooden table. On it also might be fresh onions, carrots, and lettuce from his garden. Other salad ingredients—sea rocket, cattails, pennywort, wild mint—were plucked from the wild. Helping Jessie gather the items was one of Jimmy Carter's favorite activities on the island. At the center of the table would be a box of saltines and a bowl of sauce made from ketchup, horseradish, lemon juice, and Worcestershire. A soufflé of fresh squash, bacon, cracker crumbs, and butter might be a side dish. And there would be a big cooler of beer packed in ice. Using an awl to open the oysters, the guests would gorge themselves.

Jessie lived in two different cabins, each twelve feet by twelve feet, at the Candler place. One was what he called his "summer house," the remains of an old cottage at the former resort. The other, which had a cozy fireplace and was the old hotel's laundry room, he called his "winter house."

He knew all the gossip. "He always seemed to know what was going on. He was like Oley in that respect, only more so," said Howard Candler III.

"Jessie was well read," Oley's daughter Sonja Kinard recalled. "He read every magazine Daddy had, whether it was *Motor Boating, Yachting,* or *Time*—whatever Daddy read."

As Jessie grew older, his thirst for liquor rose. "My only objection to Jessie was that he would drink too much, too easily," Howard Candler III said.

Jessie got most of his liquor from Beulah Alberty. When she died in 1969, he had to turn to other sources, including his employers and neighbors. "If he couldn't get a drink from me, he would try to get it from you," Candler said. "If that didn't work, he would go down to the Settlement and try to get it from somebody down there, or go to anyone else who was available."

"Jessie made the rounds," said Thora Kimsey, another of Oley's daughters. "In order to get his drink, he would probably tell you what you wanted to hear. He was the island gossip. It just got to be a regular thing—Jessie coming around in the evening for his evening shooter. Then he took to coming around in the mornings, too."

A favorite stopping-off spot was Carol Ruckdeschel's. He often walked the mile or so to her cabin, where she kept his whiskey and doled out shots morning and evening. That way, she believed, she could help control his drinking. Occasionally, she sat him down and trimmed his gray, kinky hair and beard. In turn, Jessie brought her venison, clams, oysters, squirrels, and marsh hens. He would sit on her back porch with his drinking glass cupped in his gnarled hands. Carol would offer him food, and he would nibble something if he knew what it was. If he didn't, he turned her down, afraid she would serve up horse meat or armadillo pâté. He thought her culinary habits strange.

Once, a gnat landed in his bourbon. "Oh, God," he said with disgust.

Carol said, "Take it on the end of your finger and eat it. It's sweet." She showed him how to do it.

He stuck a stubby finger into the amber liquid and got the gnat on his fingertip. He studied the tiny bug a minute, then flicked it toward her. "You eat it," he said. Then he drained his glass, got up, and headed home.

Oley's son, his two surviving daughters, and their children regarded Jessie almost as a brother.

"He considered us his family, and we were his sisters, and my brother was his brother, and our children were his nieces and nephews," said Thora Kimsey. "They called him Uncle Jessie."

"But like a brother, sometimes Jessie made me so mad," said Sonja Kinard. Once, after he had done some small chores for her, she gave him money instead of a couple of drinks, his preferred payment. "That was a mistake because what he did, he went and bought a fifth of whiskey," she said. "Now, where he found someone on this island to buy a fifth of whiskey from, I'll never know, but he did."

The incident might have been forgotten except that Sonja that afternoon accidentally set fire to a grassy field on her family's plot next to High Point while trying to burn some trash. Her husband, her two children, and a nephew were there. They ran out with whatever tools they had to snuff out the fire.

"It was late afternoon, and we didn't have a telephone, so I got into our truck and hurried up to the Candlers' and used their phone to let Mother and my sister and brother on the mainland know that there was a fire. They thought the house was on fire. I ran up to Jessie's house to get some fire tools, and I tried to get him to come with me, but he was out like a light. I was so mad at him. I made him get in the car, and he didn't have anything on but his underwear and shirt, and I ran back and got his pants and threw them in the car. And his dog Jessica hops into the car, too.

"And I raced back. My husband and the boys had been fighting the fire. They were using plastic trash cans to haul water from the well to the fire. And Jessie didn't do a thing. He sat in the middle of the road. I ran the truck back and forth from the well to the fire, and Jessie was sitting in the way. I said, 'Damn you, Jessie, get out of the way.' But he didn't do a thing. He just sat there and watched us try to put that fire out. And we got it under control."

There was something about Jessie and fire—a special intuition perhaps. Like the time in July 1981 when there was a really big lightning-set fire on the north end. The woods were dry because of months of sparse rain, so the fire took hold quickly. Carol and some other turtle people who were on the beach just before dawn spied the blaze, an orange glow in the woods. By then, the fire already was out of control and was spreading rapidly, whipped by high winds.

"The amazing thing to me was how calm Jessie was," said Zack Kirkland, a park ranger. "Everybody else was frantically moving their TV sets and taking stuff out of their houses. Jessie wasn't doing anything. Somebody asked him, 'Aren't you going to save any of your personal belongings from your house?' Jessie said, 'No, it will stop when it hits the big oak trees.' And he was right. The fire roared up like it was going to race right through High Point, but when it hit the big live-oak trees, it stopped like Jessie said. And the next day, when we went up in the helicopter, it was just black ground everywhere you looked except these green oases of big oak trees. They didn't burn in the fire. Most of them served as a natural fire barrier for areas on the north end. I was surprised. I had no idea the trees would do that. Jessie knew it, though."

When the fire was finally doused, seventeen hundred acres of the north end lay blackened.

In later years, what people remembered most about Jessie was his spiritual side. After Oley died in 1967, Jessie said he would "have to talk to the cap'n 'bout sump'n." He would go to the dock or sit on the porch steps of Oley's old house and talk as if the captain were there. He said the tiny red freezer light in the kitchen reminded him of Oley sitting at the table smoking a cigarette. "Oh, how I miss that man," Jessie would say.

When his friend Beulah Alberty died in 1968, he dug her grave in the rich black dirt of the cemetery at High Point. She had tenderly mothered him, serving as a confidante in his small island world. "After she dead, I go down to her house and talk to her, too," Jessie said.

On a warm, sunny Saturday in October 1982, Jessie went out in his bateau like he had done so many times to gather a load of oysters for a hunting party staying at one of the north-end homes. He never showed up with the catch. That was not like him. He might be unreliable in many ways, but he always could be counted on for bringing in the catch from Christmas Creek. Some of the folks drove down to the creek and saw his empty boat bobbing in the water. That was very strange. They went over to the cabin of Jesse's fellow employee George Merrow and asked if he had seen Jessie.

"They said they had looked all around for him but couldn't find him," George said. "I said, 'I'm gonna look for him, too, 'cause that ain't like Jessie.' I had a dog named after him, Jessico. That dog loved Jessie and would stick right with him. So I said, 'Come on, Jessico, let's go find Jessie.' And me and him went down to the creek where the boat was, and he stands up there and bark three times—*Arf, arf, arf* —like that. And I said to myself, 'Jessie's in that water somewhere.' "

Carol found Jessie. He had drowned in his beloved creek doing the thing he loved most—gathering its bounty. Nobody knows exactly what happened. He may have fallen out of the boat and drowned. Or he may have had a heart attack. Possibly, he got out of the boat and slipped while trying to climb back in, catching his heavy boot in the oyster shells and becoming trapped in the water. Carol found his body stretched out on the oyster bed.

He was buried at age sixty-five where he was born, on Sapelo, laid to rest in its oak-shrouded Behavior Cemetery, where so many of his relatives and other Hog Hammock people had been interred before him. His casket was an old-fashioned type made of pine boards. "Jessie always told me how he longed to go back to Sapelo," Carol said. "And he did, but, unfortunately, in a casket."

The casket was brought to Sapelo in the stern of the island's ferryboat, accompanied by the Candlers, Oley's family, and several of Jessie's other friends, black and white. Bags of groceries from Piggly Wiggly were stacked around the casket, for it was the same day that Hog Hammock residents did their grocery shopping on the mainland.

Many well-known politicians and VIPs who had stayed with the Candlers and other families on Cumberland flew in for the funeral, landing on Sapelo's airstrip. They had to wade through the cemetery's uncut grass and poison ivy to get to the grave site. Gogo Ferguson bore in her hands a plant she had plucked out of the salt marsh. "I wanted Jessie to have something that reminded him of the marsh and the island," she said. "I remember him in his boat with a smudge pot going on the bow, fishing and throwing his cast net."

Many of the prominent people eulogized Jessie. "I don't know anyone who had a greater love for coastal Georgia than Jessie," said Joe Tanner, then commissioner of the Georgia Department of Natural Resources. He read letters from Jimmy Carter, still smarting from his defeat by Ronald Reagan, and George Busbee, who had succeeded Carter as governor.

Jessie was buried the old-fashioned way, his friends and Sapelo's elders throwing shovelful after shovelful of the island's rich black loam onto his casket. Then they planted bright-colored flowers on the grave.

After the funeral, when his friends went through his meager belongings, they found all the worn magazines Oley had given him over the years. They were stacked neatly by month and year. That may have been the only thing neat about Jessie, his friends felt.

"Cumberland just wasn't the same after his death," Thora Kimsey said.

Audrey and George Merrow were the last of Cumberland Island's African-Americans to leave. George was a handyman and Audrey an occasional cook for the Candlers. They left the island when George's leg had to be amputated because of diabetes.

George, who lived in the Settlement for more than fifty-one years, had a simple philosophy: "I just tried to work hard, do right, and love the Lord." When he was a young man, a preacher dipped him in the salty water of the Brickhill River and pronounced him saved. His baptism, he confessed, saved him from a world of boozing, gambling, and chasing loose women.

He and his daddy helped build the First African Baptist Church. When all the other members died or moved away, he and Bobby Rischarde kept it clean and painted. "I just loved that church," he said.

He was born in 1916—the year of Jessie Bailey's birth and Lucy Carnegie's death—in his daddy's cabin in the Settlement, the youngest of nine children. The cabin, people said, was so open to the elements that snakes crawled across the rafters. The granny midwife who delivered George put a sharp ax under his mother's bed to cut the labor pains, after an old sea-island folk belief.

George's father, Nelson Merrow, was an original purchaser of a lot in the Settlement. Nelson always went barefoot, no matter the season. The bottoms of his feet were thick, the calluses tough as leather, just as protective from thorns and broken glass as a shoe. He was a stable boy, among other things, at Dungeness. When a Carnegie or a guest of the family wanted to go riding, he would lead a steed to the mounting block in front of the mansion. The man in charge of the horses was particular about their cleanliness. He would wipe down each animal with a clean white glove. If a speck of dirt was on it, he scolded the stable hand and dispatched him back to the stall to wipe down the horse again. Nelson later worked for the hotel, then for the Cumberland Island Club, then for the Candlers, who bought the club and its assets when it fizzled. He planted fields of potatoes, tomatoes, beans, greens, corn, and other vegetables for the Candlers and kept their place tidy.

George's mother, Catherine, died when he was still a boy. Her mother and father—George's grandparents—were the ex-slaves Primus and Amanda Mitchell. George's paternal grandparents were Quash Merrow, also a former slave, and an ex-slave woman simply known as Chaney. She was owned by the Bunkleys, one of the white families on Cumberland's north end. When the Civil War ended, she continued working for the family, who called her "Maum Chaney" out of respect for her age. Quash worked awhile for the Carnegies on the south end, then fished and hunted hogs and deer for the hotel at High Point. He died at the incredible age of 110.

George's working life differed little from his father's and grandfathers'. Before he was seven, he was picking up trash at the club for a nickel a day. "Ain't that something? A nickel a day," he would say when telling the story.

"Maum" Chaney, who was born a slave on Cumberland Island
Courtesy of the National Park Service

While still young, he was employed by the Carnegies. "I started working for them when I was around eleven years old," he recalled. "I was a caddie for Mr. Andrew Carnegie at Stafford. I stayed at the quarters there, but I could walk back and forth to High Point if I wanted to. I had to keep the putting green mowed at the golf course. They had a tractor that mowed the fairways. They didn't let me run it. I used to take care of Mr. Andrew's car, wash it. He liked to keep things in very good condition."

George hardly ever saw the inside of a school. For a short time, the Settlement's inhabitants tried to maintain the semblance of a school in the church, but there weren't enough children to support it, and it closed.

"I didn't get no learning," George said. "Some people said I did, but I didn't. I was the baby of the family, and my mama had died, and my brothers and sisters was all gone, and some had died. One of them drowned, and one had died from a fever when he was little. My daddy didn't want me out of his eyesight. If you went to school, you had to go to Brunswick. My family took me over there one year, but by the time I get there, they tell me my daddy is sick and he wanted me to come home. They brought me back, but he wasn't sick. He was there working in the garden when I got back. It was just his way of getting me back on the island.

"The way I learned my letters and numbers and things, I just thought it out. Figured it out, I guess. I did go through first grade, but nothing after that.

"We lived in the Settlement on the other side of the church," he said. "We had a hand pump in the backyard to get water out the well. We killed deer and squirrels to eat, fished out the creek. We butchered hogs and had a smokehouse to smoke the meat—make bacon and other stuff out of it.

"I met Audrey when I was working for the Carnegies. She was working for them, too. She was a maid for Mrs. Nancy Johnston at Plum Orchard. Her daddy was Chester Holzendorph, who was caretaker for Plum. We got married in 1942. Two months after we was married, the army had me gone. They sent me to Fort Benning, Georgia, on June 25, 1942. I spent three years, three months, and thirteen days in the army. They [the

452nd Antiaircraft Battalion] sent me to France and Germany, and I was in seven battles over there. Bombs was falling like firecrackers. But the Lord brought me out without a scratch.

"After the war, I came back to Cumberland. The Carnegies wanted me back, but Cap'n Olsen talked me into coming to work at High Point for the Candlers. So me and Audrey moved up to High Point. They built a house for us on the property. I kept High Point up for them—mowed the lawn, cut wood. I used to go out practically every day catching bait for them when they was up there. They didn't have electricity in the beginning. They had these generators, and I had to keep them going. Them things liked to work me to death. I would go down and meet the Candlers at the boat and bring their stuff up when they came. They treated us very well."

Audrey Merrow had a more vivid recollection of meeting her future spouse: "When I first met George on Cumberland, I was sixteen years old. The first time he seen me, he said he knew I was gonna be his wife. It took us a real long time before we was married in Fernandina, at the courthouse. I was twenty-four then.

"My daddy was caretaker for Dr. Marius Johnston at Plum Orchard, and I maided for Mrs. Johnston," she recalled. "She was very nice to me. I had to make up her bed, clean her room. And at nighttime, I would have to turn her bed down, get her gown, put it out on the bed laid out, get her house shoes, and put them under the bed, right down by the bed for her to have when she get ready to go to bed. And in the morning time, I would get up and go downstairs and help straighten out the living room from overnight. And I would work in the kitchen sometimes, or the pantry.

"In her bedroom, Mrs. Johnston had a button thing hanging on the wall that hooked up down into the pantry. She used it if she wanted anybody. Each button matched a different person. The butler would know when he was wanted. I'd know when I was wanted. And you had to do *everything* for them, hand and foot. They was just like babies. You had to pass the food around at the table so everybody could take what they wanted.

"I stayed right there at Plum Orchard," she said. "Everybody on Cumberland had a place for their help. Cumberland always has been a great place. The south end and the north end—I worked both ends. And they had plenty of everything.

"After the war, when we moved up to High Point, I cooked for the Candlers when they come down from Atlanta. Lord, I cooked a lot of biscuits. They loved my biscuits. They liked Swedish meatballs and roast beef. They liked ham. Shrimp, too. I fixed venison for them, and they took to eating venison.

"When we had a day off, Mrs. Candler let us use her car. We would have picnics. We'd go to the High Point dock and fish. We'd have little cookouts. We had a coal pot with a grill over it, and we put steaks and things on it to cook.

"We always went to our church in the Settlement, the First African Baptist Church there. Them homemade benches was hard, but we got used to it. There wasn't no organ, just music from the mouth. And there was no electricity, just kerosene lamps and candles. After services and at breaks in the service, we would stand around outside and exchange news and just generally gossip. Then we'd go back inside and study the Bible and sing. We sang a lot."

The music, people recalled, would well up and joyously spill out the windows and doors. In a great hosanna, the voices embraced the houses of the Settlement, echoed across the cemetery, and rose heavenward from the surrounding woods.

But the most famous resident of the Settlement was not black. She was Carol Ruckdeschel, an exceptionally strong woman. When she shot and killed a man there, it was all over the newspapers, and the spotlight shone on the Settlement for the first time.

CHAPTER TEN

ONLY CAROL and a lonely backpacker from upstate New York know exactly what happened on that late Thursday afternoon in April 1980. In her statement to the Camden County Sheriff's Department, she admitted blasting away her drunken boyfriend, Louis McKee, age fifty-two, as he tried to stomp down her locked cabin door in the Settlement.

"At about 6 P.M. there was a knock on my back door," she told police. "I was sitting at the kitchen table with a recent acquaintance named Pete DiLorenzo. I opened the door but saw no one, so in fear quickly shut it and locked it. Key was in door because it had been my habit of late to keep it locked when I was in house. I looked out the window adjacent to the door, but by that time he [McKee] was beating on or kicking the back door. I ran for the shotgun and by the time I returned the door had been smashed in, and though I remember hearing his voice, I can't remember what was said, but the tone was threatening. After suffering beatings by this man, I was terrified and was determined not to go through it again. I pulled the trigger and collapsed."

DiLorenzo corroborated her statement: "While I was sitting in the kitchen talking to Carol, I heard someone walk on the porch and start to open the door. Carol jumped up to see who it was and shut and locked the door very swiftly. I saw and heard this man breaking in the door, angrily yelling something, and by the time he had broken the main panel on the door I heard a shot behind me and he fell. Carol and I spoke for a moment. Somewhat shaken, I went and looked at the man on the porch and figured he was dead because he was not breathing."

Carol and DiLorenzo gingerly stepped around McKee's bloody remains and, with evening shadows descending, quickly walked a mile up the dusty dirt road to the Candler compound. She used the crackling radiotelephone there to summon authorities.

The call reached Camden County sheriff Jimmy Middleton about six-thirty. "Good Lord, what has happened out there now?" he remarked. He and his chief deputy, Harvey Amerson, flew in a light plane to the island, where they landed at the airstrip next to the Stafford mansion. They commandeered a Jeep from Greyfield Inn and quickly drove the twelve miles up Grand Avenue to Carol's cabin. Park Service rangers and Cumberland superintendent Paul McCrary already were there.

"It was a pretty somber scene," Middleton said.

Camden coroner Danny Saturday, a plumber by trade, arrived about ten o'clock to take charge of the body, as required by Georgia law. Covered with a dingy brown blanket, it was loaded in the back of a green Park Service pickup truck. Carol and DiLorenzo got into the cab next to McCrary, who drove the vehicle slowly down the dark Grand Avenue. The others, riding in the Jeep, followed the makeshift hearse to the Dungeness dock, where the body was placed aboard a Park Service boat and transported to Woodbine, Camden County's seat.

"It was the strangest, most perplexing, spookiest experience of my life," McCrary later said of that night.

Carol Ruckdeschel on her ATV
Courtesy of Atlanta-Journal Constitution

He had gotten hold of his boss, Bob Baker, director of the regional Park Service office in Atlanta, to ask if the FBI also should be brought in, since the shooting had taken place in a national park. Baker advised him to let the local authorities handle it.

In Woodbine, which bills itself as the "Crawfish Capital of Georgia," Middleton offered to put Carol and DiLorenzo up in a motel for the night, but Carol declined. He then said they could stay in one of the empty jail cells, so they would at least have a roof over their heads. Carol liked that idea even less. If it was all right with the sheriff, she said, she and DiLorenzo would camp out on the courthouse lawn under a big, spreading live oak.

The coroner's inquest was held at two o'clock the next day at the glass-and-brick Camden County Courthouse Annex in the usually quiet Woodbine, named for a vine that grows in the area. Word of the shooting had spread, and the hearing room's gallery was packed with curious locals, many of whom had heard tall tales over the years about the "nature woman" on Cumberland. "They say she eats snakes, possum, horse meat, anything," said a lanky, white-haired man with gaps among his remaining teeth. Also in the audience were Carol's parents, Earl and Anne Ruckdeschel, who had driven up from their home in Atlanta to comfort their only child.

Deputy Amerson offered the only physical evidence—a broken canoe paddle and pieces of molding from Carol's kitchen door. He said that McKee apparently used the paddle to break out the door's thin center panel. The gray molding that held the panel in place had two shotgun-pellet holes, he pointed out. The panel itself had no such holes—an indication that Carol had fired the weapon after McKee busted out the panel. It also was evidence that Carol had pulled the trigger from the point where the gun was found—"near the bathroom door, about sixteen feet from the kitchen door." In addition, Amerson said that "a strong odor of alcohol [was] about the victim's body."

Park Service ranger Harold Wood then testified that "McKee had a drinking problem" and that McKee and Carol were romantically involved. McKee, he also noted, "had beaten her up some, the last time in December '79, when he gave her a black eye and threatened her."

The inquest was over in half an hour. The killing was a justifiable homicide, the coroner's jury ruled. Carol was free to return to the cabin where less than twenty-four hours earlier she had taken the life of her former boyfriend.

———— • ————

Carol spent the first dozen years of her life in Rochester, New York, where her father worked for Eastman Kodak. He moved his family to Atlanta to manage Kodak's processing plant. Their home was on tree-shaded Northside Drive in Buckhead, one of Atlanta's most desirable neighborhoods, known for its bridal-white dogwood blooms and gorgeous azaleas in spring. Carol attended nearby Northside High School.

From the get-go, she took a great liking to the vine-festooned woods near her home and the creatures slithering and flitting through them. She fascinated neighborhood children. "She was always dragging us kids around and teaching us things about dead or alive animals," said Debra Sams Stegman, who lived next door to Carol. Carol called her Tootsie. "I can remember many a time picking up road kill and taking it back to her 'lab' in the basement of her home to dissect it. One time, she was raising mice for her snakes that she had, and they all got loose and ended up in our house. I can remember my father beating them with a small Coca-Cola bottle on our back porch. He was so mad at her."

After high school, Carol worked odd jobs—she fixed car radios once—and wandered. She married a divorcée and amateur pothunter named James Kemph, who owned a radio and television repair shop. He and Carol went around the state searching for arrowheads and Civil War artifacts. They divorced after two years.

Carol then went to Georgia State University, which spreads like an octopus over the heart of downtown Atlanta, to study biology. Her professor in a vertebrate zoology course—and chairman of the Biology Department—was tall, lanky, slow-speaking Charles Wharton, one of Georgia's most respected naturalists. His specialty was cottonmouth snakes, but his knowledge of the state's natural areas was unsurpassed. His book *Natural Environments of Georgia* is still the bible for biologists and naturalists who study the state's landscape. Considerably older than Carol, Wharton developed a keen fondness for his bright, eager, good-looking student.

She went on field trips with him. One was to Cumberland Island. It was the first time she had ever laid eyes on it. It was, in fact, her first time seeing any barrier island. "It was just so captivating with its wonderful beach," she recalled. "I fell in love with it. It was just very different to me."

Wharton and Carol married in May 1968. But that union, too, quickly petered out. Wharton went on to author or coauthor several more books on Georgia's natural history. When he retired, he moved to a house at the end of a long, steep, gravel road on the edge of the Chattahoochee National Forest in mountainous Rabun County in northeast Georgia.

Even after they divorced, Carol and Wharton continued traveling together on field trips. She stayed on for a while at Georgia State as a biology researcher, living in a cramped, four-room house in Atlanta with a red-tailed hawk, a Rhode Island Red rooster, an eastern diamondback rattlesnake, a black widow spider in a mayonnaise jar, and an assortment of other creatures.

In the early 1970s, she volunteered to work for the Georgia Natural Areas Council, a small government office set up by then-governor Jimmy Carter to inventory wild places in the state. In one of her forays in north Georgia's rugged mountains, she discovered a salamander species previously unknown to science. It came to be called the Pigeon Mountain salamander for the remote mountain on which it was found. It is now on Georgia's rare and protected species list.

Another volunteer was Sam Candler, great-grandson of Asa Griggs Candler of Coca-Cola fame. He lived with his wife and four kids on a farm in Coweta County near Atlanta but spent considerable time at his family's High Point estate on Cumberland.

Sam and Carol ended up roaming the state together to assess the landscape. Occasionally, they picked up road-killed snakes, turtles, possums, and other creatures to study and perhaps to roast and eat. Sam's friends said he had opted for rambling back roads and studying swamps over leading the life of a wealthy socialite.

During their travels, Sam and Carol developed a dislike for the Army Corps of Engineers and what was then the Soil Conservation Service. The agencies, they discovered, had tampered with at least 166 of the state's watersheds in an ill-advised effort to practice flood control on small streams and rivers. The effects were devastating. The waterways could no longer support more than half the native plants and animals that were there before the alterations. In addition, the valuable cleansing function of the swampy areas along the streams was destroyed. No longer were the wetlands able to clean pollutants—human waste, pesticides, oil, and grease—from the water. In one report, Sam and Carol, backed by her ex-husband Charlie Wharton, showed that six miles of a typical Georgia coastal stream had the same cleansing power as a sewage treatment plant serving fifty thousand people. They also showed that the swamps were natural flood-storage areas and served to recharge the aquifers that supplied water to much of south Georgia.

A couple of times, Jimmy Carter paddled a canoe with them down stretches of the Chattahoochee River. They wanted to call his attention to the flagrant abuse of the river by the city of Atlanta and other municipalities that dumped their treated sewage into the water, and to convince him of the need for land-use planning and other measures to protect the river.

Sam also was a longtime friend of Pulitzer Prize winner John McPhee. He invited McPhee to come to Georgia and knock around with him and Carol as they collected skulls and animal skins, chowed down on road kill, and preserved natural areas. The result was McPhee's memorable "Travels in Georgia" in the *New Yorker* in 1975.

By that time, Carol had met another of Sam's friends, John Pennington. John was divorcing his wife, Marilyn, at the time. They had sent announcement cards to their friends and John's close coworkers at the *Atlanta Journal* saying they were separating.

John became Carol's new beau. Sam Candler told his siblings about them, and they agreed to hire the couple as caretakers of the High Point estate. John would pursue his novel and Carol her career as a naturalist.

"Caretaking was the perfect job," Carol said. "We thought, 'Well, we've got time enough besides regular duties to do what we want to do.' I gave up my Atlanta base and just decided that this was the place. I always thought I wanted to live in the mountains, but when I first saw Cumberland, I knew this is where I wanted to be. I didn't ever mind leaving Atlanta. I wanted to live where I could see the stars at night. I knew I would never stay there. I just didn't know where I would go."

John first observed the island from the air. "I saw Cumberland as the migrant terns and plovers see it in the fall," he wrote in *National Geographic*. "Sam Candler flew [us] to the island in his small plane. He swung across the north end and put the entire island under the wing. From a clear October sky

I saw beaches of fine, firm sand, rumpled dunes bordered by live-oak forests, marshes and estuaries and a few buildings and ruins."

He set about trying to write his book on a battered old Royal typewriter he lugged to the island. Carol started down the path toward becoming a renowned island naturalist. Along the way, they met Louis McKee, who in April 1974 had acquired a plot of land with a dilapidated shack from one of the north end's white families. It was about a mile from where John and Carol stayed in the Candlers' caretaker's house. McKee's shanty offered a spectacular view of the salt marsh bordering Christmas Creek and the magnificent high dunes along the beach in the distance. He, wife Betty, and their friends spent weekends and holidays hammering and sawing and painting to make the shack habitable.

The county engineer for Clay County, Florida, McKee had made a pot of money from his surveying business in Orange Park, near Jacksonville. He was a dark, brooding man who spoke in monosyllables. Slender, rough-cut, and gregarious, he would go out of his way to help other island people by lending them his Jeep or hauling goods for them from the mainland.

"He was just one of the nicest, soft-spoken, honest, well-meaning kind of people I've ever met," said Grover Henderson, who was Camden County's attorney and one of McKee's closest friends.

Before long, John and Carol were going to Louis's place almost every weekend for dinner and cocktails. Louis and Betty also had a friend named Ebby, an accomplished violinist who entertained for hours at the get-togethers with his large repertoire ranging from bluegrass to classics. Joining the group occasionally was Grover Henderson. Sometimes, Jessie Bailey came to listen and sip a drink or two.

In the summer of 1976, Louis and Betty's marriage began to sour. As part of their divorce settlement that November, Betty deeded her interest in the cabin to Louis. Despite their breakup, they remained friends. She kept coming to Cumberland to be with Louis and their mutual acquaintances.

About that time, John Pennington also was having second thoughts about his situation. It began to dawn on him that caretaking for the Candlers was not the idyllic job he had envisioned. He was not making progress on his book. Worse, his relationship with Carol was on thin ice. He decided to quit.

Actually, the Candlers were getting ready to fire him. John never got the hang of watching over an estate, they felt.

"John came walking across the lawn with his letter of resignation," said Howard Candler III, Sam's brother. "[He] was being fired, matter of fact, but he quit first. He was hard to learn the ins and outs of the operation of the island and what it involved. We had an old landing craft that we plowed back and forth in between Cumberland and the mainland. He use to run that landing craft for us, and talk about how wet he use to get because the seas would wash over the bow, and [there were] no windshield wipers, and he was just sort of out in the open."

Claire Candler, Howard's wife, recalled, "He was busy writing his novel. He always said, 'I have to get back to my desk.' And of course, he and Carol were supposed to be married, and it turned out they weren't married."

"We hired them as a married couple because John had told me that, yes, they were married," Howard Candler said. "As it turned out, I found out through a friend of mine in Atlanta that they weren't married."

Apparently, Sam Candler never told his siblings that fact—if he indeed knew it himself.

Soon, there began a series of soap-opera events. Carol left John. John found new love with a young woman who was working at Greyfield Inn. And Carol and Louis became close friends.

Carol, about to lose her employment with the Candlers, desperately wanted a place of her own on Cumberland. With the help of his lawyer friend, Grover Henderson, McKee began working on a deal to fulfill Carol's desire. They obtained a place in the Settlement—an acre or so with a sagging shanty—from the last of nine heirs of one of the original lot owners, a black man named Charlie Trimmins. The son of a freed slave, Trimmins had built the shack in 1895 from boards and other items washed up on the beach.

Carol would be a neighbor of Grover Henderson. In 1974, McKee had helped Grover take over Beulah Alberty's deteriorated old house in the Settlement. Beulah's home was in the best shape of any still standing there. It was roomier and a tad sturdier than the cabin Carol moved into a few hundred feet away.

"Carol's Place," as her cabin came to be known, was not entirely hers. McKee retained a half interest. They both knew, too, that the Park Service sooner or later would condemn the property to make it part of the new Cumberland Island National Seashore. Carol hoped to work out a deal with the federal government for a lifetime estate on the island in exchange for giving up the property.

McKee, ex-wife Betty, Ebby, and other friends transported building materials from a dismantled house in Orange Park to Cumberland to make Carol's cabin habitable. She replaced joists, repaired the chimney, and strengthened the roof. Then she turned every board on the outside backwards so the original pink paint would not show and the cabin would have a weathered look. Inside, she covered the walls of the three rooms with plywood and then with cypress paneling to make the cabin cockroach proof.

As a sort of housewarming gift, McKee gave her a sawed-off twelve-gauge shotgun. He had an inordinate fear of backpackers. He thought that Carol, alone by herself on the remote north end, might be easy prey for a deranged camper. Carol laughed. It was a silly worry, but she took the weapon to make him happy.

Then, somewhere along the way, her ardor for McKee began to ebb. He grew jealous and started drinking heavily, to which Carol responded with contempt. He began to beat her. For perhaps the first time in her life, she knew real fear. "When you're afraid, it's a whole new ballgame," she once told an interviewer for *Atlanta Weekly* magazine. "You don't know what it's like to know there is someone out there who is determined to hurt you."

Louis beat her for the last time in late 1979, bruising her face and making her black and blue. A few weeks later, shortly after Christmas, perhaps in an effort to make amends, he deeded his share of the cabin and the acre it sat on to her. Now, she had full title. Two months later, she deeded it to the National Park Service in return for forty-five thousand dollars and a written guarantee that she could live there and have the right to go about the island until she died. Now, she had what she desired most— a place of her own on one of the world's most beautiful islands, where she could continue her turtle studies and the untrammeled life of a naturalist.

One morning in mid-April 1980, she was on the beach slitting open the gut of a putrefying loggerhead. As her hands groped around in its gut, Pete DiLorenzo, a lean, sandy-haired camper strolling on the sand, came up and asked what she was doing. Carol explained her turtle research. It turned out that DiLorenzo was seeking solace after wrestling for months with personal problems. He was from near Rochester, New York, Carol's hometown. They chatted for more than an hour, and she invited him to her compound, where he could pitch his tent in her yard.

A day or so later, about a mile away, the brooding McKee drank for hours with Jessie Bailey. At some point, he fell into a rage and set off in his wobbly Jeep toward Carol's place. Some said he was insanely jealous because he had learned she was entertaining a backpacker. Others said he was sulking over not getting any of the forty-five thousand dollars the Park Service had paid Carol.

Whatever the reason, he went up to her back door bellowing like a wild bull, trying to smash it in. That's when Carol, fearing for her life, picked up the shotgun he had given her for protection and fired a deadly load of buckshot into his chest.

The shooting made all the newspapers and evening newscasts. It thrust the Settlement into the public spotlight for the first time. But it would not be the last time. To understand how a peaceful, isolated, lonely place like the Settlement emerged from obscurity and became a bitter bone of contention, it is necessary to go back to the beginning, to the time when the National Park Service first showed up on Cumberland.

CHAPTER ELEVEN

ENSCONCED OVER AT THE GRANGE, next to boarded-up Dungeness, was "Aunt Floss," as the family called Florence Nightingale Carnegie Perkins. She was the last survivor of Lucy and Thomas Carnegie's nine children. Her dozens of relatives kept close tabs on her frail health and speculated on how long she might live. Their interest was not so much out of compassion as it was out of concern over what would happen when she died, for the rigid trust Lucy Carnegie had set up for Cumberland would end with Floss's passing. Once the trust expired, no longer would Lucy's vast estate—which still included all the mansions and the other property—be so bound up. Cumberland finally would be in the hands of her descendants, who could do as they wished with their property.

Despite her delicate condition, Floss lived more years than any of her siblings. She was born in 1879 in Pittsburgh, Lucy and Tom's

215

seventh child. Attractive, the tallest of the Carnegie sisters, she had tresses of blond hair and big, expressive, brown eyes in an angel-like face. She married Frederick Perkins, a lawyer of elegant manners, in an elaborate ceremony at Dungeness in April 1901. After first living in the luxurious Plaza Hotel in New York, they moved to the Grange with their three children in the 1920s. The Grange, controlled by Lucy's estate, had become vacant after William Page, Lucy's estate manager, died. The family said Floss wanted the Grange mainly as a haven for her alcoholic son, Curtis, the one who drank by himself in the woods.

Frederick Perkins fell victim to the curse that had plagued other men on Cumberland. He died within a few years of moving there. He was cremated.

Floss was unpredictable, edgy, a flighty sort of woman. She smoked long before it was acceptable for women. Family members said they didn't know how Frederick put up with her. A story says that she once papered a bedroom in the Grange in dollar bills and that her relatives made her take it down because it defaced government property. She would invite her grandnieces and grandnephews to the Grange "to see my husband," whose ashes were kept in a ceramic urn near a downstairs fireplace. When she tantalized them with tales of candy-filled closets, the youngest ones believed her.

She wept uncontrollably when Dungeness burned in 1959. She had talked about restoring it, although she had not the slightest idea where the money would come from. Even in its derelict state, the big house was the symbol of her family's former glory. Some relatives said she lost her gusto for living after Dungeness's demise. More likely, heavy smoking, overindulgence, and old age caught up with her.

Her family told the trustees that she needed a place where she could be near doctors and hospitals. They found her a new house overlooking a golf course in Coral Gables, Florida. "After she left Cumberland, she never came back, but she always wanted to talk about it," Polly Stein Carnegie recalled. "When we visited her, I always brought a sprig of palm or some other plant from the island, and that would make her happy."

Toward the end, Floss moved one last time, into the comfortable Hotel Windsor in Jacksonville to be near her specialist. She died there of cancer at age eighty-two on April 15, 1962. She was buried in the Carnegie cemetery on Cumberland next to the graves of son Curtis, daughter Peggy, who had died in 1957, and husband Frederick.

With Floss's last breath, Lucy Carnegie's ironclad grip on Cumberland loosened.

———•••———

Even if they had wanted to—and several did—none of Lucy's children or grandchildren could have disposed of their Cumberland land or done much else with it as long as the trust was intact. Even when some of the grandchildren went nearly broke because of sour business deals and heavy taxes, the trust and its trustees allowed little leeway in exploiting Cumberland's natural riches to make money.

About the only source of revenue the trustees permitted on the island was timber cutting. One summer, most of the big pines around Plum Orchard were cut. But that was about it. Carter Carnegie's tung-oil venture failed. In the 1950s, several heirs backed a plan to strip-mine portions of the island's north end for lucrative titanium ore, even though it surely would have ruined half the island's natural beauty, leaving huge gashes in the fragile soil. The trustees approved the proposal. But other family members were outraged. They feared that the island would never recover. They protested all the way to the Georgia Supreme Court, and the plan fell through.

"I spent my all to stop it," said Lucy's granddaughter Nancy Carnegie Rockefeller. "Mining the island would have desecrated it."

By the time Floss died, there were numerous grandchildren and great-grandchildren of Lucy and Thomas Carnegie. Since four generations now had a voice in Cumberland's future, it was obvious that a scheme was needed to divide the island.

"The problem facing us was frightening. Everyone had different wants," Nancy Rockefeller said. "Selling the island was impossible, as some of us insisted on holding on to our inheritance. Some, though, could not financially afford to hold on to their pieces."

The only way out seemed a division of the island into five shares for the clans of the five children of Lucy Coleman Carnegie. Relying on help and advice from lawyers and financial experts, the heirs in 1964 concocted a rather simple plan. The island first would be split into two parts—a northern half, where the titanium ore was, and a southern half, where the big mansions were. Then each half would be divided into five strips. Each of the five clans would be given a north tract and a south tract. In essence, each clan would get roughly one-fifth of the island. To be absolutely fair in the division was nigh impossible, for some tracts were more valuable than others for various reasons: river frontage, houses, location. The family decided, however, to go ahead with the scheme.

The grandchildren of Morris Carnegie, Andy and Tom Carnegie, got as their south tract a strip between Dungeness and Greyfield, including the area where their grandfather's mansion, the Cottage, once stood. Their north tract was a strip near High Point.

Floss's heirs took the Grange as their south tract and the old hunting area called Squaw Town as their north tract.

Margaret Carnegie Ricketson's descendants got Greyfield as their southern holding and a tract just north of Stafford as their northern strip.

The Johnston clan of Kentucky got Plum Orchard in the south and took over old hunting areas known as Dilworth and Banks Fields in the north.

Andrew Carnegie II's grandchildren got Stafford House, the Chimneys, and 250 acres between Dungeness and Greyfield in the south, as well as a tract that stretched up to High Point in the north.

The court approved the division, which became effective in 1965. "It was done in an orderly fashion," said Thornton Morris, who represented some of the heirs. Even so, squabbles erupted within some of the clans as they started subdividing their tracts into specific parcels for each heir.

Andrew II's share of the property was divided between his two daughters, Lucy Carnegie Rice and Nancy Rockefeller. Nancy took the southern 250 acres between Dungeness and Greyfield. "Lucy wanted not only her house, the Chimneys, but Stafford House also, and as she was ill at this point, and [had] been through so much heartache, I agreed to give up Stafford House and take the [250 acres]," Nancy said. "This portion had smaller acreage, but it had river frontage. Access to the river and its transportation benefits made up for giving up much of the ancestral home. Times had changed."

————•◦•————

They had changed indeed. Powerful outside forces were about to snatch control of Cumberland from the Carnegies and the Candlers.

One force was Charles Fraser, the crafty builder of fashionable Sea Pines Plantation, carved from a jungle-like maritime forest on Hilton Head Island, South Carolina. He envisioned a similar project for Cumberland— marinas, hotels, manicured golf courses surrounded by subdivisions of luxury homes on winding streets.

Another force was the Park Service, which wanted to make Cumberland the nation's next national park.

As early as 1950, Cumberland's primitive beauty and rich history drew scrutiny from state and federal government agencies and conservation groups, who wanted the island and its magnificent beach set aside for public use. Georgia eyed it as a possible state park. The state legislature, in fact, created the eighteen-member Cumberland Island Study Committee to examine the park idea.

But that notion appealed little to the Carnegies, who instead favored a national park to ensure as far as possible that the island would be protected. In the end, the Georgia legislature decided the state didn't need another island park after all—Jekyll Island, the former home of the fabulous millionaires' club, already had attained that status. And it had a causeway and a bridge to boot. The state concluded that since the National Park Service was casting its covetous eyes toward Cumberland, it would be foolish to spend Georgia tax dollars for a park.

Prompted by Congress, the Park Service in the early 1950s embarked on a study of the remaining unblemished areas along the Atlantic and Gulf seaboards with the idea of preserving some of them. In 1955, the report placed Cumberland second—after Cape Cod—on the list of sixteen areas of national significance.

"Cumberland is a choice example of a natural resource that elsewhere is fast giving way to commercial and residential development," the report said. "It deserves to be preserved in public ownership so that it can be enjoyed by the greatest number of people."

The report gushed over Cumberland's beauty: "It is here, the same as at Cape Hatteras National Seashore and a few other places along the coast, where natural values are being preserved, that one could come to know and enjoy to the fullest degree the allure of the sea and rolling surf, the invigoration of salty breezes, the sense of freedom beneath a limitless vault of blue, the fascination of clean sand beaches and broken grass-topped dunes and the solitude of ocean front that stretches for miles without clutter of man-made developments."

The feasibility studies that followed the glowing report recommended that Congress make Cumberland either a national recreation area or a national seashore.

At first, the Carnegies were tepid to the idea of a national park. Some wanted no truck with the Park Service. The government was poking its big nose where it didn't belong, they said. But after dividing Lucy Carnegie's estate, her heirs, knowing they lacked the money to keep up their portions of the island and pay the taxes, took a second look. A federal park, they surmised, could keep their beloved isle unspoiled forever. In the bargain, they could work out a deal to still live on the island and have the government foot most of the bills. With the backing of conservation groups, some of them even began courting the Park Service, suggesting that the family sell, under certain conditions, its northern tracts to the feds for a national seashore but hold on to the ancestral homes in the southern half.

Lucy's granddaughter Margaret "Retta" Johnston Wright, who had inherited a portion of Plum Orchard, was one who early saw the writing on the wall. If an outside foundation or government agency didn't buy the island and pledge its preservation, Cumberland sooner or later would be developed, she warned her family. Early on, she went to New York to make exhausting rounds of foundations and private trusts—the Old Dominion, the Ford Foundation, and others—to interest them in Cumberland. She toted an album of stunning black-and-white photos to show foundation bigwigs the beauty and serenity of the island. The foundations professed interest but did nothing. It became apparent to her and the others that the safest course was going to be the National Park Service, which would have a legal mandate from Congress—and federal tax dollars—to preserve and protect the island in perpetuity.

To that end, she tugged some well-connected strings. Stewart L. Udall, then interior secretary under President Lyndon Johnson, agreed in 1965 to come to a luncheon at Plum Orchard and a quick tour of the island. He liked what he saw.

Discussions between the family and the Park Service about a national seashore on Cumberland began eagerly enough. Just as quickly, they slumped. Then what the Cumberland boosters feared most happened: strapped for cash, and with the Park Service in no apparent hurry to make a decision, half-brothers Tom Carnegie IV and Andy Carnegie III made a deal with a buyer willing to put a pot of cash on the table. That buyer was Charles Fraser. Tom and Andy sold their fifth of the island—about thirty-one hundred acres—to him for $1.5 million in 1968. The land included their south tract between Dungeness and Greyfield and their north tract near High Point.

When the other Carnegies were apprised of the deal, they trembled with rage. It was as if someone wielding a club had stomped into their mansions and smashed their precious heirlooms. Here was what they had been desperately trying to ward off—a private developer coming in and transforming their unsullied paradise into asphalt streets, golf courses, vacation villas, marinas, meeting centers, and God knew what else. If they had the money, they would buy out the brothers themselves, they said.

Fraser, brash, aggressive, and used to getting his way, said that the lawyer for the Carnegie brothers actually approached him. "He told me he had two interesting clients who didn't have any money but had some property on Cumberland," he remembered. "He said that one needed to go back to college and the other needed a trust fund. They had received title to two blocks of property on Cumberland. I asked, 'Why was the Carnegie property divided in this strange sausage fashion?' And he said it was because everyone wanted part of the mining interest from digging up large parts of Cumberland for ilmenite and rutile [titanium ores]. And that was why the island was split in that fashion. I then began negotiating.

"I let George Hartzog, who at that time was National Park Service director, know what I was doing. He said he didn't have any money and didn't have any authorization from Congress to buy Cumberland. So I bought the property. My vision for the island was very similar to what I'd done at Sea Pines Plantation. Cumberland didn't have a bridge, unlike Hilton Head, and so that was a very challenging question of just what do you do with that."

Conservation groups agitating for Cumberland's preservation were incensed over what they regarded as Fraser's barging into a sacred domain.

The late Jane Yarn, a nationally known conservationist who was a close adviser to Jimmy Carter, once spoke of her first encounter with Fraser—and how his plans nearly made her sick to her stomach. "It was in the summer of 1968, and conservationists, Carnegie heirs, and others who had an interest in Cumberland met at The Cloister on Sea Island to discuss the possibility of Cumberland becoming a national park," she recalled. "Charlie Fraser appeared at the luncheon with plans all rolled up, and he threw them out and made this big announcement that he was going to develop a hotel and all this wonderful stuff. The electric transmission lines would be underground. It would be a good development, like Hilton Head, he told us. That shook us all up. So we started working on a plan to eliminate his grandiose plan. We formed an organization—we had a president, vice president, secretary, and treasurer. The organization would help shepherd the legislation through Congress to make Cumberland a national seashore. We would appear at congressional hearings and that kind of thing to get the enabling legislation passed."

By February 1969, Fraser was scurrying about his northern tract with rolled-up plats and blueprints tucked under his arm. He was quickly putting in place his bodacious plan for an airport big enough for corporate jets and subdivisions of expensive dwellings that would back up to High Point. The whole complex would be called Cumberland Oaks. His plan also called for Lake Whitney to be dredged and restored to its original size and made into a children's playground with canoes and docks for fishing. A marina would be built on the Brickhill River. The beach area would have fancy tiki bars and hot tubs. There would be swings from the great oaks. There would be watermelon cuttings in summer and oyster roasts in winter. In one bizarre notion, he envisioned "sky vans"—an aerial tramway—bringing in food and supplies.

He brought his ninety-foot yacht, *Intrepid*—with its five spacious staterooms and its well-stocked bar—down from Hilton Head so that he and his aides would have comfortable quarters during early construction of the resort. Yellow, mud-streaked bulldozers belching black smoke then began uprooting the lush forest for the airport.

On his southern swath of the island, he hastily built his cedar-sided headquarters at a spot he dubbed Sea Camp, almost midway between Dungeness and Greyfield. Nearby, he cleared the tangled growth for a "campsite"—a space with fifteen pop-up trailers equipped with electric lights, electric heat, and four-burner gas stoves. A central toilet facility had hot showers and an ice machine. Some of his potential buyers would be lodged in the campsite.

Political and business people on the Camden County mainland were jubilant. They envisioned Fraser's resort bringing in $140,000 a year in taxes and creating more than two thousand jobs in what was essentially a one-company county—that company being the smelly paper mill in St. Marys.

But the Carnegies' already bitter dislike for Fraser spiraled to abhorrence. It didn't help a bit that he had an abrasive personality and lacked warmth and tact and diplomacy, they said.

When Fraser came to dinner for the first time at their Greyfield Inn, just down the way from his Sea Camp, Edith Ferguson, who was running the inn with husband Rick, met him at the door and introduced herself. Instead of shaking her outstretched hand, Fraser hung his coat on it.

"Oh, Mr. Fraser was most impossible," said Nancy Rockefeller, whose inherited property now adjoined Fraser's newly acquired swath. "He continually tried to buy me out, no matter how many times I told him I would not sell. He was a most irritating man. I told him it was quite clear that he wanted the whole island to develop and make a fortune off of. I said that because we, the owners of four-fifths of Cumberland for eighty years, would not sell our homes to him, he had resorted to unethical means, even politics, to try and wrestle it from us."

She was referring to a blatant move in 1969, when a local legislator introduced a bill, reportedly at Fraser's request, into the state legislature to create a local authority that could condemn privately owned land on coastal islands and sell or lease it to developers. The bill clearly was aimed at wresting Cumberland from the Carnegies and placing it in Fraser's hands, newspaper editorials said. The bill never passed. A state senator named Jimmy Carter led the move to kill it. Later, it was discovered that the legislator who had introduced it was one of Fraser's lawyers.

Fraser met his match in Nancy Rockefeller. She was the daughter of Andrew II and Bertha Carnegie, who had lived in Dungeness for years with Mama Carnegie and then had closed the mansion and moved to Stafford after she died. Nancy was born in New York in 1900 in her grandmother's apartment, kept exclusively for the Carnegies when they went north. When she was twenty-three, she, a cousin, and her parents boarded the USS *Homeric* for Europe. Also on board was the United States Olympic rowing team, on its way to compete in the 1924 summer games in Paris. Nancy was introduced to a team member, James Stillman "Rocky" Rockefeller, a Yale graduate who was the grand-nephew of oil magnate John D. Rockefeller. She loved him at first sight. The American rowers went on to win a gold medal, and the romance sparked during the Atlantic crossing also won gold. On April 15, 1925, the vacant Dungeness mansion was reopened and aired out for the last time for Nancy and Rocky's flower-bedecked wedding. Eventually, Rocky became the chief executive of First National City Bank (now Citibank) of New York. He and Nancy had four children and spent most of their time at their estate in Greenwich, Connecticut.

But Nancy said her real home was Cumberland. When Charles Fraser showed up to build his resort on it, she went after him full bore.

On an overcast evening in February 1969, Jim Barker, a friend of both Fraser and Nancy, invited the two foes to dinner at his antebellum home on Pinckney Island, near Hilton Head, to see if they could hash out their differences over vintage wine and gourmet food. The effort was a disaster.

"Fraser and I got into quite an argument, and I remember him saying, 'Your family is the stubbornest bunch of people I've ever met,' " Nancy said.

In a letter to her relatives, she minced no words in her estimate of him: "He is a high-powered promoter—out for the dollar—and will stop at nothing to reach his end. He wanted a bridge over to Hilton Head and got the State [of South Carolina] to put it in.

"I let him talk and soon got the idea that he is dangerous in many ways. He ended up saying, 'I've never butted my head so hard as over Cumberland Island.' "

Nancy implored her kinfolk not to help Fraser in any way. "I feel nobody in the family should aid and abet him, like lending him cars and letting him land his airplane on our land," she wrote. "It's very clever of him to get in with us, and cause all kinds of arguments and confusions to our disadvantage."

That might have been true, but one family member got involved in a way she couldn't have imagined. She was Nancy Johnston of Lexington, a pretty girl in her twenties and author of a Sierra Club book. The Carnegies dispatched her to Hilton Head to eyeball how Fraser had developed Sea Pines. Fraser introduced her to a junior executive, Landon Butler. He was infatuated with her and she with him. They ended up marrying. Their wedding and reception were at Plum Orchard, all gussied up for the event. Fraser, being Butler's boss, was an invitée. He showed up at the reception wearing an ascot and lugging a large map case. To the Carnegies' horror, he unstrapped the case during the middle of the affair, laid some maps on the antique mahogany table, and proceeded to tell about his plans for Cumberland. The ladies remembered that he burped a lot as he talked.

In a near panic over Fraser, the heirs revved up their courting of the Park Service. They instructed their Atlanta lawyer, Thornton Morris, to help draw up a bill that would be introduced in Congress to make Cumberland a national park. "Charles Fraser's personality so alienated everyone on the island that they made it very clear to me that they did not want even a tiny part of his development," Morris said.

Retta Wright arranged for Stu Udall, who was then practicing law in Arizona, to come in as a consultant.

"The Carnegies' hired gun," Fraser scoffed of Udall.

Of Fraser, Udall said, "I want to push Charlie into a corner where he has to face the truth. He is good news as a developer but bad news for Cumberland. He is not interested in having a reputation as a spoiler, but he can't have it both ways. He tries to incorporate conservation with economic development, but it doesn't work."

Udall had powerful connections in Washington. His brother was Mo Udall, who at the time was a congressman on the House Interior Committee, which oversaw the National Park Service. Mo later made a brief run at the presidency. United States representative Williamson S. "Bill" Stuckey, Jr., of Georgia, who would introduce the bill to create the national seashore on Cumberland, let Mo use his airplane and pilot to fly around the country during the campaign for the 1976 election.

But even as Fraser was stalking the island and implementing his plans, some Carnegie family members still were leery of a pact with the government. "They had absolutely no interest in walking away from their heritage on Cumberland," said Thornton Morris. "Cumberland was viewed by every Carnegie member I know as a heritage. They felt they were excellent stewards and felt that they were better protectors than the Park Service."

The family wanted some strict guarantees. First and foremost was that they would still have a home on Cumberland, in retained lifetime estates, after the island became a national seashore. "Without that, the deal never would have gotten off the ground," Morris said.

Also, the family demanded that the Park Service promise in writing not to develop the island and not to build a bridge to it. A bridge, they contended, would bring over masses of people, who then would pressure the Park Service to put in restrooms, snack bars, conference centers, and miniature-golf courses.

In the meantime, they still had to deal with Charles Fraser.

———•———

George Hartzog was the director of the National Park Service at that time. Early in March 1970, he got a phone call from the secretary of billionaire philanthropist Paul Mellon, chairman of the Andrew Mellon Foundation, telling him that Mellon would like to have lunch with him at the scion's stately manor in Washington. The secretary did not know the purpose of the invitation.

On March 17, Hartzog sat down to an elegant lunch with Mellon and his lawyer, Stoddard Stevens, senior partner in the New York firm of Sullivan and Cromwell. While they were eating, Stevens turned the conversation abruptly by asking Hartzog, "How would you like to have Cumberland Island?"

"I was floored by his question, but I immediately responded, 'I can't think of anything in the world I would rather have than Cumberland Island,'" Hartzog recalled.

The Park Service was eager to acquire Cumberland and prevent development there. "We had explored several approaches to preserving it. In the absence of legislation authorizing the expenditure of federal money, however, we had no success. This offer from Stoddard Stevens was welcome news."

Stevens said that, assuming the Park Service could work out a deal with the Carnegie descendants, the Andrew Mellon Foundation would buy 75 percent of the island and give it to the Park Service. A condition was that Charles Fraser's property be acquired first, in order to zap his development plans. Another requirement was that title must be taken in the name of a tax-exempt organization, which would in turn donate the land to the United States when Congress authorized the acquisition of the island.

"We had the perfect instrument for taking title to the land—the National Park Foundation," Hartzog said. Congress had just chartered it to accept gifts and broker deals for the Park Service.

When the elated Hartzog returned to his office, he was feverish with curiosity over how Mellon had become interested in Cumberland. He put his people on it. A little checking revealed that Stoddard Stevens had visited Cumberland several times with a friend, Alfred "Bill" Jones, Sr., who had helped develop Sea Island. Stevens was so impressed with Cumberland's magnificence that, upon returning to New York, he told Mellon about it and explained the dangers it faced. Mellon himself then went to the island to drink in its beauty, which prompted the luncheon with Hartzog.

Mellon, who died in 1999, already had a deep interest in national parks, having helped the Park Service at other times and in other places acquire and protect desirable sites. For Cumberland, Mellon would provide more than $7.5 million to purchase the 75 percent of the island. It was assumed that Congress would ante up money for the rest.

In essence, Mellon's gift helped spur passage of the bill to create Cumberland Island National Seashore.

"There would have been no bill had we not had the Mellon money," said Bill Stuckey. "There was a shortage of federal park funds and renewed pressure to build a causeway to the island. There would have been tremendous pressure on us to build a causeway in order to get the federal funds freed up. And if there were a causeway, the Carnegie heirs would fight it.

"And there was never a truer gentleman than Bill Jones. A lot of people said he got the Mellon money so he would not have Charlie Fraser on Cumberland competing with Sea Island. I don't for one minute believe that. Bill Jones believed in the beauty of these islands. And a good example is Bloody Marsh on St. Simons. He went and got the money for it and called me after he had the money, and we introduced the bill to put Bloody Marsh under the National Park Service."

Bloody Marsh was where Oglethorpe's forces defeated the Spaniards in 1742.

"Bill Jones was doing this out of his love for the Golden Isles," Stuckey said. "He took Stoddard Stephens over to Cumberland and showed it to him. Of course, once you see Cumberland Island, that's it."

———•◦•———

"Stoddard Stevens came to me and said that Mr. Mellon would fund the takeout of Charles Fraser if we could deliver two major tracts owned by the Carnegies, in addition to Fraser's," Thornton Morris remembered. In other words, Mellon wanted to be assured that at least three-fifths of the island would be acquired for the money he would put up.

Morris immediately began fretting over whether he could get the three-fifths. "One major tract, Plum Orchard, was now the property of the Graves family, who, of course, were descendants of Nancy and Marius

Johnston," he said. "They had always wanted a national park there, so there was no trouble getting that tract."

Heirs of some small tracts were willing to sell, but their properties would not make up the required three-fifths. The only logical thing to do was go after one of the two remaining big tracts, either of which would give Morris the necessary acreage to satisfy Mellon. One of them was a seventeen-hundred-acre swath belonging to Aunt Floss's descendants, represented by her son Coleman Perkins. He said his family was not interested in selling. The other tract, the thirteen-hundred-acre Greyfield property, was owned by Lucy Ricketson Ferguson, reputedly the stubbornest woman ever to live on Cumberland. "She had absolutely no interest in selling, and she wanted nothing to do with the Park Service," Morris said. "She was not going to oppose the bill creating the park, but she had no interest whatsoever in selling. And Coleman Perkins did not want to sell at all. He just didn't want to do it, and I was getting pretty worried."

He and other park boosters worked on Coleman, cajoling him, explaining the stark reality to him: if he did not give in, there would be no national park, and Cumberland would head in the direction of Hilton Head. "My job was made a little easier by Charles Fraser's abrasiveness," Morris said.

"So Coley said all right, he would sell. He did it just so that Fraser could be taken out and the Park Service could be brought in. He was an unsung hero of the Cumberland Island National Seashore. I can remember even at closing, Coley just didn't want to sell. He did it purely because he felt that it was the right thing for the island and the right thing for America."

———•—•———

Fraser was not a willing seller either—at least not at first. But then he saw that his plans essentially were doomed. With Congress inclined to create a national seashore on Cumberland, and with some of the most influential and wealthy people in the nation backing the effort, developing the island would be more trouble than it was worth. Another

Lucy Carnegie with her granddaughter Lucy Ricketson (known as "Miss Lucy" later in life) and son-in-law Oliver Garrison Ricketson
Courtesy of the National Park Service

factor may have been that Fraser was facing some financial woes at the time over a development in Puerto Rico. And so he decided to sell to the government.

Short and slightly heavyset, hair curly and light, Fraser came from a long line of coastal Georgians and South Carolinians. His ancestors arrived in the Charleston area in 1696 and came to the Georgia coast in 1752. His father was Lieutenant General Joseph B. Fraser, a lumber baron in Hinesville, Georgia. "My father was a very distinguished leader in the Presbyterian Church, the Boy Scouts, the military, the business and the economy of the area," said Fraser, who himself was the first Eagle Scout ever in Liberty County, Georgia.

General Fraser and several partners bought much of Hilton Head for its timber and its speculative potential. As a young man working with timber crews on the island, Charles Fraser successfully urged that no cutting be done in oceanfront stands of virgin pine.

It was at the Yale University School of Law where he studied how to develop a piece of property while at the same time protecting the natural landscape. In particular, a course taught by Myres McDougal, Land Use Planning and Allocation by Private Agreement, absorbed him. The gist of McDougal's message was that property use ought to be planned, because when development occurs without controls, the result can be an ugly, spirit-withering wart on the landscape.

Fraser in the 1950s became obsessed with the idea of building a resort community over which he could retain absolute control. He was in a prime position to do so because his father owned most of Hilton Head.

He burned rubber on U.S. 17, which hugs the coast from Virginia to Florida. He sought out the original developers of beachfront property, asking them what they would do differently if they had a chance to do it over again. Their most consistent message was this: Esthetic control over a development is quickly lost if it is not spelled out in written, ironclad agreements.

Fraser pored over journals and books on architecture, the environment, and nature. He looked up historical and legal documents to learn how property was used over the previous centuries. On Hilton Head, he consulted historical maps to locate old cotton fields, old forts, old plantations.

In 1956, with no development experience and modest funds but a powerful ego, he returned to Hilton Head, where he began sketching out his dream resort. When his renowned Sea Pines Plantation was built in the 1950s and 1960s, it won national acclaim. Landscape designers and urban design specialists hailed it for the way it tastefully preserved trees, natural beauty, and wildness while blending in golf courses, hotels, shopping areas, and subdivisions. The idea was that the development should mix into the environment like leaves on a tree. The roads at Sea Pines meandered among the live oaks and palmettos, bending wherever necessary to miss the big trees. Fraser spent fifty thousand dollars to save a single live oak when he constructed a sea wall for the harbor that was dredged for Sea Pines. He legally committed himself to set aside 25 percent, or one thousand acres, as a wildlife sanctuary. His restrictions on property and homeowners covered some forty pages and were attached to every deed.

Fraser made millions from Sea Pines. At the same time, he was called one of the nation's pioneering developers, a man who set the tone for others to follow. Sea Pines evolved, in a way, as a kind of monument to sensible development.

"Ecology was a word we first used in our literature around here and in conversations in 1956, and it really didn't become part of the national media until '67 or '68, so people were just beginning to hear those words," Fraser said.

Long before the first Earth Day, which took place in 1970, he was credited with stopping a giant chemical plant slated for the South Carolina mainland only three miles from Hilton Head. It would have produced, according to Fraser, unbreathable air and dirty water. Ironically, the resort was what had attracted the chemical company's officials to the spot in the first place.

Meanwhile, his development innovations snagged the attention of other powerful people. He became commissioner of parks, recreation, and tourism for the South Carolina coast. President Lyndon Johnson appointed him to the Citizens' Advisory Committee on Outdoor Recreation and Natural Beauty.

On the committee, he became acquainted with George Hartzog. "Hartzog from time to time talked to me about Cumberland Island and his frustration that he had been unable to get any support from the Georgia congressman in the district in which it was located," Fraser recalled. "I bought the Cumberland property after he told me that the Park Service had no funds to buy it."

Fraser looked around his new territory with satisfaction, absorbing its natural wonders and waxing eloquent over its possibilities. Cumberland was similar to Hilton Head in nearly every respect—terrain, vegetation, wide beach, broad sounds, extensive salt marsh. Then he looked southward at his new neighbors, the Carnegies, and sneered.

"Plum Orchard was beginning to deteriorate badly," he said. "The Dungeness mansion had burned. And in my judgment, the Carnegies had committed scandal by tearing down the remains of the old Caty Greene house, which were magnificent historic remains. There were hundreds of places the Carnegies could have built their house on Cumberland other than the site of such a notable Georgia family. So I was always provoked at the Carnegies for tearing down the structure. The other houses, except for Greyfield, also were clearly being neglected. The locals thought it was outrageous that the Carnegies were letting the houses go to wrack and ruin without repairing the roofs. I later was told that the Carnegies were waiting to see which part of the island they got in the division of the island. They didn't want to spend a lot of money repairing a house which in some future division another member of the family may get.

"The roads were in quite good shape, but the cows and pigs were tearing up the sea oats on the sand dunes, and so great masses of sand dunes were migrating back into the forest, including covering up some wonderful ponds for wading birds. I thought that was outrageous."

Environmental groups had a similar attitude toward Fraser.

Soon after he brought over bellowing bulldozers and chain-saw crews to build his project on Cumberland, members of the newly formed Georgia Conservancy, a powerful group of conservationists, drew a bead on him. They came to Cumberland to videotape the construction work.

The taping, a highly irritated Fraser claimed, was intended to alarm the public over what he was doing on the island. "They began an extremely clever, very brilliant public-relations campaign in which they would fly down and videotape our bulldozers building our runway and interview bulldozer operators—we were planning a dirt strip just like everybody else had, so that we could come in and out—and asking such questions as, 'Well, Mr. Jones, how long have you been working on a bulldozer?' 'Oh, I've been working on a bulldozer for fifteen, twenty years.' And they would say, 'Well, what are you doing here now?' 'Oh, I'm building an airport for Mr. Fraser.' 'Well, what kind of airport is it going to be?' 'Well, I don't know.' 'Well, do you think it's going to have big jet planes coming in?' 'Well, Mr. Fraser's a big man, and I'm sure he's thinking big, so I'm sure Mr. Fraser's going to have a big jetport here.'

"A few hours after the taping, that videotape would be shown in Atlanta on the evening news. It was absolutely brilliant strategy on their part because their objective was to stop me from doing anything on Cumberland."

Financially backing the Georgia Conservancy, he claimed, were the Candlers, who were trying to kick him off the island.

The conservancy's effort got attention. In Atlanta, Augusta, Macon, Savannah—all over Georgia—people were talking about Charlie Fraser. Some said they wouldn't mind shooting him for desecrating Cumberland.

Fraser said the environmentalists were treating him like a pariah and he didn't understand why. After all, he had developed Sea Pines in an environmentally sensitive manner and had gotten national acclaim for it.

About that time, he was asked by a friend to read a speech scheduled for delivery at a Georgia Conservancy environmental conference on Sapelo Island. His friend was unable to make it. "I was assigned one . . . of about twelve cots on a screen porch at the mansion on Sapelo for the men that attended," Fraser recalled. "The man on the cot next to me turned out to be Mr. Hans Neuhauser, who had been leading the Georgia Conservancy attack against me. And you'd thought that poor man had been put right next to a bed of rattlesnakes. He was absolutely petrified. I guess he figured I would strangle him in his sleep."

It was also about this time that Fraser had his famous encounter on Cumberland with David Brower, the founder of Friends of the Earth and later the head of the Sierra Club. Brower, who died in 2000, was known at the time as the world's most militant environmentalist. Writer John McPhee captured Fraser's and Brower's ramblings on Cumberland in his wonderful book *Encounters with the Archdruid.* Fraser went on about his bitterness toward the Carnegies. Despite their professed love for Cumberland and their longtime stewardship, they had been in favor of strip-mining the island for titanium ore, he pointed out. They had kept that as a dirty little secret in all their talk about creating a national seashore, in order to save their island from the likes of him, he felt. "I have no patience with the Carnegies," he said. "They think they're the only ones who can appreciate that beach out there."

Fifteen years after that conversation, Fraser had not changed his mind. In a 1995 interview with a Park Service historian, he again expounded on the Carnegies: "I have no particular warm spot in my heart for the [Thomas] Carnegie side of that family. Thomas Carnegie is *not* the Carnegie who gave the world two thousand five hundred libraries. That was Andrew. And Andrew was disgusted that this brother headed down to Cumberland and stopped working at the age of 40. Andrew thought that was outrageous.

"I greatly respect, enormously respect, the contributions of Andrew Carnegie in his own lifetime, in literally establishing the first major system of sponsored libraries ever in world history. And this from a man who came out of Scotland penniless and used his brilliant mind as many Scots were doing at that time to develop a great industrial empire. So the Andrew Carnegie side of the family I just have enormous respect for.

"But I've judged the others on a basis of what have you done for society? And if that is zero, then my regard for them is based upon that contribution."

In what came to sound like a broken record, Fraser complained regularly that he was being unfairly picked on—that the Carnegie heirs, the Candlers, the news media, the Park Service, and the environmental groups all had their big guns aimed squarely at him.

"I had proposed to the descendants of the Carnegie family and the Candlers in Atlanta that we have some minimum land-use covenants on all of our land on the island to protect the island," he said. "I was thinking in terms of permanent dedication of substantial amounts of parks. . . . They were not interested in that. I proposed that we all restrict our land as an easement, and that was rejected.

"Finally, I proposed that we all agree that we would not dump raw sewage into the waters and that we would not permit any buildings, fast food, or anything else on the main road of Cumberland, that there be at least a five-hundred-foot setback for any gas stations and whatnot that I could easily see happening if the community began to build up over there. They rejected that."

And it was then that Fraser realized it was no use: "I knew that friends of the Jones family at Sea Island were busy at work to get the Mellon Foundation, Old Dominion Fund, and others to put up money to begin buying Cumberland Island.

"George Hartzog then approached me and said, 'Charles, I think I can get some money. I want to buy your property.' And I said, 'George, you're gonna have to pay me every penny I've put into that project.' And he said, 'Including all the money you spent on engineering and other things?' I said, 'Including every cent that I've put out.' And so we then entered into negotiations."

The bill that Representative Bill Stuckey introduced in 1970 to make Cumberland a national seashore began a sluggish trek through Congress. "I loved Cumberland the first time I ever saw it," he said. "That will do it. All you had to do back then, and I'm sure now, was see Cumberland Island one time, and you're hooked. It is a unique place."

He was born in 1935 in Eastman, Georgia, the son of the man who made famous an outrageously sweet candy known as the Pecan Roll, composed of a cylinder of white nougat laced with maraschino cherries and coated with caramel and chopped pecans. Bill Stuckey, Sr., launched his Depression-era business in rural south Georgia in the 1930s, bouncing down rutted country roads to buy pecans from farmers, then selling them to a processor. In 1936, he got the idea of adding pecans to the tasty candy his wife, Ethel, made on the kitchen stove. He opened a store to sell that concoction and other items. A few years later, he had three stores. By 1960, his empire had grown to more than one hundred Stuckey Pecan Shoppes. The stores became familiar icons—and welcomed rest stops—for weary travelers on the South's two-lane highways.

Newly graduated from the University of Georgia in 1958, Bill Stuckey, Jr., age twenty-three, became the company's president. He worked hard for his daddy, but his yen for politics and his connections in high places got him elected in 1966 as a Democrat to the House of Representatives.

The legislation he introduced met most of the Carnegie heirs' demands. Shuddering at the prospect of hordes of visitors spoiling the island's primitive beauty, they insisted the bill spell out that Cumberland be a limited-access wilderness.

But other groups had their wants and weren't to be outdone. As a result, mollycoddling the bill through Congress became the most aggravating period of Stuckey's ten-year political career.

In particular, he knew that if the local county governments came out against the park, he would have an immensely hard task pushing the bill through. A main hurdle was the five-member Camden County Commission. Two of the county commissioners were committed to the park. Two were iffy. But the fifth one favored a private, tax-generating development. He was dead set against the park and vowed to stomp it into the ground.

A man named Edwin "Fats" Godley saved the day.

What Stuckey did was bring the five commissioners to Greyfield Inn one spring evening for what he said would be a fine dinner and maybe a little chat about Cumberland. Accompanying them was Fats Godley, the Camden County clerk of court. He definitely favored the park. Flashing all the charm he could muster, he grabbed the arm of the commissioner opposed to the park and steered him into the bar, while Stuckey escorted the others into the dining room for a gourmet meal. Fats proceeded to get the holdout commissioner slobbering drunk on double shots of Wild Turkey and water. In the dining room, Stuckey was persuading the four remaining commissioners to say yes to a national seashore on Cumberland Island.

"So Fats Godley took care of the only person who might have prevented the national seashore from happening," Stuckey said. "Fats got him drunk. That's one of the great unsung stories of Cumberland Island. I don't think Fats ever got credit for that, and yet if he hadn't been there, it might have turned out differently."

During the seemingly endless rounds of congressional hearings, committee meetings, and give-and-take sessions in legislative offices, the diverse and demanding forces—Carnegies, conservationists, business people, local politicians—lobbied, glad-handed, and bestowed special favors to get what they wanted from the national seashore.

"Everybody was wanting so many different things," Stuckey said. "I talked with them, or George Hartzog talked with them, or somebody on my staff talked with them. When I came home to Georgia, everybody grabbed me. Of course, Miss Lucy Ferguson was never, ever bashful. She would tell you how she felt, and in no uncertain terms. It was a constant battle, getting one to agree to something and another one to agree to something and somebody else *not* to agree to something."

Conservation groups demanded that access to the island be restricted. "You don't want to get me started," Stuckey said. "You can never please them. You never can give them enough, never do enough. The Georgia Conservancy was pushing for restrictions to where it would be virtually nobody over on Cumberland."

Despite the Carnegies' demand that there be no bridge to the island, Camden County's political and business honchos exerted big-time pressure for one. They thought their forces superior. Succumbing to the coercion, Stuckey inserted into his bill a provision that the Park Service would at least appoint an advisory committee to review the bridge issue and make a recommendation each year. That was a mistake, because lined up with the Carnegies were the powerful conservation groups and the Georgia Department of Natural Resources, newly created by Governor Jimmy Carter. Their clout proved greater, and Stuckey yanked the bridge-committee idea from his bill.

"The bridge thing was beat to death, just wore down," he said. "I think everyone came to realize that the bill was not going to go through with a bridge. Most people knew that if the island was going to be preserved, you could not have a bridge over there. If there was going to be a bridge, the bill would never have been passed."

While the legislation ran its daunting course through Congress, the National Park Foundation, well heeled thanks to the $7.5 million from the Andrew Mellon Foundation, began the delicate task of acquiring land from Charles Fraser and the Carnegies.

"The idea was to tie up as much of the seashore as possible before the park was authorized," said Tom Piehl, a Park Service real-estate expert. His job was to oversee the appraisal of island property so that the foundation could pay a fair market price for the land.

A deal had been worked out with Charles Fraser for his acreage, but appraisers scratched their heads as to the value of the island's remaining property.

"It was difficult because Cumberland essentially had been in a one-family ownership for so long, and there had not been much sales of property there," Piehl said. "We appraise property by market comparison with sales of other similar properties. It was difficult with Cumberland because it was hard to find comparable sales. Some of the appraisers we hired actually went up and down the coast—Florida, South Carolina, North Carolina, Virginia—trying to find comparable sales. We were trying to find other islands that, like Cumberland, had no bridge access. There was quite a disparity of people's opinion as to what the value of the land was on Cumberland.

"In the end, if you look back, the prices that were paid were not really too bad. It appeared to be somewhere around five hundred dollars an acre for the land acquired from the majority of Carnegie heirs."

In addition to the land they sold to the park foundation, the heirs of Marius and Nancy Johnston made an extraordinary gift, donating Plum Orchard and twelve surrounding acres, plus fifty thousand dollars in cash and the same amount in furnishings, to the foundation.

By the end of 1970, the foundation owned 75 percent of Cumberland.

In making their deals with the foundation, many of the Carnegies also won the right to live on the island for years to come. "They demanded that they be protected in their ability to have a home on Cumberland in a retained estate," Thornton Morris said. "Without that, the national seashore would never have gotten off the ground."

The foundation signed off on several retained-rights agreements, according to which family members would have a home on the island for decades to come. A major stipulation was included in Stuckey's bill—only structures built prior to February 1970 could be fixed up and inhabited. After that, no new houses or other private structures could be constructed.

The Carnegies got some fabulous deals.

"The Park Service allows the use of these retained-use arrangements as a way of motivating people to sell their land to the government," Piehl explained. "But the Park Service limits the arrangements to twenty-five years and/or the life of the owner and their spouse. But in the transactions on Cumberland, the twenty-five-year limit went to forty years, and some of the life estates were extended to children, who weren't really the owners. At that time, the foundation was negotiating with private money, and Congress had not yet passed the enabling legislation to create the park, so the foundation could make these liberal agreements.

"There's been a lot of talk about the nature of those retained estates because they are very liberal under Park Service standards, but we were not working under Park Service standards. We did not have any laws that we had to follow. And in essence, we were working for the National Park Foundation, which used a pretty liberal set of standards. I mean, whatever it was to get the deal, you threw it into the pot."

Zack Kirkland, a ranger on Cumberland for twenty-five years, said the Carnegie heirs probably could have gotten more money. "My impression was that they sold their property for much less than they could have obtained for it because they wanted to see the island preserved as a park and refuge in some manner," he said.

As the transactions were wrapped up, a scramble ensued among the heirs to secure a structure built before the February 1970 cutoff. Some of them ended up in former caretakers' homes and servants' cottages. One had to settle for a chicken coop that was converted into a cabin. A lucky few got the right to live in some of the still-standing houses. Nancy Butler, the young woman who married Charles Fraser's aide, took over the engineer's house behind Plum Orchard. It once housed the generators that supplied Plum Orchard's power.

———•+•———

In its waning days, on October 23, 1972, the Ninety-second Congress passed the bill designating Cumberland Island a national seashore to "preserve the scenic, scientific and historical character of the island."

Congress recognized the significant efforts of the families and residents of Cumberland to establish a national seashore: "We haven't seen in any other hearing a group of property owners who were so concerned that the island be preserved for the future rather than thinking in terms of economic aspects. . . . It is obvious that you love your island, and we hope that if a seashore is created that it will be handled in such a way that you will be proud of it and your children and your grandchildren will be proud of it."

President Richard Nixon promptly signed the legislation, and Stuckey breathed a sigh of relief. "If it had not passed in 1972, there was no second chance," he said. "It might have been several years before it could have been revived. But by then, the island, I'm sure, would have been developed."

Georgia's congressional districts were being redrawn. Camden County and Cumberland Island no longer would be in Stuckey's district. The man most likely to represent the new district that encompassed the island already had let it be known he would not reintroduce the bill if it failed to pass in 1972.

"It either went through or you could kiss it goodbye," Stuckey said.

By early 1973, the Park Service already was asserting itself on Cumberland. Green-and-gray-uniformed rangers in flat-rimmed Smokey Bear hats scurried around with clipboards and crackling two-way radios, scribbling notes and snapping pictures and poking into the island's musty vacated structures.

At first, Plum Orchard was the new park's headquarters. "It was certainly more of a viable mansion than it is today," Zack Kirkland said. "It was fully furnished, and people were living in it, and it had the feeling of being lived in. Flowers were here and there. It was not open to the public at that point because it was being used as headquarters and also as kind of a staging area for the park. Everything in the mansion really worked—the electricity, the plumbing. One of the maintenance workers' wives was hired temporarily to turn on and off all the spigots in the house every other day or so to make sure that they were operating, [to] keep the water running."

Then the Park Service decided to move its island base to Charles Fraser's old Sea Camp, mostly because a working boat dock was there. The Dungeness dock, which later became the main tie-up for the ferryboat, was nearly in ruins at the time. Fraser's cedar-sided headquarters at Sea Camp became the island's visitor center.

The government also preempted for the park's use many of the Carnegie-era buildings at Dungeness, Plum Orchard, and the other places. Many of the old cars—antiques by then—in which the Carnegies had gallivanted about the island were pushed out of Dungeness's carriage house, which then was christened the park's maintenance shop. The old cars, initially destined for a future Park Service museum, were lined up under the oak trees and left. Years later, they were still there, little more than rust piles—a neglect that greatly chafed the Carnegies.

That was a mistake, park officials acknowledged. But otherwise, they were pleased with their new setup.

"A far as parks go, we were very pleased that we had a relatively new park with so many buildings available to either live in or use," Kirkland said. "Many parks when newly established don't have anything. You've got to get the appropriations and money, funding for construction, from Congress. It takes years and years, and then, finally, things are built. But we had plenty of buildings at Cumberland, whole buildings, a lot that could be used for maintenance, plumbing, carpentry operations. A lot of them were still in running order, particularly those at Dungeness. They just needed some cleaning out and minor repairs to get going. Certainly, when you have as many historic buildings as we have on Cumberland, there's always something to do to them. But many of them were operational to begin with.

"So we had places where we could meet visitors. We were kind of ahead of the game on Cumberland. We even had a developed campground ready to go, the one Fraser had built at Sea Camp. He had those little pop-up tent trailers in the campground; they are all rusted away now. He really had things set up here. It allowed the Park Service to go into operation here rather quickly."

Back-country campsites with the names Hickory Hill and Yankee Paradise were opened on the high-ground areas, which were excellent spots for camping. "We never wanted to have people camping on the beach or so close to it that you could see red, blue, and yellow tents as you walked along the beach," Kirkland said.

For the first two years of its existence, the park remained closed to the public. But the superintendent was under pressure to accommodate visitors. "We were told to get the show on the road," Kirkland said.

At first, the daily visitor load was set at fifty, mainly to see how the ferryboat schedule worked and to gauge if the Park Service's plans for walking tours in the Dungeness area, on the beach, and around Sea Camp were adequate.

But in no time, a feud erupted between conservationists and Camden County's business people and politicos over how many visitors eventually would be allowed. At first, the Park Service, relying on a University of Georgia study, predicted that the island could accommodate more than ten thousand people a day—an astounding number that incensed environmentalists. They threatened a great uprising to prevent hordes of people on the island. The higher the number of people, they argued, the more facilities would have to be built for them. More people and more facilities would work against natural preservation, they said.

The Park Service retrenched; it never had a good idea anyway of how to handle ten thousand people daily. The professor who came up with the figure said his study was misinterpreted. He never actually estimated how many people *should* visit, he said. Rather, he was simply stating that a national seashore like Cumberland would attract that many people if access to the island were unlimited. "After we got into it, we simply determined the island could not accommodate that many people," said a Park Service official.

The Park Service then came out with a slimmed-down plan. Cumberland would be limited to 1,460 visitors a day. More campgrounds would be added, although it was expected that most visitors would be day-trippers who would restrict themselves to the island's southern half. The more primitive northern half would be reserved for backpackers and serious nature lovers.

The decision pleased no one.

The Camden County people complained that the number was still too low. Their county, they said, badly needed the dollars that hordes of camera-toting tourists would bring in.

On the other side, the conservationists said the number was still too high. Robert Coram, an *Atlanta Constitution* reporter who once was a ranger on the island, waged war on the visitor number in several articles. The newspaper's editorial staff also came out squarely against the figure, claiming that masses of people would trample the island's precious vegetation, upset its wildlife, and intrude on the solitude of wilderness-worshiping hikers. Accurate or not, this generated a great outpouring, especially in influential Atlanta. More than fifteen hundred letters were delivered to the Park Service, the vast majority of them dead set against more people on Cumberland.

In the end, the conservationists won. In fact, to their great surprise, they got an even better deal than anticipated—the Park Service set the daily visitor limit at three hundred.

It was the first time the agency had ever set a visitor limit in a national park.

There was little scientific method to the formula. "Actually, it was the maximum number that the ferryboat could accommodate," said former superintendent Denis Davis. Visitors would need reservations to get on the boat because of the strict limit.

Camden County's honchos remain irate over the three-hundred limit. They never accepted it as permanent. Every now and then, they make excursions to Washington to urge Park Service VIPs and members of Congress to boost the limit.

As it turned out, setting a visitor limit was one of two rancorous disputes confronting the park in its early days. The other concerned the place on the mainland from which the Cumberland-bound ferry would depart. The Park Service initially preferred a remote peninsula called Point Peter, six miles from St. Marys. A highway would be built to it, and a mainland visitor center and dock would be constructed. But folks in St. Marys insisted the departure point and ticket booth be in their town. The matter was settled when Point Peter's owner declared that "only over my dead body" would the government get his property. The Park Service then opted for St. Marys. And that was that.

But just as soon as these disputes were settled, others rose to take their place.

CHAPTER TWELVE

THE NATIONAL PARK FOUNDATION'S duty on Cumberland was done. It had acquired 75 percent of the island from Charles Fraser and the Carnegie heirs who were willing to sell.

Until now, the acquisitions for America's newest national seashore had been relatively smooth. But from this point, the process of adding more acreage to the seashore, as Congress had authorized, would be a bureaucratic minefield. Tempers would flare, and things would get downright nasty. Cumberland once again would teem with rumor, paranoia, outrage, and comic relief. With the National Park Foundation gone, the Park Service would have to negotiate on its own with the remaining landowners — and it would be at the mercy of Congress for the purchase money.

Some of the remaining landowners were Carnegie descendants who, unlike most of their kin, sat tight on their property, holding out for more cash. Some swore never to sell to the government, no matter what the price.

Other owners had not a drop of Carnegie blood but had somehow come to own a piece of Cumberland. Several were Camden County officials—a virtual who's who list of county bigwigs—who had heard through the courthouse grapevine that several small lots on Cumberland's south end were for sale to outsiders. They rushed to buy them.

The lots were in what was known as "the OGR tract," formerly owned by Oliver Garrison Ricketson, who had married Retta Carnegie. One of Ricketson's heirs, strapped for cash, offered the lots for sale. The new owners vowed that come hell or high water, the government would pay them big for their land. The Park Service even accused some of them of swapping their parcels back and forth to drive up the price. In an urgent memo to his superiors, Bert Parks, Cumberland's superintendent in the 1970s, warned that such sales might be considered bona fide in a sympathetic court, forcing the Park Service to pay more than what the land really was worth.

His words were prophetic.

Ultimately, the demand for exorbitant prices dragged the Park Service through several costly and embarrassing land-condemnation lawsuits. The outcomes sowed a bitterness that remains today between the agency and former owners.

The agency's most devastating setbacks came at the hands of Grover Henderson, Carol Ruckdeschel's old neighbor in the Settlement and the late Louis McKee's lawyer friend. "I guess I represented about 90 percent of the people who had a beef with the Park Service," he said.

One was Phineas Sprague, Jr., nephew of Nancy Rockefeller and grandson of Andrew Carnegie II. He received two hundred acres of high land in the vicinity of Stafford when his immediate family divided its share of Lucy Carnegie's estate. While Congress was mulling Stuckey's legislation, Sprague sold five lots of less than a half-acre each along the beach dunes to friends, allegedly for sixteen thousand dollars apiece.

Government land dealers cried foul. They said they couldn't believe someone would pay that much for such a small lot. They suspected the deals actually were orchestrated to drive up the land price in anticipation of the time when Sprague would negotiate with the government.

When that day came, Sprague scoffed at the government's offer, which was the appraised value of his land. The government offered him $2,750 per acre, but he demanded $16,000 an acre. The rejection irked the Park Service, which said it would not stand by while Sprague developed land on the island right under its nose. Fearful of his intentions, the agency exercised its eminent-domain authority and condemned his two hundred acres and the five lots he had sold to friends.

In such cases, when the owner refuses to accept the government's offer, the case is turned over to the Justice Department, which sues the owner in United States District Court. When the case goes to trial, the only question for the jury is the value of the land. The value the jury establishes is what the government must pay.

Sprague hired Grover Henderson to represent him.

Government lawyers tried to discredit Sprague's price by citing sales on other islands as comparisons. The lawyers posed a question: Why in the world would anybody pay sixteen thousand dollars for such a small parcel of land, if not to drive up the price so the government would have to pay more?

"But the jury leaned to Sprague's side, and the Park Service took quite a beating," agency real-estate man Tom Piehl said.

The government maintained that Sprague's two hundred acres were worth only about $550,000, but the jury set the figure at $3.2 million. And that's what the government had to pay.

"It was a bur in our saddle that we had to pay that kind of money," Piehl said. "Sprague had his day in court, and we lost."

It was only one of several cases the government would lose on Cumberland.

Grover Henderson also represented James Stillman "Pebble"

A "retained rights" resident bikes down present-day Grand Avenue.
Ordinary visitors cannot ride bicycles on the island.
Courtesy of *the* Atlanta Journal-Constitution

Rockefeller, Jr., one of Nancy Rockefeller's four children. Despite her fervor in stopping Charles Fraser, she and her children balked over making their own deal with the government. The agency then threatened a forced takeover of their island holdings. "The condemnation threat was a great blow to us," Nancy said.

In July 1971, she, her two sons, and two daughters met with George

Hartzog in Washington to make what they said was a "generous" offer—they would donate their share of Cumberland to the Park Service, effective twenty-one years after the death of the last child. That meant the Park Service would not have the land until probably well into the twenty-first century, if even then. In the meantime, the Rockefellers would have the right to build new houses and barns and swimming pools on their land, to run their cars over the island and the beach night or day, and to use the Dungeness dock.

The Park Service declined. Instead, it proffered its own deal—it would give the Rockefellers a forty-year estate on twelve acres if they agreed to sell for the appraised value of five hundred dollars an acre.

"We said *no*," Nan recalled.

Then Pebble's land was condemned. The Park Service said that Pebble, who lived mostly in Maine, had agreed previously to an appraisal of his sixty acres on Cumberland. Moreover, he had made a verbal agreement to negotiate a sale, the agency said. When it tried to consummate the deal, he had backed down, it maintained.

"We really don't know for sure to this day why my piece was picked on," Pebble said. "I think it was a test site because my mother had gone ahead and passed on her land to us four children, and it was divided into four tracts. And I said, 'Ma, you should retain one piece for yourself so you can build your house.' And nobody else wanted to give her a piece of land. So I said, 'You take half of my piece or whatever you want, and you build a house, and when you pass on, you can will it to me.' And so that left me, of the four children, with a smaller piece of land here, which was a little piece going from Grand Avenue over to the beach.

"And so I think the Park Service said, 'Let's try and see what kind of price will be set to take this place down here'—my property. And so it finally came to a jury trial in 1978. My lawyer in Maine, who was very astute, realized that since the case was going to be tried in a courthouse in Georgia, we should have someone who knew his way around in Georgia. So we got Grover Henderson to orchestrate it. And Grover went out and got a second lawyer, whose name was Bobby Lee Cook."

Henderson and Cook latched on to the condemnation suit like a couple of attack dogs.

"I don't know why the Park Service singled out sixty-odd acres that belonged to Pebble Rockefeller," Grover said. "I do know why they singled out two-hundred-odd acres that belonged to Phineas Sprague. It was because he had engaged with another man, named Robert Davis, to develop it. They'd cut it up in lots, sold some lots, recorded the plats in the courthouse. So I know why they got Phineas, but why they added Pebble Rockefeller to it I have no idea. My guess is that they couldn't find anybody named Carnegie who still owned any property over there. So they said, 'Well, the next best thing would be a Rockefeller, to show that we deal even-handedly.' That's speculation; I don't have any proof of that one way or the other."

Pebble and his lawyers banked on ordinary people's outrage over the government's snatching a private citizen's land. "We had an appraiser who had wonderful charts and figures and everything else based on what was maybe a little, flimsy premise," Rockefeller said. "The main thrust of it was that here was the poor Carnegie family, who'd had the place all of their lives, and the big bad government was coming down and taking away their land.

"This played very, very well with the jury. I can remember when we went to have lunch, and the jury walking past and patting me on the shoulders, and saying, 'It's gonna be all right.' "

The jury brought back a price of roughly eighteen thousand dollars an acre.

"The government was aghast, the verdict was so large," Grover said. "They had brought in two *expert* condemnation lawyers from the Justice Department in Washington. And only Bobby Lee Cook and I represented Mr. Sprague and Mr. Rockefeller."

Pebble Rockefeller said, "It was a silly way for the Park Service to do it with me because if they had done a little research, they would have known that our family, above all the families here, were gonna take care of the place. We were never gonna develop it. We had the island at heart. We would never, never, never harm it. And so condemning us was just silly.

"So maybe it's a lesson about life, the way they go about things. Don't be confrontational, but say, 'Okay, we'd like your place. We'll give you a fair value for it, and we want it for such and such.' After my mother passed away, I'd probably have given my parcel to the Park Service."

————•◦•————

After that, Grover and Bobby Lee Cook won case after case against the government.

Cook was no ordinary country lawyer, as Grover made him out to be. At the time, he was rated the second-best trial lawyer in the United States, the top one being F. Lee Bailey in California. Cook, who lived in the town of Summerville in north Georgia's mountains, certainly was Georgia's best-known and most-feared criminal lawyer. Prosecutors and judges alike stood in awe of him. Murder cases were his specialty. He had represented more than two hundred clients accused of murder and had gotten more than 90 percent of them off. Sporting a square-cut goatee and clad in tailor-made suits, he was legendary for his snazzy appearance and down-home manners in the courtroom. He had a habit of looking directly at the jurors with his piercing eyes and pointing at them with his forefinger. He supposedly was the model for the TV lawyer show *Matlock*, which starred Andy Griffith. *People* magazine once declared that "if the Devil ever needed a defense, Bobby Lee Cook would take the case."

"I took the bar exam in 1976 in Atlanta and passed," Grover recalled. "I studied for it while I was surf-fishing on Cumberland. And in January of 1977, I went to Atlanta at a hotel there to attend a 'Bridge the Gap' seminar that was required of new admittees to the Georgia Bar. Hundreds of other people were there.

"And I found some of the seminar programs a little dull, and I went outside and smoked a cigarette. I saw this gentleman who was obviously nattily dressed in Brooks Brothers clothing and Brooks Brothers shoes and Brooks Brothers tie, with a goatee, and smoking a pipe. And I had on ratty blue jeans and a ratty shirt and ratty shoes because that was all I could afford.

"I went over there and struck up a conversation with him, he and I being the only two out there. And that was Bobby Lee Cook. And he and I enjoyed an instant affinity for one another, and we got to be friends. I visited him at his mountain house on Lookout Mountain [near Chattanooga, Tennessee], and he would come visit me at my house on Cumberland.

"So Pebble Rockefeller's personal lawyer in Maine called me up and hired me to represent Pebble. I didn't know the first thing about condemnation. And since this was obviously an important case involving a lot of money, I called Bobby Lee, who is an expert on many things, including condemnation.

"The jury in the Rockefeller case brought in the verdict on a Friday, and the next Monday, I began another two weeks of jury trials with the same judge on smaller parcels, ten acres and less, owned by other people. The judge sealed the verdicts, so no jury would know what another jury had done until it was all over.

"So my next two weeks with juries brought in the same per acre within a few thousand dollars as the Rockefeller jury—eighteen thousand or nineteen thousand dollars. So all my clients were deliriously happy."

But they didn't get their money right away. The Park Service was broke. It had to go to Congress for more appropriations for Cumberland to pay off the condemned landowners, a process that took about two years.

"After that, I don't think there was too much talk from the Park Service about condemnation," Henderson said.

Grover also handled condemnation suits for some of the owners in the OGR tract.

When it became obvious that Cumberland was headed to national-park status, some of the tract's lot owners began erecting cheap A-frames and other flimsy structures on their parcels, Park Service officials complained. The agency warned that the cabins quite likely would be condemned, but the owners proceeded anyway, apparently banking on the probability that their quickly built cabins would drive up their property values.

"They maybe spent six thousand or seven thousand dollars on a shack," said Zack Kirkland. "And when they were condemned and taken to court, they were awarded five or six times as much money as they spent on the place.

"So it's nice guys finish last. It's the same old story."

———•◆•———

A place called Davisville particularly aggravated the Park Service. It was named after Robert Davis, an uneducated but adept jack-of-all-trades who endeared himself to the Carnegies because he did nearly anything they wanted, from house building to cattle herding. He worked nearly all his life for the Carnegies, most of the time for Lucy Ferguson, Cumberland's legendary matriarch. She was particularly fond of him. He rode a fast horse for her once at a racetrack on the mainland. He more or less grew up on the island. Perhaps because of his steadfast devotion to the Carnegies, one of them, Oliver Garrison Ricketson III, sold him a strip of land eight hundred feet wide near Greyfield in 1968. The parcel ran from the island's marsh side to the beach. Ricketson had inherited it as his share of the island split-up.

Some Carnegies saw Davis's strip as a buffer between them and Charles Fraser. But they soon realized that selling to Davis had been the wrong thing to do. He divided most of his land into lots of about a third of an acre to half an acre and sold fifty-four of them. Quite a few were snatched up by local folks on the mainland. Fraser bought several of them.

And when Davisville's owners had their property condemned, several of them called on Grover.

It was Davisville that ushered Grover to Cumberland. A stout man with a receding hairline, he was born in Dunn, North Carolina, and served a stint with the United States Navy and a tour in Vietnam before going to work in Fernandina. There, he found out that his mother had purchased one of Robert Davis's marsh-front lots on Cumberland. He asked Davis to show him the property. "I immediately fell in love with the island," Grover said in his thick Southern drawl.

Then he learned that passage of the Cumberland Island National Seashore Act was imminent. "It had an interesting provision in it—that in order to get a retained estate, construction of the house had to have begun before February 1, 1970," he said. "Well, we missed that.

"But I was of the opinion, as was most people in this part of the country, that the government would never condemn land for a park. They would for military bases, they would for highways, but certainly not a park. But I wasn't aware of any history that led me to that conclusion.

"So I built an A-frame on the marsh in Davisville [with his mother's permission]. I had First Federal of Jacksonville finance it because I didn't have any money at the time. I was broke—not broke, but genteelly impoverished. And interestingly enough, I was the first one the government condemned. They paid me fifty-five thousand dollars for it. Other people were building houses on their lots, too. My friend Louis McKee had built a house there, too.

"I had met Louie a year or two previously by taking his deposition in a lawsuit in Orange Park, Florida. He was a surveyor in Orange Park when it was bursting at the seams, and he was the *busiest* surveyor in that part of the world. He and his wife, Betty, and his friend Ebby and I got to be good friends. Louie for some reason did not like where he was in Davisville. Apparently, he had a neighbor there who liked to play loud music at night, and Louie went to bed early. He was a very quiet, mild-mannered man. And Louie didn't like the loud music, so he bought an old fishing shack from Larry Miller up on the north end of Cumberland at High Point, on a little creek that came off Christmas Creek. He fixed it up. He literally rebuilt it. He had plumbing and electricity and a bathroom and air conditioning and heat and that sort of thing, a kitchen, too. And he left the south end of the island.

"But I think I was the first one the government wanted in Davisville because I think they saw me as a threat. Understand, at this point in time, the government was planning to bring ten thousand people a day over to Cumberland. I thought that was *absurd*. Ludicrous. And I told them so. So I got my fifty-five thousand dollars from them for my house. I had to pay the bank off, so I think I netted forty thousand.

"About this time, my friend Louie also had been looking on the north end for me to buy a place. He found Beulah Alberty's old house in the Settlement there. When I say he found it, he went to the county courthouse and checked the records. He found me this heir of Beulah's who lived in Miami, who was a teacher. [She was Peggy, the niece Beulah had put through school.] And I paid forty thousand dollars for Beulah's house in '74. It was fee-simple property; you can do anything you want with it, so long as the laws of the state of Georgia aren't violated.

"I started fixing up Beulah's old house. I'm convinced that it was built at night because there wasn't a square corner in it. It did not have plumbing, did not have electricity. The roof leaked. It was falling in the middle because it hadn't been supported correctly.

"I had never plumbed before. I had never fixed roofs. So there were a lot of things I couldn't do that I had to contract out. I did do the plumbing. Some friends in Jacksonville put a new tin roof on it. I hired an old gentleman to do the wiring. And then I hired a friend from Jacksonville to bring some four-by-twelve creosoted timbers that came out of a warehouse, and jacked up the house so it was close to being level. I lived there, and I did paneling on the inside.

"And I started corresponding with the Park Service, telling them I wanted a life estate. Well, the newspaper archives will tell you I was very active politically against whatever the Park Service was doing, because whatever they did, I thought was wrong. And I made the front page of the

Atlanta Journal and the *Jacksonville Times-Union* and the local papers.

"The bottom line is that the Park Service hated and loathed and detested me. And they refused to give me a life estate. They went so far as to have Beulah's house put on the National Register of Historic Places so they could have a reason to condemn it from me, even though it was built before February 1, 1970, and qualified.

"Well, at that time, junior senator Robert Morgan of North Carolina was one of my mama's best friends. Jimmy Carter was president. Mother and I flew to Washington and met with Senator Morgan. And we met with whoever the secretary of the interior was at the time; I don't remember who it was.

"With the good help of Senator Morgan, the government decided that it was in their best interests to give me a life estate. They'd given everybody else a life estate who met the criteria. It was not an easy thing, but I got my life estate.

"By that time, Louie McKee had got killed, and I convinced the Park Service to exchange houses with me."

Actually, he was nervous about staying in the Settlement. That was because he and Carol Ruckdeschel were neighbors. The cabin that McKee had obtained for Carol was only a couple of hundred feet from Grover's house. He could look out the window and see the back porch where Carol had shot McKee. He had not been there when it happened, but the porch was a grisly reminder of what had taken place.

"I told the Park Service—this was about in '81—that they were hoisted by their own petard, because I said, 'I'm gonna give you a historic house. Y'all made it historic to try to circumvent giving me a life estate. So I'm gonna hoist you by your own petard, and I'll swap houses with you, and I'll get Louie's old cabin 'cause I like it better.' It had plumbing, bathrooms, air conditioning, heat, a kitchen."

The Park Service very reluctantly agreed to the swap, and Grover moved to the retreat once occupied by his deceased friend. He began making alterations appropriate to his needs.

Then, in April 1984, four years after McKee's death, Grover received a blow from another side that was completely unexpected. In an audacious move, Carol filed a $350,000 lawsuit against him, claiming that she had "only recently" learned of provisions in McKee's will that left her $10,000 in cash and all of his Cumberland Island property.

Before she sued, she told lawyers for McKee's estate that she would relinquish her claim to the money if the estate would give her quit-claim deeds to any property McKee possessed on the island. The lawyers readily agreed, surmising that the property was the possession of the National Park Service anyway, and that McKee's life-estate interest in it had expired with his death. Carol apparently had made a bad deal. But she hadn't.

Her lawyers then sent Grover a certified letter saying that McKee's old shack—the one Grover had moved into after giving up Beulah Alberty's house—actually belonged to Carol. The lawyers demanded he vacate the premises and pay her back rent and damages as a result of his modifications to the structure.

It was Grover's turn to be aghast. Mad as hell, he refused her demands. Carol sued.

To defend himself, Grover called again on his buddy Bobby Lee Cook. He fully expected to win, as Bobby Lee loved the challenge when the odds seemed stacked against a client. Cook reportedly would base Grover's case on the fact that Georgia law precludes one who has intentionally killed another from benefiting as a result of the death. He would have to prove, though, that Carol had shot McKee on purpose, which was contrary to what the coroner's jury had ruled.

In the end, the National Park Service decided the issue. The day before the case was to be heard in court, the Park Service filed a quiet title action on Louis McKee's former property. The court entered an order staying the proceedings until the action was concluded. Then the Park Service and Carol and Grover brokered a settlement. The government paid her thirty-five thousand dollars and gave her the right to occupy McKee's shanty for the rest of her life. She now had two lifetime estates on

Cumberland. She presented McKee's former cabin to her parents to use. When the Park Service later told her she had to move her muddy hog pen out of the Settlement because it might offend visitors to the nearby First African Baptist Church, she relocated the stock to McKee's old place. Grover was awarded twenty-seven thousand dollars and attorney's fees.

But to him, that was only a starter. He wanted another house on the island and a lifetime estate and lots of other things to boot.

"When we were still litigating Carol's lawsuit, I got a call from Bob Baker, the regional Park Service director in Atlanta," Grover remembered. "That's like getting a call from your banker; it's never good news. And Baker said, 'We're gonna lose the lawsuit with Carol. It's her house. You've got ninety days to vacate it.' And I said, 'Now, Mr. Baker, what about this contract I have with you people?' He said, 'Contract disputes with the United States of America are brought in the U.S. Court of Claims in Washington.' So I said, 'I don't want a lawsuit with you people. I want another house.' And they said, 'Well, that's just *too* bad. Ninety days to vacate the island.' And I said, 'This is just not right.'

"Baker now has told me to get out in ninety days. This is about in 1982 or so. Fortunately [in 1980], I had supported U.S. senator Mack Mattingly, who was a Republican, against Herman Talmadge, who had held that Senate seat forever. Mattingly went in on Ronald Reagan's coattails, as many other people did. And Senator Morgan was now the senior senator in North Carolina. So I called Mama, said, 'Mama, you call Senator Morgan, and I got a friend who is a U.S. senator from Georgia.' And I said, 'I want the government to gimme another house on Cumberland Island. They got a whole bunch of them in their inventory, and it's the right thing to do.' So Mother called Senator Morgan. I called Senator Mattingly. Senator Mattingly's administrative assistant in Washington was my accountant for twenty years.

"So Mother and I flew to Washington to meet with Senator Mattingly and Senator Morgan. We had a meeting in Senator Morgan's office because he was senior. Senator Morgan, Senator Mattingly, the secretary of the interior, and my poor ol' widowed mama were all in there. And I'll never forget it because we had lunch in the Senate Dining Room, and Mother met Teddy Kennedy and thought that he was the most wonderful thing she's ever seen.

"That afternoon, I gave them a little slide presentation about Beulah's house and Louie's house and the fact that the government was just letting everything on Cumberland go to hell, and the government was targeting me and trying to make my life as difficult as possible over on Cumberland. And the bottom line was that the two senators advised the secretary of the interior to give me my house.

"And when I got back, I told the park superintendent at Cumberland, 'You'll be getting a letter from Bob Baker saying, "Give Grover Henderson a house."' So I told the Park Service people, 'I want you to take me around and show me all the houses in your inventory on the island.' They had just about condemned everybody but the rich people. People from Davisville were the first to be condemned. But yet Lucy Ferguson at Greyfield wasn't condemned, and the Rockefellers weren't condemned, except Pebble.

"So anyway, the only place that the park superintendent took me was Davisville. And he said, 'You can't have Kenneth Harrison's house because the new chief ranger has just moved in it, and I promised him he could stay there for two years. You can't have that.' And I said, 'Well, that's the house I want.' And he said, 'You can't have it.'

"Then I said, 'Well, I want Wilbur Reddick's house.' He said, 'You can't have that either because that's in the wilderness area.'

"I said, 'I want Duck House.' He said, 'Can't have that either. It's in the wilderness, too.' I said, 'You got people in the wilderness, what difference does it make?' He said, 'The parameters I was given by Bob Baker is that you can't have anything in the wilderness.' I said okay.

"Then I said, 'How 'bout the brick cottage up there by Dungeness?' He said, 'Can't have that.' I said, 'Why not?' He said, ' 'Cause I live there.'

"And then I said, 'You haven't left me much choice. I'll take Cap'n

The "Duck House" was used by guests who wanted to be out on the sloughs hunting ducks by daybreak.

Dickey's old house.' And that's the house I got. Then I said, 'But I'll only take it under certain conditions.' I said, 'Louie McKee had his house, and he built a barn with an apartment in it. That's two houses. I want two houses.' The Park Service said, 'Okay. You can [also] have a little house on that road where Cap'n Dickey's is. It was built by Marvin Wilhite. And you can have that house.'

"So I got both those houses. I said, 'Well, that's not all I want.' Nobody had lived in Cap'n Dickey's house in ten years. The plumbing was a mess. I said, 'I need some money to fix the house up.' And we settled on an amount of money. It's confidential—I can't say.

"I said, 'Well, I want more things.' The superintendent said, 'Whaddaya want?' I said, 'I want the right to add on as much as I want to. I want the right to tie my boat up at Dungeness dock.' He said okay. I'm the only person that's got that right.

"Then I said, 'I want the right to use a chain saw in the wilderness to harvest pinewood. And I want the right to close Davisville Road from the main road to where it turns in from Goodsell's. I want the right to block that off. And I want a further assurance that you can't ever build anything on that road, any encroachment on my property.' He said, 'Okay, we'll give you that.'

"And I said, 'I want the right to drive on the beach.' And he said, 'Oh, no, you can't have that. Nobody's got that right but Mary Bullard, and she's got it because she's handicapped.' I said, 'Hell, that's not exactly right. Others on this island have that right.' And he said, 'No, I'm not giving it to you under any circumstances.' I said, 'Fine. I'll go see Judge Anthony Alaimo [of the district court] and the U.S. attorney in Brunswick.'

"And I called Eddie Booth, who was the U.S. attorney. I said, 'Eddie, meet me in Judge Alaimo's chambers because we got a few matters to iron out.' And I explained to Judge Alaimo about how the Carnegies and the Rockefellers and all these other people had the right to drive on the beach, and I want it, too. And Judge Alaimo looked through those reading glasses of his with a stare that would open a oyster at twenty feet. And he said, 'Eddie, is what Grover's saying the truth?' And Eddie said, 'Yes, sir.' And the judge said, 'If they've got it, Grover can have it, too.'

"So I got the right to drive on the beach. And I got all of this until I die. If I'm married when I die, my wife can stay there when she dies.

"And I didn't just wake up one morning and somebody said, 'Wouldn't you just love to have a house on Cumberland?' I have fought, kicked, litigated, spent money. Had I not been a lawyer, I could not have afforded to pay a lawyer to do the work that I've done—probably half a million dollars in time."

A sign in front of Grover's cottage reads, "Groverville." "I own one acre," he says, "but I use a lot more than that."

———————

On the north end, the Candlers at High Point also were set to make a deal with the National Park Foundation in 1971, but as their lawyer, Thornton Morris, put it, "the foundation screwed up." The Candlers, he said, stood ready to donate a substantial portion of their two-thousand-plus acres at High Point. "All that was needed was $550,000 to close out the deal, but the [foundation] and the Park Service felt that was too high," Morris said. "The family had signed an option to sell, but the park people let it expire."

A little more than a decade later, in 1982, the Candlers were no longer feeling so charitable. The Park Service, though, still wanted their land. But now the price had gone up. This time, the Park Service had to fork over $9.6 million for the property.

"The National Park Foundation screwed it up; they just screwed up the deal," Morris said. "There was just incompetence. The Park Service could have gotten the Candler property for $550,000, but ended up paying $9.6 million for it."

Billy Warren, a member of the Candler clan, remembered that the original sticking point was over retained rights. "We were going to donate the whole [High Point complex] if they would give us retained rights on certain parts," he said. "We wanted ten- or fifteen-acre lots there to build houses at some time. The Park Service was unwilling to do that. Then we got away from the out-and-out gift when they said it was out of the question about getting these lots to build on."

When the Candlers finally inked their deal with the Park Service in 1982, they got not only the $9.6 million but also some of the most liberal retained-rights agreements on the island. The Park Service waived its 1970 cutoff to allow the Candlers to take any existing house or structure in the High Point compound, no matter how dilapidated, and rebuild it or add on to it to make it habitable. They would have five years to do that, after which they could do nothing else with the structures.

"A lot of the Park Service's standard language is that you can't modify a building [as part of a retained estate] beyond some minor putting it back together," said Tom Piehl, the agency's land expert. "The Candlers just went one step further. They were allowed to rebuild."

They looked around at what remained at High Point. Howard Candler III substantially redid the house that was built for George and Aubrey Merrow. Sam Candler chose the old caretaker's quarters where Carol Ruckdeschel and John Pennington had lived when they first came to the island. Relative Billy Warren and his family took over a former servant's dwelling that had been a garage with an apartment on top and essentially built a new house there. Howard and Sam's sister, Kitty, got one of Jessie Bailey's old shacks, which she tore down and replaced with a new dwelling of more than twenty-five hundred square feet. The old hotel that was part of the bustling resort of the late 1800s and the old Candler house built in 1941 were made into time-share retreats for other family members and guests.

Thornton Morris figured a way for the Candlers to have a presence on Cumberland for decades to come: they incorporated as High Point, Inc. In their agreement with the Park Service, they obtained retained rights on thirty-eight acres until the death of the youngest shareholders, some of whom were still unborn when the deal was struck in 1982.

"The park, then, is going to be with these people for another sixty or seventy years, or even beyond that," Tom Piehl said. "It's going to be a long time to clear out all those people."

In 2000, there were still twenty-one retained rights on Cumberland. Several are supposed to be up as early as 2010. When they expire, the property will be vacated and turned over to the Park Service.

Thornton Morris got a retained estate on the marsh side of Cumberland. "It's called Morristown," he said. "I got it directly from my good friend Coleman Perkins, who named it Morristown after me."

Ann and Richard Goodsell of Atlanta got their retained estate because of Richard's former business dealings with Charles Fraser. A developer, Goodsell had completed a three-building office complex on Hilton

Head. Fraser's Sea Pines Company was the sole tenant. A financial setback in the mid-1970s caused Sea Pines to default on the lease, which had to be renegotiated at a considerable loss of revenue for Goodsell. In return for the loss, Goodsell obtained a 38 percent share of Fraser's old Cumberland Island Holding Company. Goodsell discovered that it still owned two acres on Cumberland. Fraser never had let go completely of the island. A decade later, Goodsell bought the balance of the holding company when Sea Pines' assets were sold in bankruptcy court in South Carolina.

"So then I had full ownership of the two acres on Cumberland," Goodsell said. "I hired a lawyer to effect a swap with the Park Service for a retained estate. They didn't want us to build anything between Sea Camp and Dungeness on the bluff, and we didn't particularly want to be in that location because it's a very active area for backpackers. So we swapped those two acres for a place over in Davisville."

Dr. Ben Jenkins, a cigar-chomping eye, ear, nose, and throat specialist from Coweta County, near Atlanta, got his lifetime estate with help from Thornton Morris, who arranged for him to take possession of a small lot from one of the Carnegies in the early 1970s.

In 1976, Jenkins was a senior member and a former president of the powerful Georgia State Board of Medical Examiners when a stunning investigation by the *Atlanta Constitution* alleged he had used fake documents to get his medical degree. Jenkins later admitted that he received his degree from the University of Nuevo Leon in Monterey, Mexico, "through unusual circumstances." But he said he had done nothing wrong. The newspaper report touched off a sensational investigation by the medical board. After a year of sleuthing and holding hearings, the board in 1977 decided not to take any disciplinary action against him. "Inasmuch as the board and the University of Nuevo Leon did not rely on the fraud to issue the diploma or license, then no action should be taken," it concluded.

Jenkins's retained right expires in 2010, when he will be eighty-seven. "I'll guarantee you one thing," he said. "If I'm still living, they'll get me off this island kicking and screaming. They'll probably bring in the army with guns to get me off the damn thing. I hope that the government'll make some provision in the future for us."

Lawrence Miller, Jr., a descendant of one of the north end's white families who refused to sell to Lucy Carnegie, obtained a retained estate, but only after a bitter battle with the Park Service for condemning his property.

A civil engineer, Miller already was battle-scarred from run-ins with Charles Fraser. "Fraser tried his best to buy our property, too, and we wouldn't sell to him," Miller said. "He kept saying, 'Well, I'm *not* gonna develop the property next to you and let you reap the benefits from it.' And I said, 'Yes, you are.' I had several confrontations with him. We had no intention of selling to him. We didn't want him there in the first place. But since he was gonna be there, we were gonna reap the benefits of whatever he did; we weren't going to let him have it. You see, if he developed a tract of land right next to ours, and ours was right over the fence, then our property would immediately enhance in value. And he knew that. I knew that. That wasn't hard to see."

Fraser, though, was in tight with Miller's father, an engineer and architect. He had hired Lawrence Miller, Sr., to do the engineering for his Cumberland Oaks project. "My father took this job. He needed the work," Lawrence Jr. explained. "He wanted the job and the money."

When the elder Miller died, Lawrence Jr. inherited his father's engineering plans for Fraser's project. "And then I went out and destroyed them," he said. "Everybody was bothering me about them. So one day, I just got everything out and destroyed it—burned it all as a way of saying [it was] the end. I didn't see any point in saving Charlie Fraser's work.

"In later years, after Fraser was gone, I subdivided some of our land and made lots, building lots out of it. [Prior to that, he had sold a plot to Louis McKee—the one Carol got when McKee was killed.] We knew the national park was coming, and we had no value on the land. You know, land is valued according to what is sold in the area, and nothing had ever been sold in the area. So in order to establish the value of the land, I subdivided some of it and sold seven lots. By so doing, I established the value of the land. And we got more for our land when the Park Service took it.

"The Park Service condemned all of us. They made us several offers which we wouldn't take, and they filed condemnation proceedings against us. We got a lawyer and fought them, went to court. And we pretty much got what we wanted. We couldn't keep the land. We knew they were gonna get it. But we wanted to get as much as we could."

In settling with the government, Miller got a retained estate.

"I foresaw this whole thing coming, and I deeded part of what I own to my grandchildren. And my youngest grandchild at the time was a wee little baby. He now owned part of it, and thereby his name was put on the life estate. So at the time we settled with the Park Service, we had seventy-eight years on the life expectancy, based on the mortality tables. We have used up some of it, but those grandchildren have got it, and they're gonna have it well into the twenty-first century.

"I don't like the national park. We don't have the same freedom and liberty. We don't have any land. We had land before. We could hunt and do what we wanted to do on our own land. We don't have that anymore. All we have is a life interest in a house and one acre. And we can't even do anything with that. It belongs to the national park."

----◦-◦----

Charles Fraser never got over his bruised feelings. In an interview a few years ago, he accused the Park Service of managing Cumberland mainly for the benefit of the Carnegies and the Candlers, at the expense of ordinary Americans. "It's a perfect thing for them," he said. "They've transferred security costs to the government. The government keeps the American public away from the government lands, and it's a scandal. But it's part and parcel of the pattern of American life of the last thirty years. It's as though the government was an imperial king, a situation like the Waldorf hunting lands of the kings of Europe, where peasants were hung if they were caught with a rabbit in their hands in the king's woods.

"And I think it remains an open scandal that a few families able to manipulate the media are able to keep the level of use on Cumberland pegged at such a limited number of visitors—three hundred, last time I heard. It's a scandal, and at some point, someone is going to spend money to publicize that scandal and bring pressure upon whoever's in charge of the Park Service to do something about it.

"After we sold our property, others on the island began to ask extraordinarily high prices for their property. The Candlers eventually got five or six or seven times as much per acre as we sold for. And the Park Service was utterly terrorized by Miss Lucy Ferguson.

"Had Cumberland been privately developed with taste and with sensitivity and with large areas set aside as conservation areas and parks, a lot more people would have benefited very richly."

———————

Former Cumberland superintendent Denis Davis, driving a green Park Service truck down Grand Avenue in the central portion of the island, points to the roofs of some large houses barely visible through the spring foliage. "That property is still owned by the Rockefeller side of the Carnegies," he says. "If they wanted to, they could build a hotel or subdivision there, and there's nothing we could do about it."

Georgia Rockefeller Rose, daughter of Nancy Rockefeller, sold her eighty-two acres adjacent to Sea Camp in 1997 to an Atlanta buyer who remained anonymous. Some outsiders speculated it was John Kennedy, Jr. Whoever it was, the sale sent shivers up the spines of the Park Service and conservation groups. This was the advent, they feared, of the development they so long had tried to forestall.

Thornton Morris, who represented Rose, tried to calm the jumpy nerves. "I can assure you that the buyer has every intention of protecting this property and not developing it," he said. At the most, he added, maybe one house would be built on the property.

"But truth be known," Tom Piehl says, "we're really at their mercy. If they want to sell their property, we don't have the money to buy it. We can't prevent them from selling it. We can't prevent them from developing it. If in fact there was some large-scale development planned, the park superintendent would have to declare that it was a resource-damaging action, and we would have to notify Washington with the stipulation that we don't have the money to do anything about it. So we would ask Washington for something, to reprogram our money or some kind of special permission, to try to buy these properties or file condemnation on them. But we really couldn't file condemnation without having money to pay for it. So we would be in a bad situation.

"Of course, we could implore Congress to appropriate money. They have done it on other occasions. They've done it where there has been an emergency; they have made special reprogrammings or special appropriations. But you hate to be the one asking for it because the people who give you the money are looking for something in return later on. So it's the old trade-off up there."

———————

Lucy Ferguson was more stubborn than all the Carnegies and Candlers together. She had inherited most of the Greyfield tract on Cumberland. She battled the Park Service at every turn. She swore that as long as she breathed, the government would not get one square inch of her property.

It didn't.

CHAPTER THIRTEEN

OF ALL THE WOMEN who dominated Cumberland, Lucy Ricketson Ferguson was the toughest, the bossiest, the orneriest of them all. Of all the people who lived here, she is the one people remember—fondly or not so fondly—the most vividly. She was Cumberland's empress, its very embodiment. The island was her life.

She had the will, the fortitude, the courage, and the stubbornness of another strong Lucy, her grandmother Lucy Coleman Carnegie, for whom she was named.

Of all Thomas and Lucy Carnegie's grandchildren, Lucy Ferguson was the only one who made Cumberland her home. The others came and went. Lucy Ferguson not only lived here, she possessed the island as no one had before her.

Known universally as "Miss Lucy," she dared the National Park Service to lift a finger against her or her property, the eleven-hundred-acres known as "the Greyfield tract"—the island's largest swath of land still in private ownership. Lucy had inherited it as well as the imposing Greyfield mansion in the Carnegies' division of

Lucy Ricketson (later Lucy Ferguson) at age eight
Courtesy of the National Park Service

Cumberland. The Park Service did not take her dare.

Her enmity toward the agency was legendary. She derisively called park rangers "Smokey Bears." She made it clear to anyone listening that the island had spiritual significance for her family, that five generations of Carnegies were buried here, and that her family had been good caretakers of the island and could protect it better than the Park Service.

"I'm not going to sit by and watch the Park Service ruin this island," she once said. "They can't do anything to me except condemn my property. And I told them, 'Go ahead and do it.' They've done nothing. They think that when I pop off, my nineteen grandchildren will get in a devil of a fuss, and then it will be easy to acquire."

After she ate her evening meal on the rainy September 11, 1989, she announced, "I am going to die." A few hours later, she was dead, three days shy of her ninetieth birthday.

Her passing marked the end of an era. Never again would there be a single owner, outside the National Park Service, who would reign over Cumberland as Miss Lucy had. Only Lucy Carnegie and Caty Greene Miller before her attained such eminence on Cumberland.

With her final breath, the winds of change began swirling on Cumberland. This is Lucy Ferguson's story.

Some saw her as a woman of heroic dimensions, a tiny, wispy widow fighting the United States government. She had a rare ability to command respect and affection from the people of rural Camden County, as well as from members of Congress. In many people's minds, she was a one-woman police force who chased off developers for the better part of the twentieth century.

Because of her formidability, relatives, friends, and the Park Service knew that her opposition to a national park on Cumberland could derail the plan. Thornton Morris said he was hired by the Carnegies to help push the legislation through Congress mainly because he was Miss Lucy's lawyer. "It wasn't because I was any great person to put this together more than probably some other people could have," he said. "The family felt I had the added benefit of Lucy's ear. If she opposed it, we would not be able to get a bill through Congress.

"At that time, and I would say this was in the 1960s or 1970s, Lucy was probably one of the five or six most politically connected women in

Georgia. Her husband, Bob Ferguson, who died in 1968, had served in the Georgia legislature. He was probably the first Yankee freely elected to the general assembly after Reconstruction. He was immensely popular. Because he had been in the legislature, he knew people like Herman Talmadge and Richard Russell, both former governors and U.S. senators from Georgia, and the other powers of that period. We needed their help to get the bill through Congress."

In the end, Miss Lucy softened a tiny bit. She still was not in favor of the Park Service coming to her island, but for her family's sake and for the sake of the island, she would not oppose a national park.

Nevertheless, she wrung a big concession from the Park Service. When legislation setting up the park was passed in 1972, the government promised that it would not acquire her land in her lifetime if she pledged not to develop it.

"Lucy said, 'I'm a full-time resident. It's unlikely that any of my kids will ever be full-time residents,' " Morris recalled. "She said, 'I'm a farmer, and I want to live on my land the rest of my life.' And the Park Service said, 'Okay. We won't bother you again in your lifetime.' "

That is not to say that Miss Lucy didn't bother the Park Service. "If you ask me what the park superintendent's job was, I'd say it was rushing over to Lucy's every few minutes," a resident once said. Park rangers said she was responsible for having more than one superintendent transferred from her domain.

———— · ·• ————

Her physical appearance gave little clue to her great strength of will. She was a mite of a woman, weighing only about eighty pounds. If she stood on her toes, she might reach five feet. She rode a horse like an Indian and looked like one as well, with her olive complexion, high cheekbones, and straight, dark hair pulled into a bun at the back of her neck and tied up in a kerchief.

"She had the most expressive face I've ever seen because when you first talked to her, her eyes would get real wide and her mouth would narrow," said writer Robert Coram, who knew her when he was a park ranger. "Then her sense of humor came out—her dark brown eyes would crinkle shut, and her mouth would just explode with laughter."

When she was riled, it was best to stay out of her way. She once shot at a low-flying airplane she thought was buzzing her, though she didn't come close to hitting it.

She had to battle deafness all her life, a legacy of the scarlet fever she caught at age thirteen. Nevertheless, she could charm a roomful of guests at Greyfield as easily as she could track an illegal hunter or strip a rattlesnake of its skin.

Though she could have worn finery—her estimated wealth was $30 million—she instead dressed as if her clothing came from a thrift shop.

"She wore some of the oldest clothes I've ever seen on anybody," said Jack Horne, who wrangled horses for her. "If you saw her in the street, you'd think she didn't have a dollar to her name. She always drove an old car, most of the time without a muffler. She had an old felt top hat. She liked sweaters. She had an old gray sweater she wore for years. She wore overalls, the old dungarees type. And she'd wear little old tennis shoes. She would buy two pair for a dollar in them little dime stores.

"She was like one of the old-timey people; you'da thought she was ready to go out there and plow a hundred acres, the way she dressed and looked."

After Bob died, she moved a few miles away into a two-story, frame farmhouse on Cumberland Sound, on property that was once part of Robert Stafford's old plantation. The original occupant was Henry Miller, the former Stafford cattle manager who helped Bill Carnegie dig up his wife, Gertrude, so Bill could snip a locket of her hair. Lucy called her new abode Serendipity. It became as much a natural-history museum as a home. She had more bones, skulls, rattlesnake skins, arrowheads, shells, and other island relics—including a stuffed pelican and a tapir skull—than furniture.

———•·•———

She was born on September 14, 1899, in her grandmother's apartment in the Life Building in New York City. Her parents were Oliver Garrison Ricketson and Margaret Florence Carnegie "Retta" Ricketson, oldest daughter of Lucy and Tom Carnegie. Oliver's family owned an iron foundry in Pittsburgh. He married Retta in the soot-covered town on a cold, wintry, rainy day. Retta squeaked and slogged up to the altar in her galoshes, hidden by her beautiful white satin wedding dress, the same one Miss Lucy and her granddaughters would wear years later at their own weddings.

Oliver was handsome, debonair, always impeccably dressed. The ladies had an eye for him, which probably contributed to the undoing of his marriage. On his prized schooner, he and his friends traveled to plantations along the tidal rivers to hunt quail.

Mama Carnegie built Greyfield in 1901 for Retta and Oliver. The graceful, three-story stucco mansion overlooked a high bluff on Cumberland Sound two miles north of Dungeness. Its wide verandas faced a broad lawn shaded by live oaks, whose heavy branches twisted into the ground. Across the lawn was Grand Avenue. Oliver, a man of high refinement, was the inspiration behind Greyfield's design. He wanted it built like a large, eighteenth-century coastal plantation house, raised on a high basement. Greyfield's kitchen and dining room were thus on the ground floor. A door led from the dining room to an ivy-covered pergola running across the lawn to the children's playhouse. In the mansion's upstairs were a well-stocked library, an elegant living room, spacious bedrooms, and servants' quarters.

Oliver and Retta brought little Lucy to Cumberland for the first time when she was six weeks old and lying in a laundry basket. She, brother Ollie Jr., seven years older than she, and their parents lived with Mama Carnegie at Dungeness until Greyfield was ready for occupancy.

The Ricketsons spent only the winters at Greyfield. Lucy and Oliver had French nurses and German governesses on the island. When they turned school age, they were privately tutored in the little schoolroom connected to the pergola.

Lucy was a precocious, rambunctious child from the start. It was she who, as a little girl, caught Marius Johnston holding hands with Nancy Carnegie under a blanket before Nancy's first husband, James Hever, died. She snitched to her family, whereupon her grandmother dispatched Marius on the extended African safari.

On trips with their parents to New York or abroad to London and Paris, Lucy and Ollie Jr. found ways of getting into great mischief—like when they dropped wet toilet paper from hotel windows onto people walking below. The hotel people told their father, who put a quick end to the

Lucy Ricketson and her brother Oliver Ricketson, Jr.
Courtesy of the National Park Service

shenanigans. When they were visiting Skibo Castle in Scotland one year, Uncle Andrew Carnegie caught Lucy and a girl cousin tussling in a hallway. He pulled them apart and chided them: "Scottish lassies should not play like boys." He may have been the only man she was ever afraid of. She told friends and family in later years that she had an intense dislike for her great-uncle.

On Cumberland, her cousins adored her, although she sometimes mischievously shoved them into ponds and indoor swimming pools with all their clothes on. She rode her sprightly, crop-tailed pony, Coxie, in a beautiful riding habit and hat that made her cousins jealous. Oliver Sr. rode his steed next to her, chicly done up in a white shirt, a smart riding jacket, and occasionally a derby hat.

Oliver and Retta separated before Lucy turned a teenager. Retta had become an alcoholic. She and Lucy moved to Washington so Lucy could go to the private school picked out for her there—the exclusive Holton Arms School for girls.

"I was just terrified on my first day there," Lucy recalled. "I will never forget the first lunch. Great, long tables. The girl on one side of me asked, 'Who's your father?' And I answered, 'Oliver Ricketson.' She replied, 'I don't care about that. *Who* is he?' I replied again, 'I told you, he's Oliver Ricketson.' 'My father is Admiral Wood,' she said. I was so flustered that I drank the cups of cocoa at my left *and* at my right. One of those cups was the girl's.

"But I loved school. Mrs. Holton was still there. I loved being called a schoolgirl, with my books under my arms."

She and her brother spent most summers at their grandparents' compound at Ricketson Point, near the old whaling town of New Bedford, Massachusetts. It was there as a teenager that Lucy met and courted Robert W. "Bob" Ferguson, whose family was in the lumber business in New Bedford and whose grandfather had quarried granite at Mount Desert Island in Maine.

He and Lucy were married at Ricketson Point in 1920. By all accounts, it was an excellent match. They seemed made for each other. They both loved animals and cherished Cumberland. Early on, they decided to make the island their permanent address and raise their kids there. Through an arrangement with the trustees of Mama Carnegie's trust, Bob and Lucy were given the use of Greyfield.

They had four children. The oldest, Robert Jr., known as "Bobby," was born in 1921. Then came Margaret, whom they called "Retta," then Ricky and Cindy. All of them were born in Massachusetts. Ricky was Gogo Ferguson's father.

Lucy was quite pretty in those days. She stayed brown as a nut because she lived outdoors most of the time. When she washed her hair, she would go outside and lie in the sun to dry it.

When Bob was puttering around somewhere else, she would stuff a couple of bottles of beer in her knapsack, climb on her horse, and be gone all day. Sometimes, she went down to the beach, peeled off her clothes, and skinny-dipped. Sometimes, she shot a rabbit with the pistol she al-

Lucy and Bob Ferguson with three of their four children (l to r) Bobby, Retta, and Ricky. Ricky was the father of Gogo Ferguson.
Courtesy of the National Park Service

ways packed. She would stop in a clearing, skin the creature, and cook it over a fire. When she boasted she could survive in the woods if she ever had to, no one doubted her.

In their early years, Lucy and Bob explored nearly every square foot of Cumberland. They gigged flounder at the south end's jetties and cooked the fish at home. They hunted ducks in the sloughs. They frolicked in Dungeness's big indoor pool and somersaulted from the big rings dangling from the ceiling. Sometimes, they would dare each other to swing across the pool. Lucy would start from one end and Bob from the other, and they would meet in the middle and playfully kick out to try to make the other lose hold and tumble into the water.

After learning to fly, they kept a two-seat plane in a Quonset-hut hangar at Stafford, where they converted the old golf course into a landing strip. At Kingsland on the mainland, they helped build an oval racetrack, where they raced their fast horses against steeds of other well-to-dos on the Georgia coast. In the main events, Lucy rode Marius Johnston's thoroughbred mare Sandi, pushing the horse hellbent around the turns and down the backstretch as if it were the Kentucky Derby. People lugging picnic baskets and bottles of wine came from as far as Savannah and Jacksonville to see the races.

Lucy was one of the most savvy horsewomen on the Georgia coast. During World War II, when Coast Guard and United States Army personnel patrolled Cumberland's beach on horseback, she sometimes went down to the barracks and taunted them: "Why don't you boys bring your horses to the beach and see how fast they are?" They would take her up on it. Her horse often won. The military men took quite a liking to her. It was in her honor that they named their Cumberland encampment Lucy's Village.

Bob flew a military spotter aircraft during the war. Their two sons also served in the conflict. Like many other women of that era, Lucy rolled bandages and darned socks and uniforms to support the soldiers at the front.

To serve in the war, Bob resigned his seat in the Georgia legislature, where he had represented Camden County for six years. "Bob would've been reelected, but he felt he had to go to war because our two boys were both there," Lucy said. "I couldn't say anything because if anything had happened to one of them, he wouldn't have forgiven me."

When Bob first ran for office, Lucy, who tilted toward the Republicans, reluctantly turned Democrat to help him win. At that time, a Republican—or even a person married to one—stood about as much chance as a goat of getting elected in Georgia. Bob also had another drawback—he was a Yankee by birth. Nevertheless, he won the election and became the first Yankee ever freely elected to the Georgia House of Representatives. "When we got up to Atlanta and they realized they'd elected a Yankee, they were very good sports," Lucy said. "They thought they'd just elected a regular man from Camden County." Not only did his fellow lawmakers accept him, they introduced him and Lucy to the state's power clique. Those heady connections helped propel Lucy into the ranks of influential women.

She never hesitated to use those contacts. Once, when the Army Corps of Engineers was dredging across from Cumberland to build the Kings Bay Ammunition Depot on the mainland, the work caused the creek behind Dungeness to silt up. The Carnegies no longer could get their boat up the creek. When they protested repeatedly to the dredge-boat captain, he said there was nothing he could do—his orders were from Washington. Lucy then put in a call to her friends up there. The next day, a hopper dredge arrived to clean out the creek.

On Cumberland, Lucy and Bob viewed themselves as genteel farmers, laid-back country folk raising horses, cattle, and a menagerie of other animals. They built another herd of free-roaming, white-faced Herefords, although their fifty or so cows were only a fraction of the five hundred head that had roamed Cumberland during Mama Carnegie's era. Every so often, Lucy and Bob, their workers, and some of Lucy's kin, all on horseback, rounded up the herd—just as in Mama Carnegie's day—and drove the animals through the cattle dip at Stafford to treat them for screw worms and other parasites.

Not everyone on Cumberland appreciated the cattle. Some Carnegies complained that the animals attracted hordes of flies and spread ticks. More than one relative demanded that Lucy get her cows off their land. At Stafford, Bertha Carnegie said the bovines caused her allergies to flare up. She protested to the trustees. Lucy and Bob got fed up with the nagging and had most of the herd barged to their three-thousand-acre farm on the mainland just across the Florida border. They had bought the place, called Woodstock Farm, during the Depression. After Cumberland was divided among the various clans and Lucy got clear title to Greyfield, she had the animals brought back to the island.

She never made much money on the cattle. She probably broke even at best. Roaming freely on the island, the cattle weren't the fattest and the healthiest of their kind. But the idea of a cattle woman had a romantic appeal for Lucy. She loved the cattle drives and the auctions and the haggling over prices at market. No one was going to tell her that maybe she should try a more profitable venture.

———————

Lucy dearly wanted her four children to be as passionate about Cumberland as she was. She wanted them to be accomplished riders and outdoor types. They were given the freedom to wander the island as soon as they learned to swim, which was at an early age. Stodgy old Andrew Carnegie II over at Stafford was shocked when he heard that the Ferguson kids didn't always wear bathing suits when they swam.

"My childhood was almost magical," said Retta Ferguson McDowell, Lucy's oldest daughter. "Mother was very active. We went riding often. We helped milk the cows every morning and every evening. We were raising chickens and pigeons. Hunting. Duck hunting. Deer hunting. Busy every single minute. Mother organized our lives.

"A typical day started off when an older black man named Lee, who lived in a little corner house, would come into my bedroom at Greyfield and light the fire. This was princess treatment. He'd say hello. Then I'd watch the fire and wait 'til the room got a little warmer because we were cold in the winter. Then I got up and got dressed.

"My brother Rick and I would be out of bed at the crack of dawn. We would run out to see if our hens had hatched their eggs or if there were any new calves born. We would help milk the cows. Then we'd come back to breakfast, which usually was oatmeal and the thickest cream you'd ever seen from these cows. We'd separate the milk, and the cream was so thick you could dip it out. We had three square meals a day. We had hens and eggs and chicken and pigeons and venison, beef, and pork. And there was a wonderful garden at Stafford, which had a big, big garden with a caretaker. The produce from Stafford was delivered every day to our house. Beautiful food, fresh and ample.

"Our friends were those who did the wash, cleaned the stalls, cut the wood, and put it in a shed. They were mostly black. I became very, very comfortable with them. There was a governess from Germany who boxed our ears, not a very pleasant person."

Like their mother before them, Retta and her siblings were tutored in a little house behind the Greyfield mansion. One tutor was Harvard graduate Lynwood Bryant. "It sounded adventurous, and I was fed up with the academic world, so I accepted the job when Miss Lucy offered it," he said in explaining why he came to Cumberland.

The kids stayed in class until noon. There were no grades.

"I learned to read when I was four or five," Retta recalled. "Robert read at three."

Even before they could read, Lucy tried to teach them to ride. There certainly was no shortage of horses on which to learn. In the spacious stables and corrals Lucy built at Greyfield were wild horses right off the range. They were not broken until they were two years old, but that was two years too late. Horse experts opine that if a horse isn't touched all over at a very young age, it will be much more difficult to train later.

Some people said that Lucy's horses never were broken completely.

"Mother expected her children to love to ride," Retta said. "But the two boys lost interest immediately when one of the ponies that was brought from the stockyard ran under a low barn door with my oldest brother, Bobby, on him. Bobby was knocked off and nearly scalped. Both brothers then said, 'Phooey, no more riding for us.'

"I was continually being bucked off. The horse would shy at everything, even a little leaf wiggling in the wind. A pig would jump out of the bushes, and the horse would jump like a rocket, and off we'd go. But I was always willing to please. I was not afraid of being scalped or bloodied or anything and wanted to go right along with Miss Lucy. I was her shadow. Did everything with her. She and I would ride every day. She would arrange for Nana, our cook, to fix a picnic lunch, and we'd stop somewhere in a sunny spot out of the wind and build a fire and roast oysters and eat whatever else we had for lunch. Then we'd sleep in the sun for a while. Sometimes, we'd ride up to Plum Orchard for lunch or for dinner. We might stable our horses at Plum Orchard and spend the night."

During those rambles, Lucy told Retta tales about her girlhood on Cumberland. The past was vivid for Lucy, and she kept it alive and magical through her stories. She told of the golfer who came over from Scotland to design Stafford's course, only to be thrown from his horse and killed. She told of the beautiful Gertrude and how Uncle Bill went nearly crazy when she died. When she and Retta rode along the old telephone line strung between Plum Orchard and Greyfield, Lucy recalled how the families called each other about parties and dinners. "Once when I was a little girl, there was a marvelous party at Plum Orchard," Lucy told Retta. "In those days, the women wore beautiful slippers dyed to match their dresses. The guests were in the dining room, and I crawled into the room and under the table to look at all those wonderful shoes. Nobody knew I was there."

When it was time for her kids to go to school up north, Lucy took them to the tiny whistle stop of Yulee on the Florida mainland. She stood along the tracks and waved a handkerchief to stop the train. The kids rode by themselves on the thirty-seven-hour journey to Massachusetts, where their school was.

Lucy stood by the tracks long after the train was out of sight. Because of her deafness, she could not hear it, but she could feel its vibrations from miles away.

Her family said she developed superb senses of sight and smell to compensate for her hearing loss. She once told a grandchild that other people might be able to hear a shrimp boat coming up the river, but she could smell it before they could see it. She wore a hearing aid, but, to her annoyance, it squeaked a lot. She would say, "Oh, blast this trumpet. I'm turning it off." But even when she shut it off, she seemed able to hear, "especially if you said something you weren't supposed to," said granddaughter Jesseca Ferguson, who spent summers with Lucy. "She could lip read, I know that. She would also say that she could hear a high-pitched whistle, so that if I was ever lost or something, she would say, 'Just whistle, and I'll hear you.' Maybe she was trying to reassure me, but I believed her."

Those who knew Lucy well said her deafness contributed to her sense of self and her judgment of others. She could talk with you for five minutes and tell if you were a good or bad person. She had the spiritual intuition to understand whether she could trust you or not.

Sometimes, she had a little fun with her hearing. "Lucy and I were on the mainland once to make a telephone call to Atlanta because we could not call from the island," Thornton Morris recalled. "She kept one piece of her hearing aid in her ear and the microphone in her bra, between her breasts. So when she talked on the telephone, she didn't talk with the receiver in her ear. She talked with the telephone upside down. The mouthpiece was at her mouth, and the receiver was between her breasts. And there was this guy standing behind her while she was talking, waiting to use the phone when she finished. He just couldn't believe what he was seeing. She turned around and saw him staring at her. She said, 'I'll be through in just a moment.' And when she hung up, she turned to him and said, 'I so wish I could hear out of here'—pointing to one of her ears—'but I can hear only out of here'—pointing to her breasts. The guy was dumbfounded.

"Lucy was always doing little things like that, and she got a kick out of it."

But sometimes, she got into an awful blue funk, at which times she would seek solace in an employee's cottage across the big lawn from Greyfield. The cottage was occupied by Greyfield's maintenance man, James Douglass. His daughter Gloria remembered a bedraggled Lucy coming around from time to time. "She would come over and go into our bathroom and take a bath," Gloria said. "And Mother'd give her a clean gown to put on, and she'd go get in Mother's bed. I remember her saying to my mother, 'Geneva, you're one of the few persons I can trust to have a clean bed.' And she'd go right in that bed and sleep for hours. Mother told me later, 'I didn't know what to do. I couldn't figure out what to do except just let her do what she wanted to do. 'Cause after all, this was her place.' And Miss Ferguson would rest and rest just for hours at a time, and when she'd get up, she'd look and feel a lot better, and she'd put on her old clothes and go on back up to the mansion."

———————

By the time Lucy packed her kids off to school in the early 1930s, she had become Cumberland's czarina. Like her grandmother before her, she put her indelible stamp on the island. Her close cousin Nancy Rockefeller once quipped that Lucy thought she owned just about everything that walked on Cumberland. Lucy herself believed that. She occasionally employed wranglers from the mainland to round up and break in wild horses. They were sold to buyers on the mainland. Some horses she sold unbroken to rodeo promoters. She declared that she was the owner of the island's wild hogs, which her workers trapped and sold.

The island's unfettered spaces provided Lucy ample opportunity to indulge her great interest in animals. She loved all kinds—great and small, cuddly and slippery, cute and repulsive. "I never did discover my love for animals," she remarked once. "It was just something that happened. We had as many as thirty dogs at one time."

Those would have been the Dalmatians she raised. Over the years, she had a variety of dogs, including twin Labrador retrievers and a little mongrel she called Ugly. She had a pet deer named Dinah that would come into the house. One summer, she took it up north with her on the train in a Pullman car, like a pet dog.

She kept numerous chickens and dozens of cooing pigeons, cackling guineas, strutting bantam roosters, and squawking peacocks, all of which roved Greyfield. The peacocks made a peculiar, high-pitched sound resembling a human screaming "Help!" This sometimes caused visitors and employees to come running, thinking someone was in distress.

Once, when Lucy was driving a dirt road on the mainland, she spied something fluffy in the road—a baby black vulture, or buzzard, as people in Georgia called it. She brought it over to Cumberland and raised it. It would flap from one end of the island to the other but always would return to Greyfield. Lucy giggled when it landed gently on her thin shoulder. Her family and visitors loved photographing the ungainly creature on its shoulder perch. Sometimes, it landed on the back of one of Lucy's old nags, which didn't seem to mind the bird. The vulture refused to conform to the dietary habits of its breed, eating only the choice-grade hamburger and beef tips Lucy tossed its way.

She traveled the world and brought back exotic animals from places she visited. She had ostriches, which laid their big eggs around Greyfield, and kangaroos, which were cared for by Greyfield's servants, who really had no notion of how to provide for the strange creatures. Her miniature Sicilian donkeys roamed the island at will. Once, in a trade with a veterinarian friend who worked for Ringling Bros. and Barnum & Bailey, she swapped some of the donkeys for a stallion name Rex, which she set free on the island. One donkey, Spencer, was Greyfield's yard pet. He would come to the mansion's back door or up to the windows of servants' cottages and bray shrilly, a signal he wanted something to eat. Some of the servants fed him cigarettes, which he found delectable.

Lucy had two tapirs, big, hog-like creatures from the South American rain forest. When one of them died, she displayed its skull on her coffee table at Serendipity. The surviving tapir, a female named Tippy, lived in a fenced-in, swampy area near Greyfield. Lucy would go to the fence and call it, and the animal would come lumbering from the woods. Others could call and call, but the tapir never responded to them, only to Miss Lucy.

Her great love of animals extended to those in the wild. Family members said her sharp eye for the critters of the woods, the marshes, and the fields compensated for her deafness. When she found a dead animal, she sometimes cut it open to see what made it tick.

She was especially protective of the loggerheads that crawled up the beach to lay their eggs in the spring and summer. "Don't ever mess with a turtle nest," she warned. She was fond of cakes made from turtle eggs when she was young, but in later years, she was liable to shoot anyone caught robbing a nest.

Alligators fascinated her. She went down to Lake Whitney and sat and watched them for hours. She worried that the sand dunes building up from the beach would fill in the pond, or that salt water would get into it and push out the fresh water and make the gators leave. Some of the scaly reptiles were as long as fourteen feet. When she made the sound of a baby alligator, the eerie eyes and snouts of big gators would emerge from the water, a scene that made some visitors a bit nervous. She found great delight in taking guests to the lily-covered pond behind Plum Orchard, where she stood on the cedar-railed bridge and called up the reptiles.

Another reptile, the rattlesnake, did not get as kind a treatment. She had great respect for the venomous creatures, but she never let one get away if she could help it. She carried a forked stick and a knife strapped to her hip in case she ran across one. When she spied a rattler coiled up

Lucy Ferguson on Cumberland Island's beach
with a sea turtle in the 1940s
Courtesy of the National Park Service

or slithering across her path, she deftly pinned it to the ground with her stick, jerked out her knife, and sliced off its head. Then she relieved it of its hide. Occasionally, she took the snake meat home and cooked it and ate it. The skins were given to a black servant named White, who cured them and fashioned them into wallets and pocketbooks and belts. She kept some of the bigger ones to adorn Greyfield and Serendipity. One of the largest rattler hides ever taken on Cumberland stretched for years over a Greyfield fireplace.

There was only one four-legged animal she could not tolerate—the wild hog. The grunting, beady-eyed animals stalked the beach at night, rooting up sea-turtle nests and slurping the eggs. Sometimes, even before a turtle had given up her last egg, the hogs already were cracking open the newly laid ones. Lucy and some of her workers would get their strongest and bravest hunting dogs and walk down the beach at night, trying to catch the marauding swine. The rest of the island suffered just as badly from them. They rooted up the entire island, destroying vegetation and making life hard for other animals. Everywhere Lucy went, she saw the damage. Particularly worrisome were the huge holes they gouged on Stafford's landing strip, where the dug-up ground could wreck an airplane taking off or landing. Several times, island workers had to rush to Stafford to fill in hog-made holes so that Lucy or Bob or others could land their planes.

But if Lucy disliked wild hogs, she downright despised the two-legged kind of predator—the poachers who trespassed on Cumberland to hunt without permission. Lucy's abhorrence of them bordered on obsession. When they shot and killed her pet deer, Dinah, she loathed them. When they killed Spencer, Greyfield's lovable old donkey, she swore to eradicate them.

Her vow caused consternation among family members, who were afraid that one day one of the "rednecks" would blow Lucy's head off. The trespassers were tough and felt no qualms about shooting first, the family warned her. But just as she showed no fear of rattlesnakes, she exhibited no alarm over poachers. Lucy wasn't scared of the devil, it was said. Although they would readily shoot a deer on someone else's property, she didn't believe they would shoot her or any other person. She said she knew who many of them were, though she rarely was able to catch them in the act.

She enlisted her children, her employees, her guests, her cousins, her in-laws, and even her grandchildren to help track down poachers. She kept an eye out for strange lights at night and told her workers to listen for gunshots. When a light appeared or a gun went off, she and the men hopped into a car to see who it was.

During the 1940s, when her cousin Pebble Rockefeller was stationed at Turner Field at Albany, Georgia, he and a friend spent a weekend with her at Greyfield. At breakfast, Lucy told the young men she wanted them to go poacher hunting with her that evening. "We will hide under the bank along the river and catch them when they come back with the deer," she said.

The three of them crouched under the bank while infernal sandflies nibbled unmercifully at them. Then a boat came up the river and anchored. Half a dozen men with guns hopped ashore. They lit a fire, then melted into the woods. The sandflies became intolerable, but Lucy insisted that she and her two allies stick it out until the trespassers came back. When they did, they had no deer. They squatted around the fire and sipped from whiskey jugs. Then Lucy went after them. "I caught you this time!" she yelled as she charged out of the dark. They jumped to their feet, guns cocked and ready to fire. It was a grim situation: a tiny woman and two very nervous partners, the three of them unarmed, facing six rough-looking men with guns.

Then Lucy said to her adversaries, "Why, Harry, how could you? And Tom and Jack, you really know better. I would not have thought of you doing a thing like this. I hate to have you arrested."

The six men put down their guns. The man called Harry said, "Oh, no, Mrs. Ferguson, don't do that. You see we have no deer. We were just sitting and talking."

They offered to pass their jugs around, and everyone relaxed.

"There are no deer, but you meant to get one, and I know that you are poaching, but I'll give you another chance," Lucy said. "Come back with us to Greyfield, and we'll have some breakfast."

The trespassers looked relieved but turned down her invitation. They suspected she would have the sheriff waiting on them when they got to Greyfield.

Gogo Ferguson was pressed into poacher patrol. "We'd stake out their campsites," Gogo said. "If Grandmother saw a fresh campsite, we'd go back that night. We'd all be in our pajamas, and we'd sneak out into the woods and try to catch them. Most of the time, we didn't."

Polly Stein, wife of Lucy's cousin Carter Carnegie, went with Lucy on a poacher adventure once. "My husband told me that if I went poacher hunting with Lucy, he'd never bring me to Cumberland again," she said. "Well, one night, I came to him, and I stood over his bed, and I said, 'Lucy's here, and she wants me to go after poachers with her.' I told him, 'Now's your time to show me whether I'm considered an equal in this house.' I was a great believer in women's rights back then. So he said, 'Go ahead.' "

She climbed into Lucy's old, battered Jeep. Half an hour later, the vehicle's motor conked out on a back road that was hardly more than a path. "It was pitch-black dark in the woods, and I was scared," Polly said. "I thought we could retrace our steps on the road, but it was so dark you couldn't see the road. So we got down on our hands and knees to try to feel the road's ruts in the ground. Finally, by the grace of God, I found the ruts. We felt our way up the road for a few minutes, and then we saw a glimmer of light, and we headed towards it. And then we had the most thrilling surprise—the hunters were some players for the Brooklyn Dodgers. My husband and I were avid baseball fans, so this was an immense surprise. They had come over to the island in a little putt-putt boat. They got Lucy's truck started. They climbed into the back of the truck, and we took the whole bunch to the Cottage. Carter got up, and Eddie [the Cottage's butler] gave them breakfast.

"They told us that they had paid a man on the mainland, who told them he had made arrangements for them to hunt on Cumberland. They were embarrassed when we told them that the man had suckered them in, that they were hunting illegally on the island. They told us they had done well. They were getting two or three deer a week, and they were paying this man by the week. Lucy called the sheriff and had him pay a visit to that man, and that put a stop to that. Carter said that if the Dodger players wanted to go hunting on the island, they could come next time as his guests."

Lucy's closest employees were not above suspicion of poaching. She wanted to make sure they were not shooting illegally. Geneva

Hungerford, whose first husband was Greyfield maintenance man James Douglass, heard Lucy poking around her family's cottage at night. "We would be in bed and hear the garbage cans rattling," Geneva said. "Jimmy would say, 'Be quiet. It's Mrs. Ferguson looking to see if we are killing deer, to see if we are honest.'

" . . . When I was away, she even went inside our cottage. I could come back and see where she had gone through my things. I never took anything, so she learned to trust us, and that was a star in my crown. If they ever found you with anything that didn't belong to you, they would fire you right there."

Geneva said she learned to drive taking Lucy rattlesnake hunting in the afternoons.

What particularly galled Lucy and Bob were the visitors other family members allowed on the island to hunt, and who let their bagged game spoil. Lucy and Bob believed in consuming what they shot. To them, it was a great transgression to let game taken during the hunt go to waste.

Once, a hunter brought Morrie Johnston at Plum Orchard some whiskey to get his permission to shoot on the island. That man killed two sacks of mallards near Lake Whitney and hauled them around in the truck he borrowed from Morrie so long that they spoiled.

As J. H. "Smitty" Smith, who worked for Lucy and Bob, remembered, "Miss Lucy somehow heard about it, and she and Mr. Ferguson got down fast to the manager's office at Dungeness. When the hunter came up, Miss Lucy and Mr. Ferguson started raising Cain with him about how he was letting them ducks go to rot. They were yelling, and both Mr. Ferguson and that hunter grabbed their shotguns. Then Miss Lucy stepped back in and made them put their guns down. And I guess they would have had a shootout if it wasn't for her."

Lucy told the man who managed Greyfield for Bob and her to stop the poaching. He became overzealous at it. Some family members maintain that his relentless pursuit of poachers doomed the Dungeness mansion.

His name was J. B. Peeples. He was rough, gruff, and sun-blasted. He had an incredible mean streak when he was drinking. Most of the people who didn't have business with him avoided him.

"He scared all of us," Gogo said. "He drank a lot, and he had cut most of his fingers off on one hand. He used to smoke a cigarette between his stumps and smoke it right to the end and then put that one out and light up another."

Lucy and Bob hooked up with J. B. early on, when he was a pimply teenager trapping raccoons on the island. He became their do-everything man, overseeing their cattle and farming operations, maintaining their buildings and equipment, and supervising their farm hands. At one time or another, he was also a shrimper and a logger. He once had a timber-cutting contract with the Carnegies. He lost his fingers when he was trying to crank up a saw at the sawmill and a belt slipped.

Another sideline was making whiskey—with Bob as one of his partners. "Bob Ferguson's greatest claim to fame was that he and J. B. Peeples made moonshine over on Cumberland in the 1930s and 1940s," said George Davis, a longtime Carnegie friend. "There were two or three stills. They used to use chicken feed to make the shine. They'd get these hundred-pound bags of scratch feed, which had a lot of corn and barley and so forth, and they used that. The revenuers used to wonder why they used so much chicken feed over on Cumberland. They used it for the mash to make the moonshine. Oh, yeah. They also used chicken manure to make it hot, make it ferment faster. White lightnin'—that's what they called the whiskey they made. I know they used to drink a lot of it. Pretty strong stuff."

No one today remembers whether they sold any of their concoction. Bob did not think of himself as a lawbreaker. He was simply making a little whiskey for home consumption.

Lucy told J. B. that he should never let poachers set foot on

Cumberland. If they did, he was supposed to kick them off pronto. J. B. took it to mean that he could shoot them if necessary.

On a sultry spring night in 1959, he heard a boat coming up a creek to an island landing. He hid his car and crouched behind a tree. Two men with rifles came up the bank. His own gun loaded and cocked, J. B. stepped out from behind the tree and shone a light in their faces. "Get the hell off this island or I'll blow your goddamned heads off!" he yelled.

They turned and took off running toward their boat. J. B. chased them. He thought he recognized one of them as a man Lucy had had arrested for poaching only a few weeks earlier. He demanded they stop. When they didn't, he shot one in the leg. The man and his buddy escaped.

The doctor who cared for the injured man on the mainland also identified him as the poacher Lucy had nabbed earlier. The man, however, never owned up to being J. B.'s victim. He said he accidentally shot himself.

The Carnegies said J. B.'s victim got revenge in another way. A few weeks after the shooting, the lines of the *Dungeness* were cut from the Dungeness dock, and the vessel was set adrift. The *Dungeness* carried the Carnegies to and from the island and brought in mail and supplies. The Coast Guard found her a couple of days later, half sunk and drifting out to sea, several bullet holes riddling her hull.

A few weeks later, the great Dungeness mansion caught fire and burned to the ground. Authorities ruled it a case of arson. The Carnegies had no doubt that the culprit was J. B.'s target that night, the same person who had tried to scuttle the *Dungeness*. The sheriff's office said there was insufficient evidence to arrest the man, and he was never charged.

***

After Bob died in 1968, Lucy placed near total reliance on J. B., whose power ascended several notches on Cumberland. She told her family that he was the only one she could depend on. Whether he was butchering hogs or treating cows for cuts and bites and broken bones, Lucy was usually right there with him. She loved going to cattle auctions with him and to his father's place near Kingsland, where they watched bloody cockfights. She enjoyed that kind of life, and he was the one who enabled her to pursue it. In turn, J. B. had an almost lapdog dependency on Lucy. He was in her kitchen at five every morning, sipping coffee, dragging on a cigarette, and staring out the door into the darkness. He and Lucy often drove an old blue Jeep about the island, one of Lucy's dogs always with them.

"He had an amazing friendship with my grandmother," Gogo said. "Anything J. B. said went. All of us were a little bit frightened of him, of how he wanted things run. He managed her farm as well as he could, I guess. There was always a joke that J. B. would simply drive a bulldozer or a tractor into the marsh when he wanted Grandmother to buy a new one."

"When Miss Lucy was right there on the island, J. B. was all right," said Jack Horne, Lucy's former horse wrangler. "She would keep him straight. But when she wasn't around, he'd get to drinking, and he'd flip. When he was sober, he was a good man, but when he was drinking, it was really hard to get along with him. If something aggravated him, he'd do it in. Like he had two young puppies, and when they didn't do what he wanted them to, he took his knife out and cut both their throats."

One time, when Lucy was in Europe and J. B. was on the island nipping a bottle all day, he decided he had had enough of the old horse that Lucy's pet buzzard perched on. The horse was prone to pulling items— nails, buckets of corn, tools—out of the old Jeep that J. B. drove on the island. It made him madder than hell.

"You couldn't leave anything in the Jeep," Horne said. "That old horse would just reach in there and grab hold of whatever was in there with his teeth and just scatter it all over the place. And then you had to get in there and pick it all up. And J. B. just got fed up with it one day, and Miss Lucy was gone, and that ended the horse. I buried it with a dozer.

"A couple of weeks later, J. B. got mad at the buzzard because we was having to clean up the porch where the buzzard would leave his droppings. J. B. got rid of the buzzard, too."

When Lucy came back, J. B. said that the horse just up and died and the buzzard flew away. Lucy accepted the explanation, just as she took his word for nearly everything else.

Horne said that some of her other animals also met their end through J. B. "One of them tapirs that Miss Lucy used to keep got sick, and the vet told her that she could give it two drops of strychnine," Horne said. "But J. B. gave it two *spoonfuls* and then told Miss Lucy, 'Well, the vet was wrong about that strychnine.' But he didn't tell her how much strychnine he give the tapir. That's what killed it."

J. B.'s killing of twenty-nine of Miss Lucy's cattle was accidental. His ignorance of toxic chemicals probably was the reason for their demise. He had run the skittish animals through the cattle dip. At the same time, he fed them worm medicine. He may have given the cows excess doses of the worm treatment, or the combination of the medicine and the dipping-tank chemicals may have been deadly. At any rate, the cattle, many of them pregnant, ended up dead a short time later, lying in the woods belly up, their bloated, rotting carcasses smelling to high heaven for miles when the wind blew right. No one would go near the carcasses, not even the buzzards. It took about a year for them to totally rot, leaving behind a great pile of yellowish bones.

For Gogo Ferguson, the remains were a gold mine. "I was in heaven for a couple of years after that, just gathering cow bones and skulls," she recalled.

Gogo said her grandmother was "extremely upset" over the cows' deaths, "but she would never let J. B. know that."

———•———

In 1964, with the trust no longer in effect and no money coming in to care for the Carnegie mansions and outbuildings, Lucy and Bob confronted the stark realization that they could no longer afford Greyfield and its upkeep. The old mansion was falling apart. A grandchild was nearly hit by a big chunk of stucco falling off it.

In a firm tone, Bob would ask Lucy, "How are you going to afford this house? What are you going to do?" Lucy's kinfolk whispered that Bob's family money had run out a long time ago, and that he had been living off Lucy's inheritance all these years.

When they had needed money before, Lucy and Bob had sold some of their cattle, or rounded up the wild horses and sold them, or sold some of their land up north. But that was not enough now. They needed steadier money, and more of it.

At one point, Lucy saw the plan to strip-mine half the island for titanium as the answer, even though her close cousin Nancy Rockefeller vowed to kill the proposal. To this day, some family members puzzle over why Lucy, who had an abiding love for Cumberland, backed the strip-mining idea.

She explained her position in her memoirs: "We considered the titanium mining a wonderful thing. They were never going to do over a hundred acres at one time. And when they finished, they were going to re-plant, and we would be quite well off. Nan was against it. There was one other place outside of Jacksonville that had been mined. I assume Nan went to visit there, but there, they had not replanted. We were the first that Glidden [the company that wanted to mine Cumberland] offered to replace the topsoil and replant. If they had done all that, we would have been rich people. I thought it was a wonderful offer. It wasn't going to ruin the island at all and we would have a good income. But the family got very divided about it."

Nan took the battle to the Georgia Supreme Court, which quashed the venture.

Lucy and Bob had to think of another plan. What they and son Rick came up with was to turn Greyfield into an inn. To that end, they extensively renovated the old mansion, most notably closing in the porch to create more bedrooms. In some people's minds, it ruined Greyfield's architectural beauty.

The inn opened in 1965. Rick and wife Edith were tapped to run it. They lived in the attic the first summer. Family and friends who inhabited the little cottages around Greyfield pitched in to polish furniture, brew coffee, and make up beds. Some of Lucy's grandchildren went to the north end and picked scuppernong grapes from Bobby Rischarde's arbor to make jelly, which they served on pancakes to the guests.

There was no advertising; notice that the inn was up and running was spread by word of mouth. Immediately, guests started making reservations. They were picked up at the Carnegies' private dock in Fernandina and shuttled to the island aboard the *R. W. Ferguson*, named, of course, for Bob.

At first, the inn was formal. Men wore black ties and women evening dresses at dinner. The guests spent the day roaming the island, mucking about on the beach, squishing through mud in the marsh, or digging for clams. In the evening, when the big gong—the one that had once summoned Dungeness guests to dinner—was sounded, the bar was closed and patrons came downstairs to the ground-floor dining room for dinner. Sitting around the table, they talked about their adventures during the day. On summer nights, they might go back to their rooms, change clothes, and tromp down to the beach to see what generations before them had witnessed—loggerheads crawling on to the beach to lay their eggs.

All this time, Lucy was right there, voicing opinions, bossing people around, actually trying to run the place. Though she had moved to Serendipity, she still kept a tight rein on the inn, located a few miles away.

Rick did the best he could, but Lucy was always second-guessing. She refused to buy a dishwasher for the inn because she thought it engendered laziness. The first sight of her Jeep rolling through Greyfield's north gate was enough for the staff to issue a "Fergie alert."

"Greyfield was her home," Gogo said. "She could care less whether it was an inn. It was her home, and we were not allowed to change any of the bedspreads. Everything had to be exactly as it was when she was living there. She was very difficult to work with. She used to come by on a weekly basis to do a bra check to make sure we were all wearing bras. We'd all run out on the back porch and rip our shirts up. And she'd go by for inspection and proceed on."

Then Lucy fired Rick. No one ever said publicly why she relieved her own son of the manager's position. She reportedly told him not to come back to the island. Her daughter Retta speculated it had something to do with Lucy's never-ending craving for control, and perhaps jealousy that someone else could do something better than she on Cumberland. "As Rick and Edith became more and more popular running the inn, Mother got crosser and crosser," Retta said. "We're talking about a power struggle. A worker at the inn told me, 'You know, the more successful you become, the madder your mother is going to get.' Which was exactly right. You're talking about a woman who had been raised on Cumberland, who had become the queen in charge. And with a little point of her finger, sort of like the Red Queen in *Alice*, she could command, *boo*, something get done. She just couldn't stand having somebody else do something and have it become successful.

"How did she solve the problem? Rick was fired. That solved it for a while. And she became queen, which she really liked very much."

Shortly after that, Lucy hired a new manager, John Frank Fox III, an experienced hotelier who was the son of a good friend. "I didn't see how the inn could make any money because it was so small and out of the way," said Fox, whose stocky frame and bald head made him resemble the old actor Broderick Crawford. "All Miss Lucy wanted was to make just enough money to keep the place in good shape. That's all she wanted. She didn't want it to get run-down."

But there was not enough money to keep it intact and pay the bills. There was a lot of mold in the house, for instance. Fox spent a full year trying out new paints and other schemes to get rid of it. "We needed to keep the house up and keep the paint on and get rid of the mold and pay the light bills and stuff," he said. "We had to have more income, so I was looking for certain things here and there."

He raised the room fee from thirty-five to fifty dollars per person and started charging guests when they used Greyfield's vehicles to ramble about the island. Lucy and her family feared the higher prices would discourage people from coming, but that never happened, and Fox began whipping the inn into better financial shape.

But he also didn't last long. When he kept getting sick to his stomach, he thought it was stomach flu. Lucy arranged for him to see her doctor friend in Jacksonville. Tests revealed that he had pancreatitis. He was told that he must avoid alcohol. He was an alcoholic, but he was in denial.

"Miss Lucy said, 'John, I've smelled alcohol on your breath several times during the day,' " he recalled. "And I said, 'Well, that's part of my job, to deal with the guests and everything.' And she said, 'Yes, but I smell it during the day. I'm letting you go, giving you a couple of months' pay.' And I was very upset."

When he left the island, Lucy rode on the boat with him to the mainland. "She said, 'I know you're mad at me, but I just want you to know that I want you to get better,' " Fox remembered. At the dock, she handed him an envelope with his name on it. "She said, 'Take care of yourself, and remember me, and someday I hope you come back and visit me on the island.' "

At the time, Fox still did not believe his condition was serious. "It took me about seven more years of drinking and misery to figure out that I was an alcoholic, and I went into treatment and have been sober since 1980," he said. He did not open the envelope Lucy handed him until years later. In it was a check for $450.

"When I became sober, I wrote to Miss Lucy and made amends for anything I could have done wrong on the island," Fox said. "I told her, 'I really want to thank you because you really did care for me.' She said, 'I've been around a lot of alcoholics, and I know that sometimes it takes a shock or two to get better.' Miss Lucy was a dear, thoughtful, kind, considerate lady, who also could be tough. She could be tough as nails."

Today, Greyfield is one of the most exclusive inns in America. Rooms start at $290 per night. It is owned by the Greyfield Limited Partnership, made up mostly of Miss Lucy's descendants. The black-tie-at-dinner rule has been relaxed, although gentlemen still must wear jackets.

───────·◆·───────

When Bob died, Lucy, like the strong women who preceded her on Cumberland, was left to run the island in her own fashion.

"It was a given that, while she was alive, nothing would change on this island," Gogo said. "Her life would not change, and the Park Service would not try to move in or do anything to disturb her. She was really the matriarch."

When the Carnegies, the conservationists, and the politicians were working to get Cumberland into the national park system, uppermost in their minds was that Lucy's blessing was vital if they were to succeed. If she opposed the park, it would be an insurmountable hurdle to pass a bill. Without her say-so, the Georgia delegation would not support the legislation. Her powerful friends in Atlanta and Washington would quash the deal in a hurry if she asked them to.

That's why the bill's supporters turned to Thornton Morris, her lawyer. She would pay attention to him. "The thought was that the way to shut her up was hire her lawyer and get him behind the deal," Morris said.

Then it became Bill Stuckey's burden to deal with Lucy. "I did everything I could to work with her to get this bill through," he said. "But she was part of the reason the House Interior Committee and the Park Service had a problem with the bill. The problem was that the Interior Department didn't want what Miss Lucy wanted."

In particular, she was hellbent on making sure there would be a hands-off policy toward Greyfield. She demanded the Park Service promise in writing that it would not try to acquire Greyfield during her lifetime. The agency reluctantly agreed.

Another problem was the wild horses.

"In the bill, I made quite a determination that the park become not only noncommercial but open for agriculture as well," Stuckey recalled. "That was because of Miss Lucy and the wild horses. I'm not sure anybody knew whose horses they were. The Park Service wanted to remove them. But Miss Lucy said they were hers. Nobody but nobody was going to tell Miss Lucy they were not her horses. They just roamed the whole island. She would bring the people over from [the Georgia town of] Waycross, and they would break the horses for her, and she would sell them. That was income for her. She wanted to make sure she kept those horses. And we put that in the bill."

Gradually, Lucy came around. She said she was not in favor of a national park, but that, to appease her kinfolks, she would not fight it.

That did not mean she wouldn't bug the hell out of the Park Service. The squabbles started almost the day Cumberland became a national seashore. She was on the backs of superintendents, rangers, secretaries nearly every day. When Park Service archaeologists wanted to excavate an Indian shell mound near the runway at Stafford, she wouldn't let them because she was afraid the Indians' spirits would come out.

For embattled superintendent Bert Roberts, who was in charge of the park in the mid-1970s, the biggest headache was not protecting the wildlife or shoring up the dilapidated buildings. It was Miss Lucy. "She's a slick operator," he said once in a fit of exasperation. "We have to spend half our time setting the record straight, what with those little old ladies visiting Greyfield and sending all those letters to Washington. I think she just enjoys being Miss Cumberland, playing the role of the grandmother with a gun on her knee."

Thornton Morris sympathized with the superintendents. "One issue was that Lucy said the Park Service somehow did not understand that the cows were her cows," he said. "And the wild pigs. The Park Service wanted to get rid of them. I was getting calls from these poor superintendents, who were just getting flogged by this little mother hen because they had penned up some of her pigs down at Dungeness. And they said, 'Well, Miss Ferguson, you're supposed to keep your animals on your land.' She said, 'I've never done it that way.' And they said, 'Well, this is our land now. The feral-hog law says that if a pig is found on our land, it's ours.' And she said, 'We don't do it that way on Cumberland.' I'd have to call Lucy and say, 'Okay, Lucy, they'll give you the pigs. Your pigs [are] what's on your land, not what's on their land.' 'But you don't understand, Thornton,' she would say. 'We don't do it that way on Cumberland.' "

What they worked out was that Lucy would remove the remaining cows—those that J. B. Peeples had not poisoned—from the island if the government would acknowledge the hogs were hers. Actually, the Park Service's ploy was that it would not argue whether the hogs were Lucy's or the government's. "We worked it out so that we would trap the hogs, and we would give them to Miss Lucy in return for her hauling them off the island," Zack Kirkland said. "She would sell them and get whatever she could for them. Some fetched as much as a hundred dollars apiece. It was good for us because we were having to pay somebody five dollars a head to haul them off. The only part of the deal that worried me was transporting the hogs to Miss Lucy's ferry. We wanted to make sure that none of the little hogs didn't get tossed back into the woods to grow bigger and be captured again. So we always escorted them into the sunset, so to speak."

Despite her cussedness, most people couldn't help liking her. Even some of the Park Service people said that. And there came a time, in fact, when some of them won her grudging respect.

John Ehrenhard was one. He was the Park Service archaeologist who excavated portions of Cumberland. "It was obvious that I didn't know anything about the island when I got there in the 1970s," he said. "I would go see Miss Lucy, not knowing you just didn't do that, especially if you were with the Park Service. I knew she had quite a bit of knowledge about Cumberland, and I wanted to ask her about some artifacts that had been found over the years. I managed to get an audience with her. It was quite a deal. I went into this large living room there on the first floor and was told that she would be in shortly. I sat there for some time.

"She finally came in and introduced herself and wanted to know what I was doing. I told her. She said, 'Oh, we've had you people before,' and went into a tirade against the Park Service. Then she handed me a long bone and said, 'What kind of bone do you think this is?' I said, 'Well, it looks like a bird bone because it's hollow at one end. It looks like it's from a pelican. That's the best guess I have.' There was silence, and then she handed me a picture of a sea turtle that looked like it was standing on end, on its flippers. She said, 'How do you think that turtle did that? I didn't know turtles could stand on their flippers.' It looked obvious to me that the turtle was in the water and just happened to be in that pose. So I said, 'I think the turtle's in the water. How else could it happen?' Then she handed me something long and sharp. 'You think this is maybe like a barb or Indian spear?' I said that it was the spine from a sea catfish. Then she said okay, and she told me where she had found these things. She said she had some Indian stuff, too.

"I didn't realize it at the time, but she was testing me to see if I had any sense. She didn't believe the Park Service had much sense. We became good friends, and she even invited us to supper at her house."

She brought Ehrenhard one of her most treasured items, picked up long ago. "She came over one day and gave us a human skull that had fallen apart and wanted to know if we'd glue it back together again for her," he said. "Since we were there, could we do it? It was the skull of an aboriginal, and I asked how she got it. She said that when she was sixteen, she was riding her horse along River Road on the island and saw the skull in the riverbank.

"It was about at that same spot in 1989, about the time she died, when Hurricane Hugo washed out several skeletons. It was possibly a cemetery, which would have been associated with a large Timucuan village or with the Spanish mission on Cumberland."

Serendipity, where Lucy lived in her later years, was dwarfed by the surrounding oaks, sweet gums, and pines. In addition to her assorted collections of bones and shells and skins, much of the house was filled with brochures, letters to Washington, petitions, and correspondence with conservation groups, lawyers, and legal societies of all kinds—matters concerning the fate of Cumberland.

Inside and outside, there were puppies, big Dalmatians, and other pets. And there was something else: a wing attached to the house was an incubator room and hatchery of sorts for baby turkeys and Egyptian quail. Though land rich, Lucy still felt money poor. She tried raising the turkeys and quail by the thousands. "I'm gonna make money; I'm gonna make a fortune on them," she said. "I'm sending all these quail over to the rich people." She stayed busy tending the little quail eggs in incubators. She would put them anywhere that was warm—even in the bed where she slept. She sold the quail to exclusive hotels like the King and Prince on St. Simons and The Cloister on Sea Island.

"The hotel people would fly into the little airport at Stafford to pick up the quail," John Frank Fox remembered. "There was one time—I'll never forget it—when she called me all of a sudden and said, 'I need help badly. I've got an order for twenty dozen quail that have to be ready to go this afternoon.' And I had to go help her. She killed the quail. I just couldn't do that. She'd take them and pinch their necks or something like that. And then we had to clean the darn little devils and dip them and get all the feathers off and get them ready to go to the King and Prince. And she would throw the innards and stuff from the quails out for the domestic hogs she kept penned at Serendipity. And I told her later, 'I'll do almost anything for you, but I'm not going to do that again.' "

In the fall of 1981, Miss Lucy spoke to the *Atlanta Journal-Constitution* in the dark-paneled living room at Greyfield Inn. Clad in old boots, stained khaki pants, an old sweater, and a knit cap with wisps of gray hair poking out, she was surprisingly lively for someone eighty-two years old. She was surrounded by memorabilia from generations of Carnegies—stacks of photograph albums of the family at play, hundreds of varieties of seashells, old bottles, and sports trophies from long-forgotten country-club tournaments. Dominating a wall was an oil portrait of a beautiful young woman dressed in a blue flapper shift with a red scarf pulled across her forehead, gypsy style. A dagger was on her belt . It was of Miss Lucy, and more than anything else, it served notice that she was the queen here.

At that time, the Candler family had agreed to sell its land to the Park Service, after which Miss Lucy would become the island's only major private landowner.

"I am not going to sell my land," she said. "I'm fighting to save it. It is forever on my mind these days. They couldn't offer me enough money to give up my land. Look around you. These things here are from generations of Carnegies. I have five generations of family buried on this island. The only thing that has held this family together is its common bonds to Cumberland. Had we not had Cumberland, we would not have held together.

"I want to save this land for my children and grandchildren. I have nineteen grandchildren. We are part of the history of the island. We are the last thing left. We're the ones who love Cumberland."

She pulled back some tall drapes to reveal ruled lines on a cypress wall—lines that marked the heights of Carnegies from the 1920s onward.

After talking for half an hour, she called her little mutt, Ugly, climbed into a Jeep, and headed to the beach.

"This is the most beautiful beach on the whole Atlantic coast," she said. "It's one of the main reasons the Park Service wanted Cumberland, you know. The only reason this island is still so wild and beautiful is because we kept it that way. If you were here a few months ago, you could see the turtles crawling up on the beach to lay their eggs. Look at those big pelicans there flying over the water. Doesn't that thrill you?"

She drove along the sandy, shell-flecked Grand Avenue. "I just think these live oaks are the most beautiful of all trees." Then she commented on the prospect of having three hundred people, perfect strangers, come to the island each day, to a place she once ruled. "I want to make sure they don't ruin what we have worked hard to protect," she said. "I will keep working and fighting the Park Service to make sure they do the right thing. I'm an old woman, but I still have a lot of fight left in me. It keeps me from getting moldy."

Ugly started yapping at the sight of three hikers—two young men and a woman—coming up the road. "Hush, shh, Ugly," Miss Lucy said, stopping the Jeep. The hikers smiled as they approached. One of the men wore earphones connected to a Sony Walkman on his belt. "How can you listen to the little birds singing if you wear that thing?" she asked, pointing to the contraption on his head.

"He can't hear you," said the woman.

Miss Lucy shook her head in disbelief. "Where are all of you from?" she asked.

"I'm from Atlanta. These two guys are from Athens," said the young woman.

"What do you do?"

"I'm a teacher; we're all teachers," the woman said.

"I'm glad to meet you," said Miss Lucy. "Are you camping out?"

"Well, my husband is doing some geology work here, and these two guys are our friends who came for a couple of days."

"Do you like it here?" she asked the man without the earphones.

"Oh, yes, ma'am. This is the first time I've been here. I think it's one of the most beautiful places I've ever seen."

"Good, I feel the same way," Miss Lucy said. "You want a lift?"

"Oh, no, thank you," said the young woman. "We're enjoying walking."

"That's the spirit," Miss Lucy said.

She stopped at Plum Orchard to sit on the dilapidated veranda and chat for a few minutes.

"I think the national parks are necessary, especially for the poor city man," Miss Lucy said. "The way I feel now about the park is that it has given many people great pleasure. When you see them, you see that many of them are enjoying the island, like those young people we saw back there. I feel good about the park being here."

Then, looking out across the Brickhill River and the great salt marsh beyond, she grew pensive for a moment. "I sometimes think back about life on Cumberland when everything was high and handsome and wonder if we were snobs," she said after a moment's reflection. "The lines then were very strict, and I remember thinking the lowest thing in life was to be a servant. I thought the rich played together. Now, there are no lines. My mother and father, I don't think they were snobs. They liked people for what they were worth."

In September 1987, thousands of people from all over Georgia turned out in St. Marys for Lucy Ferguson Day. They honored the woman who had worked many years to protect her island. When it came her turn to speak, she said, "There are too many people on Cumberland, too many cars going up and down the road."

In the last year of her life, Lucy's spunk, spryness, and cockiness ebbed away. Her sight faded; she lost weight and was frail. She sat quietly and serenely for hours, meditative, introspective, uncommunicative.

Her old sidekick, J. B. Peeples, had been dead for years, a victim of throat cancer. His widow, Lillian, and sister-in-law Oriole came over to look after Lucy and cook for her.

Lucy's family didn't talk about it much, at least to outsiders, but she somehow had alienated several of them. Toward the end, Retta said, her mother would not let her or her brothers, Rick and Robert, come visit at Serendipity. Only Lucy's youngest child, Cindy, seemed to be in her good graces.

"Rick finally said, 'This is hokum. We're going up to visit her,' " Retta recalled. "But we got hostile receptions from the people helping her. It was outrageous. I had such a wonderfully pleasant, really magical life as a kid growing up on Cumberland, to have it change so radically and feel so betrayed."

Lucy fell and broke her shoulder and had to stay briefly in the hospital. Then her family and caretakers put her in the Quality Care nursing home in Fernandina.

According to Retta, her mother loved being in the nursing home. "She was lonesome on Cumberland," she said. "In the nursing home, the people were her own age. She was pushing them around and feeding them. I mean, she loved it."

But some family members argued that Lucy really wanted to be back on Cumberland. "We don't want her in a nursing home, away from the place she loves," one of them said.

So Lucy came back to her island. On the evening of September 11, 1989, she ate a bowl of ice cream, then closed her eyes. She died in her sleep at Serendipity.

———•—•———

Gogo Ferguson is sitting in her rustic home she and her husband built near Greyfield. She is reflecting on Miss Lucy.

"There are parts of Grandma I just don't understand," Gogo says. "It was very hard for her to get very close to people. I think her deafness had a lot to do with it. And I think she hadn't done so many of the things she wanted to do in her life, and time was running out. I think there was a bit of resentment because of that. She was capable of doing it, but her body was tiring out. . . .

"She realized, and I realized, too, that we're the minority here, that nature and the naturalness of the island are far more in control. You learn to have a real respect for that. I think that kept her gravitating back to Cumberland. She spent many summers in Massachusetts, but I know this is where she was the happiest. . . .

"We'd go out on horseback with Grandma, or by foot, or by Jeep, and we were always finding skeletons of snakes or alligators or horses. I learned that there is beauty in a deer tibia, as well as in the design of a tree-snail shell. There's just such a natural beauty in the curve and design of bones in the way they fit together in shark vertebrae—or any kind of vertebrae, for that matter. The snake vertebrae, that sort of ball-and-socket joint, is just so perfect. . . .

"As we grandchildren got older, for some reason, about the time we reached puberty, she sort of disassociated herself from the women in the family. I don't know whether it was because we became much more independent than she was ever able to become, just because of society back then. It seemed like most women, especially in our family, became a little bit estranged from her. I can't remember any of the women being real close to her. She was much closer to all the men in our family because she loved doing all those manly things—going out herding cattle and riding horses. She liked to restrain all of the women.

"I think that she was just a woman who had such a young spirit still at eighty years old. I think she slightly resented the fact that she was getting old, and we were able to do the things that she really wanted to do. . . .

"My lifestyle is so similar to hers, and my love for the island so similar. I'm getting so much like her. Some of my mannerisms, all of my interests are very similar to hers. . . .

"I'm beginning to feel extremely close to her again. I wish that we had been able to be close when she was getting older. But we didn't. At least now, I can look back and see all of the wonderful qualities she had."

The Park Service had bided its time. When Lucy died, her ashes hardly had been interred in the family cemetery before the agency began making its move on her property. Park officials placed acquisition of the land as one of their highest priorities.

An agreement between the Park Service and Miss Lucy's thirty or so heirs to sell eleven hundred acres of the Greyfield tract to the government was finally struck in 1997. The Nature Conservancy of Georgia would act as the go-between, buying the property and taking title to it until Congress appropriated the money. The purchase price would be nearly $19 million, and the acquisition would be done in five steps.

It was a carefully crafted deal.

Others, however, saw it as an opportunity for getting some things of their own. They came to the brink of dismantling the deal. It is not settled yet. It is another of the virulent battles still being fought over Cumberland.

CHAPTER FOURTEEN

HAL WRIGHT HAD A CONTENTED LIFE—or so he thought. He had a successful environmental-law practice with a firm in the quaint, laid-back town of Monroe, near Atlanta. His wife recently had redone the kitchen in their two-story brick home. His five-year-old son was absorbed in tae kwon do lessons. Two lovable dogs romped in the backyard.

But he was restless. Cumberland Island was tugging at him. He had first come to the island as a University of Georgia student doing work to stop wild hogs' destruction of sea-turtle nests. Its beauty mesmerized him. "It was love at first sight," said Hal, a slim man with black, wavy hair and youngish looks. "Cumberland gripped me as no other place I'd been to before."

He remembers coming over the dunes and seeing the beach for the first time—mile after mile of white sand with no human in sight, no beach umbrellas, no tourists covered with oil, no hotels, no beach-side tiki bars. Later, he began bringing his family and visiting more often.

He also remembers the time he was strolling the beach when a Jeep driven by a kid shot from behind the dunes and nearly ran him over. "Needless to say, it wrecked my feeling of solitude," he said. "You might think this would happen on Daytona, but not on Cumberland."

He had heard of Carol Ruckdeschel and sought her out. They immediately understood they were kindred spirits. Carol saw in him someone as passionate about Cumberland as she was. She told him about the conflicts raging there and how they threatened, at least in her mind, to spoil the island's timeless beauty by inviting more human intrusion. Hal was appalled over what she told him.

Then, one day in 1995, he and Carol were scrutinizing a couple of boxes of Park Service records when they came across a bombshell—the proposed "memorandum of agreement" to allow Gogo Ferguson's group to use Plum Orchard as an artists' colony.

At first, the Park Service didn't want to talk much about it, but Hal and Carol persisted. Agency officials finally acknowledged that they had been trying for years to lease the mansion to a group or company that would fix it up and use it for small retreats. Partnerships with private parties to restore and maintain old buildings, they explained, had to be explored by national parks. "We're looking at many new ways of accomplishing our responsibilities, short of using taxpayer money," one of them said. But no one could be found to take over Plum Orchard until Gogo's group came forward with its artists' colony idea.

"Unless we get a private group in here to help keep Plum standing, it's going to be lost," Gogo said. "That would be a tragedy."

But Carol said the real tragedy would be if the colony went forward. She wanted a study first. Plum Orchard, she pointed out, was hemmed in by a congressionally mandated wilderness area, a condition that under normal circumstances would bar automobile access. A group of dancers and writers and poets would increase the number of people and cars in the official wilderness, she said.

Hal, who by now had come to see himself as Cumberland's watchdog, went a step further. He gathered some one hundred environmental leaders and grass-roots activists into a loose-knit organization, Defenders of Wild Cumberland, and became its executive director. In their behalf, he sued the Park Service for failing to protect the wilderness. Preserving wilderness, he argued, was more important to park visitors "than restoring mansions of former robber barons." By ignoring wilderness laws to accommodate an artists' colony, he explained, the Park Service was turning the wilderness into "a private playground for the rich and famous from the Northeast."

Soon afterward, the agency withdrew its proposal to Gogo and her cohorts. It was not because of the lawsuit, the government claimed; instead, it was because bureaucrats in Washington had determined that the memorandum of agreement was not the way to negotiate a long-term deal. And since the lawsuit didn't matter, the Park Service claimed that Hal was not due attorney fees or other considerations for his long hours on the case.

Hal was undeterred. There were other battles to be waged over Cumberland. He vowed to be in the thick of them. He left his law firm and moved his family to St. Marys to be near the island of his desires. He set up a new office in a room over his garage.

Strangely, Carol never joined Hal's group. She would be more effective, she surmised, if she acted individually. Nevertheless, Gogo and the others saw her as the ringleader who killed the artists' colony. They believed she was the one who got Hal Wright stirred up in the first place.

———•—•———

It was George Hartzog who may have unwittingly planted the seeds for Cumberland's becoming a wilderness area. The then-Park Service chief revealed in 1971, during a hearing on the bill to create Cumberland Island National Seashore, that the government planned to develop virtually the entire island to accommodate ten thousand visitors daily.

Conservationists and preservationists were horrified. They began

A hiking trail leading to the beach on Cumberland Island
Courtesy of the Atlanta Journal-Constitution

barraging bureaucrats, politicians, and anyone else in charge, demanding there be no development at all on Cumberland. The best way to guarantee that, they said, was to persuade Congress to make the island a wilderness area.

President Lyndon Johnson had signed the Wilderness Act into law after Congress passed it in 1964. It established the National Wilderness Preservation System to preserve some of the country's last remaining wild places as scientific enclaves and to protect them forever from human encroachment. It provided the strongest protection of land possible under federal law.

With its maritime forest, its unspoiled salt marshes, its tall dunes, and its long-as-the-eye-can-see beach, Cumberland offered a wilderness experience few places in the world could match, the conservationists said.

Hans Neuhauser, an ecologist who was an officer in the Georgia Conservancy, was one of the wilderness boosters. "At first, the Park

Service was not receptive to the idea," he said. "They probably thought that the limits imposed by the Wilderness Act would cramp their management freedom on the island."

It took years of persuasion, but the Park Service finally gave in. "Actually, it was drawn kicking and screaming into the idea that more than half of Cumberland would be designated as wilderness," Neuhauser said. He and another activist, Bill Mankin of the Sierra Club, then set about drafting a wilderness bill for Cumberland.

By then, there was an urgency. One reason was that the navy had selected Kings Bay, located only a few miles from Cumberland, as its Polaris—and eventually its Trident—submarine base. The environmentalists feared that development pressures from the base's rapid buildup would spill over to Cumberland unless it was designated a wilderness area as soon as possible. Another reason was that United States representative Bo Ginn, who had promised to introduce the legislation into Congress, was planning to resign to run for governor of Georgia.

Neuhauser and Mankin worked feverishly, and Ginn introduced the bill in October 1981. Shortly after he cashed in some political IOUs, the House passed the measure without holding committee hearings. In the Senate, Sam Nunn of Georgia pulled political strings, and it passed Congress as part of an omnibus parks bill.

There was one other obstacle—Interior Secretary James Watt, sworn enemy of tree huggers everywhere. Despite the Park Service's support of the legislation, Watt recommended that his boss, President Ronald Reagan, veto it. That's when United States senator Mack Mattingly, a one-term Republican who in 1980 had miraculously defeated Georgia's good-ol'-boy Democratic senator, Herman Talmadge, joined the fray. He persuaded Reagan to okay the measure in return for some political favors from Democrats. When Reagan, also no friend of environmentalists, signed it on September 9, 1982, it was the first conservation-friendly bill he had ever approved.

Essentially, the legislation drew a line across the island at Stafford and designated nearly everything north of that—just about the whole northern half—as wilderness. There would be 8,840 acres in "instant wilderness." Another 11,700 acres—including the retained estates and the remaining private property—would be "potential wilderness." The potential wilderness would become real wilderness when it qualified—in essence, when it became the property of the Park Service. The wilderness boundary carefully skirted Plum Orchard and a few acres surrounding it and stopped short of the Settlement and the Candlers' High Point compound.

It was an "injured wilderness area," Carol said. "But over the next century, if the Park Service does its job, the wilderness gradually will heal itself. When I die, my cabin will be torn down and plowed under."

The highest number of visitors would be concentrated on the south end, in the Dungeness, Sea Camp, and Greyfield areas. Only hardy hikers and backpackers willing to commit the time and energy to tramp the many miles to the north end would experience the wilderness—and in the process get a glimpse of Plum Orchard and the Settlement.

But the wilderness label did not sit well with the Carnegies, the Candlers, and the others who had retained estates on the island. Most of them banded together in their own group, the Cumberland Island Preservation Society (CIPS). The wilderness restrictions, they feared, would make it difficult for them to travel freely about the island as their forebears once had. Greyfield Inn would have to get another special-use permit from the Park Service to continue its Jeep tours for guests.

Basically, they were puzzled over how the island could be worthy of wilderness-area status. How can you have a wilderness area, they asked, when you have underground telephone and electric cables running through it and houses sitting in it? The island's main thoroughfare, Grand Avenue, ran smack through the middle. The CIPS members vowed that they wouldn't stop using Grand Avenue just because it cut through the wilderness. They held up a Camden County Superior Court judge's ruling and their retained-rights agreements as legal evidence of their right to drive through the wilderness.

Park Service officials scratched their heads and acknowledged they didn't have ready answers. The law, they admitted, indeed said no mechanized vehicles were supposed to be in a wilderness. Congress had seen fit to create a wilderness area on Cumberland, but the Park Service seemed to have little idea of what to do with it. There was no management plan. "Cumberland is a unique situation, that's for sure," a park ranger said.

Thornton Morris, representing some of the Carnegies, felt the whole wilderness thing was a bit ridiculous. "If you're a Park Service visitor, or even a Park Service employee, you can't even ride a bicycle through there," he said. "So visitors come over here, and they see people riding bicycles on the north end. And it has to be explained to them that these are the people with the retained rights or the friends or family of those with retained rights. But the Park Service visitor doesn't have that right.

"I was driving down Grand Avenue one day to my house on the island when a tree that had fallen across the road stopped me. Two park workers were trying to cut it up with an ax. I asked them why didn't they use a chain saw. They said they couldn't because this was wilderness area, and they can't use mechanized machines. So I said, 'You fellows wait here for a few minutes and take a rest.' And I went up to my house and got my chain saw and brought it back with me. I also brought a couple of cool drinks for them. I told them to sit in the shade and sip their drinks. And I cranked up my chain saw and had the tree removed in no time."

The skirmishes and sniping continued. If Thornton Morris's crowd had disliked Hal Wright before, they liked him even less when he fired his next salvo—a legal challenge to stop them from driving on the beach. Again, fearing that beach driving endangered nesting sea turtles and shorebirds, the environmentalists sided with Hal. "Driving on the beach is not a God-given right," he said.

But the Carnegies, the Candlers, and their friends said it indeed was their right. Five generations of their families, they pointed out, had helped protect the island from developers and preserve its natural beauty. Beach driving was a right they had earned.

"My family has been driving on the beach since the beginning of the automobile," said Candler family member Billy Warren. "We drive on the beach to get from the north end to the south end. We drive on it to go fishing and oystering. We drive on it so we can get elderly and disabled members and our children to the ocean. We have done so responsibly and with utmost concern for the well-being of the island and all of its inhabitants and its visitors."

Well, maybe not all the time, he admitted to state officials. "When I was young, we sometimes drove that beach at 110 miles per hour," he said.

In the end, Hal Wright's beach-driving challenge was withdrawn because, in his view, it was not heard by a superior-court judge in a timely manner.

Now, the CIPS members got their licks in. They sued Hal for what they said was his continual harassment of their organization and of island residents. They demanded he pay the thirty-eight thousand dollars they had incurred in legal fees and costs to defend their beach-driving rights.

Once more, the environmentalists rallied around Hal, and the court summarily denied the CIPS motion.

But by now, CIPS had someone on its side much more influential than Hal Wright on the opposing side. He was United States representative Jack Kingston.

———————

On an overcast afternoon in October 1998, Tavia McCuean, executive director of the Nature Conservancy of Georgia, was driving on I-16 through the table-flat pinewoods of south Georgia. She was headed back to her home in Atlanta after a meeting in Savannah. She had left early because a family member was ill.

Her cell phone jingled. On the line was Kingston, who said he wanted to tell her about the bill he had just introduced in the United States House of Representatives. As a courtesy, he wanted to let her know the details before she read them in the newspaper.

McCuean felt that it couldn't be good.

The congressman said his measure basically was a four-point plan aimed at "preserving and protecting Cumberland," while at the same time resolving several longstanding feuds plaguing the island.

McCuean's stomach turned queasy. The bill would unravel her group's delicate plan to buy Lucy Ferguson's Greyfield tract and add it to the national seashore.

The Park Service and Lucy's thirty or so heirs who made up the Greyfield Limited Partnership had asked the Nature Conservancy to broker the deal. According to its carefully drawn-up plan, the conservancy would purchase the tract's eleven hundred acres in five steps for $19 million. The parcels then would be transferred to the government as federal funds became available to reimburse the organization. United States senator Max Cleland of Georgia would ask Congress to appropriate the funds.

But Kingston said he had a better idea.

A father of four and a Savannah millionaire who made his money selling insurance, Kingston rode into office during the political upheaval and voter discontent of the 1990s, when Republicans gained majorities in both houses of Congress. He was an ultraconservative who believed the federal government was too big for its britches. He stridently called for President Clinton's removal from office during the 1998 impeachment proceedings. Environmentalists regarded him as a foe of just about every major measure they endorsed. In their campaign to make the Arctic National Wildlife Refuge in Alaska off-limits to oil exploration, for instance, Kingston lashed out at them, saying that too many potential oil fields in the United States had been placed off-limits in the name of conservation.

In introducing his Cumberland bill, he said it would provide funds plus a "private match" to restore Cumberland's "historic treasures." It would allow more members of the public to eyeball the north end's "historic buildings," such as Bobby Rischarde's old cabin at the Settlement. "We're envisioning for the first time in history a grandmother and a grandchild together seeing these historic sites that their tax dollars paid for," he said.

"See, if you're handicapped and you are a senior or if you're a mom or dad with small children, you can't get to Plum Orchard or the Settlement because you can't ride a bike, you can't take a golf cart, you can't drive a car or any other motorized vehicle to see these sites."

To get to those places by mechanized means, he proposed "cherry-stemming" Grand Avenue—simply removing it from the wilderness designation. It would make moot the environmentalists' arguments against operating machinery in the wilderness, he theorized, because in that little strip, you wouldn't be in the wilderness. Anyone could drive Grand Avenue without violating the sanctity of the precious wilderness, he said.

And there would actually be a net gain in wilderness acreage, as his bill would designate another two hundred acres in the island's southern tip as wilderness.

Then came the kicker: the Candler family would be allowed to reclaim permanent, private title to several dozen acres of High Point land it had sold to the Park Service in 1982. The family wanted to build as many as twenty new homes there. The acreage would be removed from the potential wilderness designation, and the Candlers would hold it in perpetuity and agree to no commercial development. They then would buy up to one thousand acres of the Greyfield tract and donate it to the American people.

"It will save taxpayers $17 million," Kingston said. "It's a win-win deal."

But environmental groups didn't think so. Hal Wright felt it was just plain dumb. "It would take land already publicly owned and create a private compound that would exclude the public," he said.

Carol said all Kingston was doing was placating his rich pals.

The Park Service also saw few virtues in the bill. If the Candlers were allowed to take back their property, it would be the first step toward dismantling the national park system, the agency said. Former landowners in other parks across the country would demand their land back as well. It would be a total mess.

In the end, Kingston removed the most offending parts from the bill.

Nevertheless, it was killed on the House floor.

But Kingston didn't just lick his wounds and go home. He turned to another tactic and fanned the feud even hotter. Until the Park Service worked out a way to provide easier access to Cumberland's north end, he intended to persuade his congressional comrades to hold hostage $5.5 million in federal money set aside to buy eight hundred acres in the Greyfield tract. He was in a position to do that because he served on a subcommittee of the powerful Appropriations Committee, which oversees funding for the Interior Department.

It seemed he would not be satisfied until the Park Service hauled van loads of camera-clicking tourists to Plum Orchard and allowed them to saunter through it to see how the rich folks once lived, or hauled them seven miles farther to the Settlement and let them peek into the First African Baptist Church, read the epitaphs on the tilting tombstones of the old cemetery at High Point, and stare at Carol Ruckdeschel's rustic cabin.

The scheme enraged Max Cleland. A feisty Democrat, he had long

A road on Cumberland Island during the early 1900s
Courtesy of the National Park Service

struggled to get funds for the Greyfield purchase. A bitter quarrel erupted between Kingston and Cleland. Kingston was accused of acting in bad faith. "He keeps moving the goalposts," Cleland said.

Hal Wright said the Park Service essentially was letting a political bully dictate how it ran one of its parks. "The Park Service is being manipulated and intimated through political blackmail," he said. When other politicians tried it in other parks, the Park Service politely told them to butt out. But as long as Kingston was on the powerful Appropriations Committee, the Park Service would cater to him, and his hand on Cumberland would be heavy, Hal predicted.

Kingston was undeterred. He said he had been sent to Washington to work in the best interest of taxpayers, and that was what he was going to do.

In the end, the feuding factions hammered out a contentious compromise behind closed doors. They publicly unveiled it in February 1999. The Park Service said it would run a van for sightseers up Grand Avenue every so often to Plum Orchard and the Settlement, even though the van would have to penetrate the wilderness. Meanwhile, it would look at the feasibility of using boats to get tourists to those places. The Park Service also would have to commit to spending $3 million over the next two years—and $300,000 a year thereafter—toward restoring Plum Orchard and the island's other historic structures. Cumberland's other contentious issues, from fire suppression to reining in wild horses, would be addressed in a forthcoming wilderness management plan, the Park Service promised.

Kingston then said he would free up the money for the Greyfield acreage and secure more money for renovating Plum and the other ramshackle structures.

But as far as the Nature Conservancy was concerned, the Greyfield deal was wrecked. Because of the political scuffle, the organization would not be reimbursed for a huge chunk of money—some $6 million—it had spent in good faith toward the purchase of the Greyfield tract. For the sake of the island, the conservancy would donate the money, rather than press its case for reimbursement from the government. If the Greyfield transaction had fallen through, the organization said, the price tag quite likely would have gone up.

The heirs insisted on one last change before the deal was closed. Sixty-five acres around Miss Lucy's old home, Serendipity, would be retained by them. Twenty-one of those acres were in the wilderness area. Environmentalists were outraged all over again. The Park Service promised to identify twenty-one acres outside the designated wilderness and exchange them for the acreage within the wilderness.

Then the deal was done. And Miss Lucy probably turned in her grave, for her beloved Greyfield was now in the hands of her old nemesis, the National Park Service.

Her Greyfield Inn, though, was still skirmishing. Early in 2002, another old adversary, the Defenders of Wild Cumberland, filed a federal lawsuit in Washington, D.C., against the National Park Service, charging that both the inn and the agency itself were running sightseeing vehicles in the wilderness area in violation of the Wilderness Act.

The inn had run daily tours—mainly for its guests—to the island's north end since the 1960s. Like the Park Service's tour van, the inn's little bus also went through the heart of the wilderness. Greyfield had won a special concession from the government to continue its tours when Cumberland's wilderness area was designated in 1982.

This time, the Defenders of Wild Cumberland had powerful allies—Wilderness Watch, based in Missoula, Montana, and Public Employees for Environmental Responsibility. "Running tour vans through a federally protected wilderness flies in the face of the law," said Wilderness Watch executive director George Nickas.

The lawsuit was still pending in mid-2002.

Whit Foster and his cousin Margaret Graves are having lunch in an outdoor café in downtown Atlanta on a day in May. They are on their way to a CIPS meeting on Cumberland. Margaret, a smiling, soft-spoken woman, is a great-granddaughter of Nancy Carnegie Hever Johnston. Her grandmother donated Plum Orchard to the national park, and her aunt Retta Wright early on urged the family to make a deal with the National Park Service to save Cumberland.

Margaret spends most of her time in Kentucky working for a land conservation group. But Cumberland, she says, is bound to her soul. At least once a year, she and relatives stroll through Plum Orchard, swapping stories about Cumberland and their ancestors' sojourns there. They want to pass the family lore on to their children.

She says that while the Park Service may be trying to abide by the mandates of the Wilderness Act in its dealings on Cumberland, it has given short shrift to another law, the National Historic Preservation Act, which calls for preserving historic structures.

"It's really hard for me when I go to Cumberland and see Plum Orchard in the shape it's in," she says. "Sometimes, I come away crying. The island should never have been classified wilderness. There are too many human alterations there. The government made a big mistake."

Even so, she says she can live with it as long as the park doesn't keep making nitpick rules at the behest of "obstructionist" lawyers like Hal Wright, who interfere with her family's enjoyment of the island. The rights of island residents should come first, she maintains. Hal, she says, insists that the park follow the wilderness law to the letter. But on a place like Cumberland, so heavily touched by man's hand, it can't be done.

"Hal is not the only one who can file lawsuits," she says. "We are also prepared to challenge the park ourselves to protect historic resources."

———•-•———

Art Frederick, who became Cumberland's superintendent in 2000, desperately wants to head off the legal head-butting.

The mandate handed him by his bosses, he says, is to manage the island's cultural resources without neglecting its natural resources. "They want to see all the structures maintained and the wilderness maintained in a harmonious fashion. I don't think the management of one supersedes the other. But it's a very complex situation."

It was his decision early in 2002 that limited park rangers to walking or riding horses—and not riding in cars or trucks—when going into the wilderness for routine matters. He says the lawsuit of the Defenders of Wild Cumberland might become moot, at least as it pertains to the Park Service, because he already plans to stop running the government tour van to the north end at some point in the future. After that, tourists may be taken up there in a boat that skirts the wilderness—or else Jack Kingston might raise hell again.

Frederick's first assignment to the island was in the 1980s as a firefighter during a severe drought. It gave him a chance to appreciate Cumberland's beauty and tranquility. "I always wanted to come back," he says. "There's something about the island that grabs you."

One of the first things he did as superintendent was take a look at Plum Orchard and Dungeness and the chimneys of Robert Stafford's old slave quarters. He had not seen any of them in two decades, and he was shocked by their dilapidated state. "I don't remember any buildings then looking the way they do today," he says. "All the buildings were in good shape. This shouldn't have taken place. Many of the problems are because of the lack of plans to manage the island. But we also just don't have the funding to do the things we were mandated to do."

Restoring Plum Orchard alone, he says, will cost more than $10 million. Kingston's efforts have helped, but the money set aside for Plum Orchard so far is only a fraction of the total needed to save it.

Over at the Settlement, Carol Ruckdeschel says one problem is that no one seems to know exactly what constitutes *historic*. Politicians, environmentalists, the Park Service, and historic preservationists all squabble, for instance, over the historical significance of the remaining houses and outbuildings at the Settlement.

"As these structures were renovated, their historic character was altered and in some cases completely lost," Carol says. Beulah Alberty's old house, for instance, sports aluminum siding that Grover Henderson installed.

"Some of these structures are not even fifty years old, and they do not offer the African-American heritage that some people have advertised," Carol says.

Yet the structures are on the National Register of Historic Places—even Bobby Rischarde's vacant bungalow that's caving in. "For goodness' sake, Bobby was a good man, but there's no way his house belongs on the National Register," Carol says.

She wrote the register's national office protesting the designations and asking that they be rescinded. As long as the Settlement is on the register, she argues, the Park Service will have to spend money to restore collapsing structures devoid of any worthy history. The genuine African-American history on the island, says Carol, is over at Stafford, with its twenty-three chimneys—mute evidence of the slave community that once existed there. But the chimneys are surrounded by private property and are inaccessible to the public.

———————

At Greyfield Inn, Gogo Ferguson has another viewpoint. Despite what Carol puts forth and what the environmental groups espouse, whatever future lies ahead for Cumberland cannot exclude human history, she says.

"In this quest for utopian wilderness, it's wiping out human presence, and I don't know where we extracted humans from nature," she explains. "We're a part of it. We coexist. We always have. We all love Cumberland Island. We just want to make sure it's preserved as a whole, not just protecting or creating this so-called wilderness."

CHAPTER FIFTEEN

CAROL HAS COME ACROSS A DEAD HORSE, a chestnut mare lying on its side in a sunny opening near Plum Orchard. Its big black eyes are open. Its brownish green tongue lolls out. Its upper lip is pulled back over its large teeth. It is so bloated its two left legs stick almost straight up. The animal is—or was—part of the herd of wild horses that roams Cumberland.

Carol circles the carcass, deciding how she will perform the postmortem. Sharp knife in hand, she slices through the animal's thick neck muscles. Then she works the knife between two verte-brae and gives a twist that snaps the spine. The big head, its glassy eyes appearing to stare at her, is free. Grabbing one of its ears, she lugs it over to her battered Jeep.

Then she turns her attention to the swollen belly. She wants samples of the stomach contents because they can provide excellent clues to the horse's diet and its life in general. She must be careful. Puncturing the swollen belly will release a huge volume of gas and rotting stomach mess that could spew all over her. So she crouches behind the horse's back, reaches an arm over its belly, and rams in the blade.

Her strategy backfires. A great gush of putrefying liquid and gas erupts, *whoosh*, hitting her in the face and nearly knocking her down. "Ugh," she says in disgust, wiping her face with a paper towel. She scoops up some of the stomach material, places it into some bags, and labels them.

She studies the carcass once more. She's deciding if the meat is still fresh enough for her to slice off some choice cuts for supper. Horse steaks sautéed in butter and olive oil and sauced with fresh garlic and sherry are delicious, she says. This horse, however, probably has been dead a little too long, so she'll leave it for the vultures.

Carol considers grilled horse meat a delicacy. But she is not as fond of the living horses roving Cumberland unchecked. "They are ecological insults of major proportions," she says. "They are not native. They belong here about as much as they belong in downtown Atlanta. They must compete with some three thousand deer and other animals for limited food. They trample on delicate vegetation. They disturb ground-nesting birds. They've just mowed down the marsh grass on the Cumberland Sound side of the island and the sea oats on the beach side. Sea oats stabilize the primary sand dunes. Without sea oats, the dunes erode and blow away. If humans pulled up sea oats, they could be arrested, but the horses eat the sea oats with impunity."

What to do with Cumberland's wild horses has become as much a hot potato as the bitter feuds over Plum Orchard and the wilderness.

At public hearings, horse lovers stand in line to warn the government to keep its hands off the creatures that buck and gallop over the beach for the pure joy of it. People tie strength and independence to the frolicking horses. Cumberland's retained-rights holders—Carol excepted—maintain that wild horses have been part of the island for centuries. So why bother them now?

"I've been here forty-four years, and I haven't seen that much destruction by them," Gogo Ferguson says.

Grover Henderson theorizes that the horses will balance their own population if left alone. "They'll die off," he says "They'll get diseases. Let God handle the horses. Not the government. I don't want the government doing anything except guarding the coast and perhaps carrying the mail. And that's about it. I'm going to do everything in my power to see that the horses are left alone. The Park Service has an egregious record. Every time they start interfering with the natural balance on Cumberland, they mess up, and I'm not going to let them do it this time."

Most likely, he would get some backing. Surveys show that the animals are the number-one reason people visit Cumberland—a fact not lost on chambers of commerce. Glossy brochures aimed at luring tourists to coastal Georgia inevitably sport shiny photos of wild horses romping and kicking on the island.

The environmental crowd cringes over such images. Equine-caused damage is so bad on Cumberland, they say, that the unrestrained animals should be rounded up and evicted. Even the mighty oaks are in danger, they say. Live-oak seedlings never have a chance to grow very high because the horses crop them as soon as they put out new shoots. When Cumberland's mature oaks die off, there might be no new oaks coming up to replace them.

That attitude riles Jack Kingston. He once sneaked a rider on to an appropriations bill that temporarily prohibited federal spending for horse control on Cumberland. Those who want the horses eliminated are "environmental extremists," he says. "The horses add to the character and mystique of Cumberland. They should be preserved."

It's not clear how and when the wild herd originated. A legend says the horses are the progeny of Spanish stock that swam ashore from foundering sixteenth-century galleons. The earliest official account of horses

Wild horses tussle on the beach on Cumberland Island
Courtesy of the Atlanta Journal-Constitution

on Cumberland was in 1742, when the Spaniards in their war against Great Britain attacked Fort St. Andrews and found fifty to sixty horses in a corral. They claimed to have shot the horses, but some biologists believe the faster ones escaped to become the nucleus of the wild herd.

When the Carnegies arrived on Cumberland in the 1880s, they encountered dozens of roving, untamed equines. They sold several of them. Over the next seventy years, they and others brought over trailer loads of Western mustangs, Tennessee walkers, quarter horses, Arabians, Paso Finos, and even retired circus ponies to blend with the herd. Someone thought that spotted horses would be pretty, so an Appaloosa stallion was introduced. Lucy Ferguson and her wranglers used to fan out across the island to geld as many wild male foals as they could find, after which they'd turn out their own stallions during breeding season to roam the island and service the wild mares. "It improves the herd," Lucy said. As late as 1992, a retained-estate holder shipped over four registered Arabian horses to bolster the wild gene pool.

So many different breeds made for some creative couplings. A horse expert once labeled Cumberland's wild herd as "Heinz horses," comprised of fifty-seven varieties.

The herd's population today hovers around 250, nearly double the number that existed in the early 1980s. But at the same time, the horses' general health seems to have deteriorated. Many appear malnourished and disease-ridden—glue-factory material. The foal mortality rate is 29 percent.

Spartina, the dominant plant of the salt marsh, is their preferred food, perhaps by necessity rather than choice. They have chewed up most of the succulent grasses on the high ground. Sea oats are their second-favorite meal. Carol says a reason Lake Whitney is filling with sand is that the horses have nibbled down the sea oats anchoring the dunes there. The horses also munch on thorny greenbrier stems, bayberry twigs, seaweed, and even Spanish moss. In heavily grazed areas, they have gobbled up 98 percent of the vegetation.

Actually, what appears to outsiders as one herd is several small bands—or harems—competing for food. The more dominant harems, made up of a mature stallion and several mares, have forced the others into areas where vegetation is sparser.

In spring and summer, when mosquitoes and biting flies plague the horses unmercifully, they take to the beach, where their droppings foul the sand. Sometimes, they wade into the surf and stand up to their withers, trying to get relief from the bugs.

From a helicopter hovering over the salt marsh around Christmas Creek, Duane Harris, head of the Georgia Department of Natural Resources' coastal office in Brunswick, looks down on five horses standing in foot-deep water, chomping on bright green *Spartina*. "Look at that," he says. "They actually have their snouts under the water, trying to get at the grass. I've never seen that before."

The *Spartina*, he explains, should be chest-high. Instead, the spot below the helicopter resembles a muddy football field. The horses are overgrazing the marshes, decreasing nursery areas for shrimp and other marine life, Duane says. More than a third of Cumberland's salt marsh is accessible to the animals. In going to and from the marsh, they have created extensive trail systems, trampling marsh plants in the process.

Robin Goodloe has seen it all from ground level. She spent five years slogging through the marshes and tramping through the woods, chasing the animals as part of her doctoral research at the University of Georgia. She saw the harm they caused. It left her with an indelible conclusion: "The horses should not be on Cumberland Island. Cumberland should be maintained as a natural area, and those horses are not natural."

The wild hogs aren't natural either. Their ancestors were domestic pigs brought over centuries ago by Europeans. The damage they cause reads like the indictment against the horses, only stronger. "They're even more destructive than the horses," Carol says.

Their constant rooting turns the island's soil with the efficiency of a rototiller. The overturned dirt is ideal for nonnative plants like tung trees—brought over by Carter Carnegie in his ill-fated moneymaking scheme—to gain a greater foothold on the island. The exotics crowd out the native plants and wreak ecological havoc.

Weighing up to 350 pounds each, the swine compete with wild turkeys, deer, and other creatures for limited food. They run off ground-nesting birds and raid loggerhead nests. On the sand dunes, they go after pennywort, a plant that keeps the dunes intact.

More than two thousand of the grunting creatures live on Cumberland. Getting rid of them is a government priority. The Park Service has allowed special hunts and hog-trappings. Park workers have been urged to shoot the creatures on sight; hundreds are shot each year. Still, they multiply. A sow can produce four litters a year.

Zack Kirkland, longtime Cumberland park ranger, doubts that wild hogs will ever be eradicated from the island, short of an army battalion combing the place. He undertook a campaign in 1975 to trap as many hogs as he could and haul them off the island. In the process, he gained a grudging respect for his adversaries—and for J. B. Peeples.

"We just trapped the dumb ones, really," Kirkland says. "The smart ones, I think, knew what we were up to. It began initially as an experiment, but we were very successful.

"It was dangerous work. One time, we had forty or fifty hogs in a holding pen. Some men were hired to take the hogs off the island. J. B. Peeples came down to watch. We didn't have the pens designed correctly. We were supposed to have something like a funnel to funnel the hogs on to the trailer that was there. We didn't have a funnel. So we tried holding sheets of plywood and trying to force all these hogs running around in the pen into the trailer. It was kind of like a three-ring circus, with us out there and the hogs.

"Two of the guys were supposed to be professional cowboys. Somebody hollered, and all the hogs went charging them. Plywood went flying everywhere. I jumped over the fence. I looked around, and the two allegedly professional cowboys were up a tree eight feet off the ground. The hogs were running around, and I thought, 'This doesn't look good. The professionals are up a tree, and we are losing it here.'

"The situation was pretty bad. These hogs were just running around wildly in the pen. Then J. B. decided he would take over. He picked up a big stick on the ground, and he saw the leader of the hogs, the biggest one in there, a big, mean boar. And J. B. said, 'I'm gonna take care of him.'

He says, 'Y'all come when I holler.' And I looked at him like he was crazy. And he hopped over the fence and marched out to the center of the pen, and the big boar charged him. And J. B. whacked him hard on the head with that stick. I swear, J. B. was acting kind of like a matador. This went on for about four passes. And each time, the hog was getting madder and madder. And I remembered that J. B. had had a heart attack. And I was trying to remember the number for the Life Flight helicopter. I was thinking, 'I'll call them and tell them to warm up their engines because somebody is going to lose here.' Finally, J. B., after stunning the hog again as it charged him, reached over and grabbed its tail. For a few seconds, it looked like J. B. was water-skiing. He reached down and grabbed the hog's leg and disabled him and then finally held him. He hollered for help, and the professionals ran over and tied up the hog. I never will forget that scene— J. B. like a matador, raging boar charging."

Another time, Kirkland and his men trapped about eighty hogs and had them penned up near Dungeness to take off the island.

"One of the rangers went down there to check on them, and they were gone," he said. "The gate was open. Somebody had opened it in the middle of the night, and the hogs were all gone. And it turned out it was one of the girls staying in one of the retained-rights houses. She was just a teenager, and she felt sorry for the hogs because she didn't know what was going to happen to them. She thought it would be a nice gesture to turn them all loose. But she wiped out about two weeks of hard work."

Kim Knight, whose family had a retained-rights agreement at the Grange, where Aunt Floss once lived, confessed to the act: "We were fifteen, maybe sixteen, years old. We decided that we would all excuse ourselves from the table and meet out in the backyard clandestinely and sneak across into the compound and free those pigs. We talked one of the little kids to go over and get on the gate and swing it open. Of course, when our parents found out what we'd done, they were furious. They had tried to maintain a good relationship with the Park Service. We apologized the next day."

Grover Henderson says that he wants the hogs, like the horses, kept free. He feels the hogs perform a useful function by giving people something to hunt and by killing rattlesnakes. He says that if he were bitten by a rattlesnake, antivenom would do him no good, since he's allergic to it.

"I don't know anybody who lives here who doesn't like the hogs," he says.

Actually, the Park Service despises them. It believes the porkers must be totally removed from Cumberland—or else the island can never return to its full natural splendor. If the government has its way, twenty years from now, wild hogs on Cumberland will be just another memory—and one less conflict.

CHAPTER SIXTEEN

The Vig

WHEN PRESIDENT JOHN F. KENNEDY was assassinated in Dallas on November 22, 1963, Beulah Alberty sent word across Cumberland that she and her neighbors in the Settlement were having a memorial service that night in the First African Baptist Church. The folks at Greyfield, Stafford, and Plum Orchard, the Candlers at High Point, and the Millers and Olsens on the north end were all invited.

The invitations were quickly accepted. It was a somber affair to reflect on the life of the thirty-fifth president. "It became quite a service for the entire island," Gogo Ferguson says. "It seemed so appropriate that there was a service for President Kennedy in a church like that."

As the group—large by Cumberland standards—held a candle-light vigil at the service's close, no one gave a fleeting thought, could even conceive the idea, that the president's then three-year-old son would choose this humble place for his wedding thirty-three years later.

—————

Gogo coordinated the extraordinary marriage of John Kennedy, Jr., and Carolyn Bessette in the little church on September 21, 1996. Tabloid writers and the paparazzi would have killed to be there. But they didn't know of the event, which was pulled off in total secrecy in a feat befitting the CIA.

John-John was a longtime friend of Gogo's. He had been coming to Cumberland since his mid-twenties, staying mostly at Greyfield Inn. Gogo's daughter, Hannah, was just beginning to walk, and he fell in love with her. He agreed to serve on Gogo's board for the Plum Orchard artists' retreat and pledged to help her raise the $10 million needed for the mansion's renovation.

"He loved to get away, loved his privacy, loved to be able to kayak," Gogo says. "He was a great athlete. He jogged every morning or swam from Sea Camp dock, which was just astounding. I don't think any member of our family ever did that. He would hike around the island or go clamming. It was obvious he loved Cumberland for the same reasons we did."

In 1992, he met Carolyn Bessette, then a public-relations executive with Calvin Klein Ltd., supposedly while they were jogging in Manhattan. They began dating. Soon, they were living together in New York. At the time, John was one of the world's most desired bachelors. *People* magazine in 1988 named him "the sexiest man alive."

Carolyn began coming to Cumberland with him. She loved it as he did. It cloaked them in privacy and gave them a respite from the photographers and the curious who forever stalked them.

"We saw a lot of them on Martha's Vineyard, where I lead a very chaotic life during the summer," Gogo says. "I have two stores up there, and it's usually seven days a week. Sometimes, we would take a Sunday off

First African Baptist Church on Cumberland Island
Courtesy of the Atlanta Journal-Constitution

and spend a day on his mother's—now his sister's—compound and play football and go to the beach and have wonderful dinners. We would play with the dogs and play a lot of tennis.

"And one night, we were asked to come out to the compound. They said they were thinking of getting married, which didn't surprise me. But they wanted to do it on Cumberland. 'Wow,' I said.

"I knew that was going to be logistically very hard to do. But I also knew that it was the one gift I could give two friends that no one else could give them. It was their privacy. To me, it was such a wonderful thing to do for people who were so constantly followed. I thought it was something that I should do."

The planning began. Carolyn started flying down quite often to Cumberland. She sometimes brought her mother or her friend Gordon Henderson from Calvin Klein, who helped plan the wedding details.

"We had to hide Carolyn because everyone down here could have recognized her and noticed what was going on," Gogo says. "We would keep her on the floorboard of the car when we were going up to the church, all the way to the north end of the island.

"We had to hire Liz McComis with a fifty-five-gallon drum to wash the entire church. The ceiling was all cobwebs and mud daubers. We oiled the floor, and we oiled the benches. That was done just before Carolyn came down one time, so she could have an idea of what it would look like. So the church got a good cleaning.

"At that point, I talked them into at least telling Mitty [Gogo's brother] and Mary [Mitty's wife] because they were running Greyfield Inn. This was a major wedding, even if it was a small one. It had to be done just the way John and Carolyn wanted it. Mary would never have forgiven me if I had not told her.

"I told Mary that we needed tables because Carolyn wanted a beautiful sit-down affair for the rehearsal dinner on the porch at Greyfield. We had to have the right tables and right chairs over here because Gordon Henderson and Carolyn designed all the tablecloths and covers for each night. They were made in New York. I mean, she really saw to every little detail. She had the most amazing taste.

"Every plate was sprinkled with gold and silver almonds and beads from Balducci's. It was absolutely beautiful. Her flowers were beautiful. Bunny Mellon [a friend of John's late mother, Jacqueline Kennedy Onassis] had sent exquisite bouquets down for Carolyn and the kids. And in all the chaos of getting truckloads of people to the church—and trying to find John's father's shirt that he wanted to wear—evidently no one was in charge of the flowers. So they got left in the refrigerator. And what you see her carrying is mistletoe and some lily of the valley that had been flown in from Holland for the rehearsal dinner. That was Bunny's gift—the beautiful flowers that they didn't use. Well, I think they used them for some of the table settings.

"Carolyn wanted circular tents and white-oak dance floors. We had them shipped from Chattanooga, some from North Carolina. Everything had to be brought over on a boat. A lot of their china and other things they wanted to use were shipped from New York.

"And I had to buy out [reservations] at the inn. It was already booked when John and Carolyn gave me the wedding date. I had only four to six weeks to do this. We found one week when those who had reservations were willing to have a free weekend at Greyfield in order to give up their reservations. We told them that a friend of the family was getting married, and everyone understood.

"John and Carolyn decided that, right from the beginning, they wouldn't tell any of their family. I didn't tell any of our family because once it got out, someone was just not going to be able to resist telling their brother or their sister, and it was just going to be a chain reaction from then on.

"Thank God we had people like [Camden County probate judge] Martin Gillette, who is very professional and did not ask any questions. I just told him that they were dear friends of mine who were getting married, and they are having a hard time getting their blood tests and marriage license done, and could he meet me at the airport in St. Marys and have that done. It was done right on the plane. Of course, they then realized what was going on, but they vowed they would not say anything until Monday. And they did not say anything until Monday.

"No regular wedding invitations went out to the guests. No one knew. No one even realized. I think John and Carolyn just sent plane tickets and said, 'Please be here at this time.' People came from everywhere. Christiane Amanpour, the big CNN correspondent, a dear friend of John's from Brown University, came over from the Middle East. People made a huge effort. I am sure it was an unspoken invitation, that everyone knew exactly what was happening but was pledged to secrecy.

"We took over every house on the Greyfield compound, and the inn. Thank God we had a security group. A wonderful man from Jacksonville who used to be with the FBI had been a guest quite often at the inn, and he had a security group that did this sort of thing. He had a laser beam around the Greyfield compound, which of course was triggered by every wild horse that went through it at night. But it kept the security people on their toes. You could see their flashlights out in the woods all night long.

"All of our staff at the inn were so honorable because they knew that John and Carolyn were friends of ours. They were friends of the [staff] as well. No one broke the silence.

"There was one paparazzi from France that did get on the compound beforehand that was removed. They just told him that he had to leave early that morning before the wedding happened because there was a problem with the boat, and he was going to have to get on the early boat, and he would have to leave. He was not happy, but he ended up leaving.

"We had, gosh, I don't know, maybe twenty or twenty-five people staying here. There weren't many plush situations for sleeping. We had people on lawn chairs and mattresses and couches. It was quite something. Everyone seemed comfortable, and everyone was just so amazed by the island that it didn't really matter."

The elegant rehearsal dinner was held on the front porch of Greyfield.

"It was like a dream, really just like a dream," Gogo says." The tents [for the wedding dance next evening] weren't even set up. Carolyn didn't want the tents set up until the next morning, so that it would be just that beautiful oak tree and the candles lit all around the porches of Greyfield.

"Then everyone retired to the beach house, the gazebo, for cognac and cigars and dessert. They walked down. And as we came over the beach dune on the beach road, there were hundreds of tiki torches all around the gazebo. It was the most spectacular sight. We had a big bonfire going, and everyone that came over the dune started screaming when they saw it.

"The way the bride got dressed for her wedding was pretty funny. I called Mary Warren, who is the matriarch of High Point, just four days before the wedding, and I said, 'Mary, you can't even tell Billy this. Someone on our board is being married, and it has to be completely quiet. Could we use the hotel at High Point or your house to have them change for the wedding at the church?' She said absolutely. We changed in her house because I believe some of the kids in the Candler family were staying at the old hotel.

"The tide was too high [to drive on the beach from Greyfield to High Point], so I had to bounce Carolyn up all the way on Grand Avenue. They had had very little sleep from the rehearsal dinner at Greyfield. She sort of slept halfway up.

"So we dressed her in Mary's house, and Mary had a high tea for them. We had gone up early with ironing boards and steamers and everything that we needed. Mary's wonderful maid, Louisa, was just so darling. She had the ironing board out and was helping iron and was serving coffee.

"John had lost half of his clothes that he was supposed to wear. He had his father's shirt and cufflinks and studs that he wanted to wear. We couldn't find those. My husband, David, was racing up and down Greyfield trying to find those, and finally he did, thank God.

"John was in one room of Mary's house, and the dress designer and the hairdresser were in another room with Carolyn, trying to get her ready. They had done the last fitting, and the dress wouldn't fit. It was just total chaos."

The dress designer was Carolyn's longtime friend Narciso Rodriquez with Cerruti 1881 in Paris. He had designed for her a forty-thousand-dollar pearl-colored silk crepe bias-cut gown with silk tulle.

"We finally got her in her dress," Gogo says. "She traveled on all fours, her hands in the front seat right next to me, while I was driving. Then she was sort of standing up in the back, so that there wouldn't be one wrinkle when she got to the chapel. Of course, she sunk down into the dirt in her beautiful white satin shoes as soon as she stepped out.

"The church was incredible. There was a butler, Efigenio Pinhiero, and a woman, Martha, who basically raised John and his sister, Caroline. They were at the wedding. It was a very well-thought-out group of friends and family who were invited—people who mean a lot to John and Carolyn.

"Effie did the church. I think he used a lot of grapevine. The Park Service would not let him do a lot, once they caught on. But he did have a beautiful arch there. I think he had white morning glories trailing along on the floor. Other than that, it was lit with flashlights. We were allowed one candle up at the front. The Park Service would not let us have any other candles. We had applied for a special-use permit through Greyfield for the use of the church, which has been done several times. I did not want to involve the park just because I knew that would start a wildfire going. And it did. The boat people in the Park Service were the first ones to let the media know what was going on."

Getting the sixty or so guests—among them Teddy Kennedy; Maurice Templeton, one of Jackie Kennedy Onassis's closest friends; John's sister, Caroline Schlossberg; and her kids, Jack, Rose, and Tatiana—from Greyfield to the church ten miles away was another logistical headache. The plan was to transport them in cars and trucks quickly via the smooth, hard-packed beach.

Gogo kept her fingers crossed that the tide would be low enough so

Interior of First African Baptist Church
Courtesy of the Atlanta Journal-Constitution

the beach would be passable for hauling the guests to the church, then back to Greyfield for the post-wedding festivities.

"In looking ahead, we could see that the tide would be low in the afternoon and would give us time enough to get up the beach and back," she says. "Otherwise, it would have been a four-hour trip getting everyone up to that church and back down again. We drove them up there at low tide and then back at low tide. Thank God.

"We had every means of transportation. I had some Greyfield employees drive some people up and down. Whit Foster drove some people in his pickup truck. And we had all the Chippendale chairs and plastic chairs and everything else in the trucks.

"John and Carolyn were like two hours late for the wedding because of trying to find his clothes and getting her into her dress. People were taking tours of Carol Ruckdeschel's little museum by then and looking for armadillos. Everyone was covered with ticks for weeks afterwards.

"We finally got to the church, but by then it was so dark that Carol loaned flashlights. The Park Service also had loaned flashlights to light it up. It was by far the most beautiful service."

Caroline's three-year-old son, Jack, was the ring bearer. He walked down the aisle, sat in the front pew, and piped up, "Why's Carolyn all dressed up like that?"

Caroline, carrying orchids, was matron of honor.

Best man was Anthony Radziwill, John's first cousin.

Readings were by his brother-in-law, Edwin Schlossberg.

Atlanta photographer Denis Reggie, brother of Teddy Kennedy's wife, Vicki Reggie Kennedy, took photos.

Flower girls Rose and Tatiana Schlossberg scattered rose petals on the carpet placed on the worn wooden floor for the wedding.

David Davis, a Baptist choir leader in Fernandina, sang "Amazing Grace" as John and Carolyn walked in. They held hands at the altar before the Reverend Charles O'Byrne, a family friend from Manhattan's Church of St. Ignatius Loyola. After John and Carolyn were pronounced man and wife, Davis sang "Shall the Circle Be Unbroken" as they walked out of the church.

"I had interviewed many, many people from Jacksonville—all over Jacksonville—people who sing in the choirs," Gogo says. "I just sat on the phone or went over and interviewed a lot of people. We wanted an untrained voice because there was going to be no musical accompaniment. Mr. Davis was just perfect. He didn't have a clue who was in the wedding. He was shocked when he got over here and I told him that the couple would come and talk to him about what they wanted him to sing. And then John and Carolyn came out, and I thought his jaw was going to drop. He was speechless for the entire afternoon. But it was just wonderful. We couldn't have found anyone better for that."

Carol Ruckdeschel, an uninvited observer, eyeballed the whole thing from her barn's doorway, where she sat and nursed a beer and munched popcorn. When the ceremony was over, Carolyn, beautiful in her sparkling white gown, daintily stepped over to Carol's fence for a wedding photo. While she smoothed some wrinkles in her gown, she absent-mindedly held up her bouquet in her left hand. She felt a tug—Carol's horse had sauntered over to the fence and decided to make a snack of the wedding bouquet. John, chuckling, went over and petted the horse and said hi to Carol.

The wedding party feasted on capon and seafood at Greyfield after returning from the church. Ted Kennedy toasted the couple: "I'd like to introduce you to Mr. and Mrs. John F. Kennedy." The newlyweds' first dance was to "Forever in My Life" by Prince.

"It was just unbelievable, unbelievable," says Gogo.

The next morning, John and Carolyn sailed off on the Kennedy family yacht, *Honey Fitz*, for their honeymoon in an unknown place.

John issued a statement: "It was important for us to be able to conduct this in a private, prayerful and meaningful way with the people we love."

* * *

The day after the wedding, word leaked out to the media. All hell truly broke loose then. Writers from every media organization from *Time* to the *National Inquirer* were furious that they had been one-upped by Gogo and her allies. In the world of celebrity reporting, stories don't get much bigger than this.

"I would have people calling me from newspapers and magazines saying, 'You owe me this interview,'" Gogo says. "The Atlanta paper said that they were coming the next day with a photographer, and I owed them an interview. I said, 'I don't owe you anything. I'm not interviewing anyone. I did this for John and Carolyn's privacy.' So I told them, 'If you come past our gates, you are in violation of trespassing.' And then they were found in the living room of Greyfield. I mean, people were just unbelievable.

"The money being offered in St. Marys and Fernandina for charters and for any photographs of any Kennedy—especially John and Carolyn—

went up to something like twenty-five thousand dollars. Just watching the flotillas of media trying to get on to this island after the wedding was horrifying. It was horrifying that our privacy could be so violated.

"The media used a lot of pictures out of context. There is one magazine that had the kids, Jack and Rose and Tatiana, supposedly at this wedding, when in fact it was some wedding way up in the Hamptons that they were photographed at. There were pictures of Greyfield with the dining room fully set for this elegant meal, and it wasn't that at all because our meals were eaten out on the porch and out under the tents. There was a picture in *People* magazine that was probably two years old. It was taken from a Georgia newspaper article.

"There were a lot of consequences. I have gotten a lot of hate mail, a lot of anonymous hate mail. Every environmental group said it was the beginning of the end for Cumberland. The crowds were going to be just unbelievable.

"It's so funny because I never once harped on the opportunity to profit from this or be recognized for this. Yet I am doing a fund-raiser for the Department of Natural Resources, and in their brochure, the first thing they do is advertise 'the famous Cumberland Island of the Kennedy wedding.' So everyone is jumping on the bandwagon to make some kind of profit off it.

"Right after the wedding, my family had a meeting at Greyfield to discuss what we want from this. And what we wanted to get from this was that our family and our inn are a place of privacy—that no matter who you are, you can come, and you can remain unrecognized and enjoy yourself in total privacy. And I think that we accomplished that. And I think that I will always go down as someone who will always honor people's privacy."

———•◦•———

A year or so after the wedding, Gogo and her husband planted two sago palms in front of the First African Baptist Church. "One palm was in memory of President Kennedy; the other was for John and Carolyn," Gogo says. "We had them sunk in front in pots until we got permission from the Park Service that we could put them there permanently."

The Park Service removed the palms because they were not indigenous to the front of the church.

John and Carolyn died in a plane crash in July 1999.

———————

Measuring twenty-eight feet by sixteen feet, the church has remained essentially unchanged since it was built in 1937. Other than what happened here, there is nothing remarkable about it. The entrance is through sagging double doors painted fire-engine red, matching the trim around the windows. Faded wooden boards laid across concrete blocks serve as steps. A sheet of brown tin nailed across the threshold prevents wear and tear on the creaking boards underneath.

Inside are eight wooden pews, paint-spattered, splintery, and cracked. Up front is a plain, rough, wooden altar table painted white and holding a Bible opened to the Twenty-third Psalm. Behind the table is a crude cross made of red cedar. On the back wall hangs a colorful, poster-sized National Baptist Picture Roll of Bible stories from 1935. The sunlight streaming in is filtered through glass windows "stained" with chalky paint.

Outside, a handmade concrete plaque in a niche near the door lists the founders and officers: "Founded 1893 by Rev. T. Lockett. Deacons: W. M. Alberty; C. Trimings; P. Mitchel. Officers 1937: C. Alberty; P. Trimings; N. Merrou; Beulah G. Alberty, church clerk; Rev. L. Morrison, pastor."

The Reverend L. C. Morrison, still remembered as Cumberland's most beloved clergyman, was invited to come here by Beulah and her brother Chester. "The church's membership had gone down. Members had moved away," says Franscena Jacobs, the pastor's daughter. "He caught the *Dungeness*, the Carnegies' boat, at Fernandina over to the island. On his first trip, he was so happy because of the natural beauty and the people.

A plaque on the outside wall of the First African Baptist Church in the Settlement lists the church's founding members.

Courtesy of the National Park Service

"When he got there, there was the old, dilapidated log-cabin church that was about to fall down. He wanted to rehabilitate the church and reorganize it. While they were building the new church, he went often to the island to see that things were getting done or help do whatever he could. Baptism was in the river, total immersion. The music was our natural voices.

"The church members had fish fries to get money for the new church. The Carnegies gave donations. The community was good to my father because they believed in what he was doing. And he believed that if you give, you will receive."

He was the pastor for fourteen years, from the Depression until World War II's outbreak.

"He had nothing but faith and hope and determination," his daughter says. "His religious philosophy was that there is some good in everyone. You find that good, and you make that relationship there. And that, through God, all things are possible."

Visitors to Cumberland now clamor to see the little church made famous by the Kennedy wedding. To Carol's great chagrin, the Settlement may never again bask in splendid obscurity.

"It is no longer the First African Baptist Church," she says. "It's the Kennedy church."

In time, the wedding will be just another part of Cumberland's lore, just another blip in its rich history. The island will endure, a place protected forever for those who cherish great natural beauty and wild places.

But Cumberland's conflicts are far from over. Islands, like mountain peaks, always have invoked strong emotions in humans. It might be that Cumberland, an almost deserted island with near primordial beauty, especially draws out primitive longings in us. What else explains why so many people spend so much of their lives locked in bitter strife over it?

"Something about Cumberland makes everybody a little crazy," Lucy Ferguson said.

As long as inholders and retained-rights holders live on the island, as long as the wild horses still roam, the dissension will continue. Decisions over Cumberland's future could very well affect the way the government manages its entire national park system. A saying in the Park Service goes that if you can manage Cumberland, you can manage any national park in the country.

Unlike most parks in the system, Cumberland is home to several endangered species, dozens of structures on the National Register of Historic Places, and a wilderness area with at least five still-occupied houses in it. Combine all of that with the wild horses, forty-eight thousand visitors a year, and twenty full-time and three hundred part-time residents, and you have a formula for a management train wreck.

In an effort to correct years of mismanagement on Cumberland, the Park Service in 2001 finally drafted a five-part plan on how to administer the island's natural and historic treasurers—the first such blueprint for the park since it was established in 1972. The lack of such a plan has made Cumberland fertile ground for lawsuits.

The new plan may be unprecedented for any national park because of the range of issues it addresses. According to the still-to-be-implemented plan, nearly every aspect of life will be affected on Cumberland. One recommendation calls—once again—for thinning the horse herd from 250 animals to as few as 60. Another restricts where residents can drive. Still another limits to 15 the size of groups walking through the wilderness area together. And if you want to get married in the First African Baptist Church, as John Kennedy, Jr., did, you'll have to walk the several miles to the church.

The plan is set to go into effect in late 2002. Whether that actually happens depends on the whims of feuding factions that in the past have sued when things didn't go their way on Cumberland.

As for another bone of contention, Plum Orchard, the future is uncertain. The money that Jack Kingston shook loose from Congress is being used to stabilize the old mansion and at least halt its deterioration. Until the work is completed, it is shut down to visitors, probably at least through the end of 2003. After that, the Park Service wants a group or an individual to lease it for a corporate retreat or a bed-and-breakfast or a youth hostel or some other acceptable purpose. But there's a big catch: whoever signs the lease might have to spend some $6 million to renovate the house's interior. They also would have to tolerate tour groups coming through and would have to abide by the wilderness restrictions. So far, only one individual has expressed lukewarm interest.

"We should have let Gogo have it when we had a chance," a Park Service official admitted.

Meanwhile, Kingston got another $450,000 through Congress to stabilize the twenty-three chimneys of Robert Stafford's old slave quarters. Some of the money could be used to build a replica of one of the slave cabins, he says.

Which leaves some people wondering who will come see all of this. With daily visitation to Cumberland restricted to 300 people, the island is one of the least visited of the National Park Services' 387 parks, seashores, battlefields, historic sites, and other units.

Of course, the low visitor limit incenses Camden County business and government leaders, who want to see hordes of sightseers on Cumberland—visitors who would buy meals, stay at hotels, and purchase trinkets from gift shops. The local governments have all passed unanimous resolutions calling for a study to see if more people can be hauled to the island. St. Marys mayor Jerry Brandon, who runs the eighteen-room Riverview Hotel near Cumberland's mainland dock in his town, complains that he has to turn away potential patrons almost daily when they learn the ferryboat is booked or the campgrounds are full. Most of his customers spend the night at his hotel before catching the ferry the next day.

But the local governments should be careful what they ask for. A study could find that the current three-hundred-per-day limit is not good for the island, and therefore reduce it. And despite what Brandon says, the Park Service people maintain that the island reaches its capacity of visitors on fewer than fifty days a year.

Perhaps the salvation for Cumberland Island will prove to be time. Time has erased evidence that the Timucuans, the French, the Spaniards, and the English were here. It has rubbed out most of Caty Greene Miller's and Robert Stafford's presence. And in a century or two, even the signs that the Carnegies sojourned here might be gone, and Cumberland may again bask in natural splendor.

EPILOGUE

ON THE DAY AFTER NEW YEAR'S, my wife, two kids, and I are in our Plymouth Voyager zipping along arrow-straight I-95 in coastal Georgia, where salt marshes and pine plantations dominate the flat landscape. We are going to Cumberland Island.

The traffic is heavy. Blurring past us are license plates from New Jersey, New York, Massachusetts, attached to SUVs and minivans driven by weary Northerners dashing home after holiday pilgrimages to Disney, Sea World, Universal. Football fans who came south for the bowl games also are in the scramble. Hooked on to their cars and flapping madly in the breeze are little rectangular flags sporting their schools' names and colors.

We veer off at the St. Marys exit and head down Ga. 40. For most of its route, it is a franchise alley of gas pumps, convenience stores, Shoney's, Burger Kings, K-Marts, Publix supermarkets, Home Depots. In St. Marys, it becomes Osborne Street, the town's main thoroughfare, lined with oaks and wind-scarred cedars. St. Marys is a quaint, old sea town occupying an eminence on a scenic stretch of the St. Marys River. Osborne

Street dead-ends at the waterfront, where the placid water reflects white-painted shrimp trawlers moored to wooden docks. The aura is that of an Old World fishing village.

Near the docks, the Cumberland Island National Seashore Visitor Center is a squat, stucco-and-shingle structure painted a drab gray. This is where we must buy day-use tickets and boat tickets—fifty-six dollars in all for the four of us—to spend five hours on the island.

Like us, the vast majority of the forty-eight thousand sightseers who go to Cumberland each year are day-trippers who stay five to seven hours. The Park Service ferry provides the only public access to the island. If the boat is full and you haven't made reservations, you're out of luck.

At the dock, the *Cumberland Queen*, a gleaming, white, double-deck boat sixty feet long, is just getting back from its early-morning run to the island. Among those stepping off are four women in muddy shorts, saggy sweaters, and wet hiking boots. They look as if they just ended a forced march—and with good reason. They spent three days roughing it on the island, they say. Their camping gear is soaked. "My pants are miserably wet," says one, her auburn hair snarled pitifully from wind, rain, and lack of brushing. "We spent New Year's Eve and New Year's Day on the island. We had nice weather until early this morning, when it started drizzling and then pouring. It's no fun taking down tents and packing gear in the rain."

Before we board the ferry for our forty-five-minute ride to the island, a park ranger warns us to be at the island dock at four-thirty for the return trip. If we miss the boat, we'll be stuck overnight. No pets or bicycles. Bring your own lunch or go hungry. A final warning: The wild horses kick, so don't bother them.

The *Cumberland Queen* is plying the twisting St. Marys River on the eleven o'clock run to Cumberland. Her twin four-hundred-horsepower Caterpillar engines push her along at a steady clip. About one hundred

The Cumberland Island National Seashore's ferry, the Cumberland Queen, transports visitors to the island from St. Marys. Here the boat is shown at the Sea Camp dock.
Courtesy of the National Park Service

people are aboard. The water is mirror calm, the sky is slightly cloudy, and the temperature is balmy for early January.

But all is not postcard perfect. Across the salt marsh loom the bland, block-like structures of a paper mill. Sitting on the mainland at the marsh's edge, the sprawling mill is an abrupt reminder that this is also an industrial area. Thick, gray plumes belch from its smokestacks. It stinks horribly.

Even on this boat headed to a pristine isle, it is impossible to escape the sulfurous paper-mill stench that some liken to rotten eggs. One writer said the odor is what mustard gas must have smelled like, billowing across the trenches of the Marne in World War I. Some people blame the mill for the air pollution that has eaten paint off houses and chrome off cars and caused Spanish moss to disappear from the oaks in St. Marys. With the passage of the federal Clean Air Act, the air around St. Marys got cleaner—or so government regulators say. Still, when the breeze wafts your way, you have to pinch your nose against the stink.

Nevertheless, people in St. Marys call it something else—the "smell of money." The mill provides good-paying jobs, benefits, and tax revenue, they say.

The view from the boat's other side reveals two more paper mills spewing plumes in the far distance. They are in Fernandina, Florida, a few miles from Cumberland's southern tip.

When I look away from the mills, the view of the winter-brown marsh with the tidal creeks coiling through it is gorgeously panoramic. Long-legged wading birds stalk their prey along the creeks. Flocks of shorebirds huddle on the banks.

Georgia's long-ago poet laureate Sidney Lanier must have had the same wonderful view when he penned his famous "Marshes of Glynn." " 'Tis here, 'tis here thou canst unhand thy heart and Breathe it free," he wrote. His marshes are farther up the coast, near Brunswick.

As the vessel turns eastward and heads across Cumberland Sound, the high, reddish bluffs, tall palmettos, and giant oaks on the backside of the island come into sight to starboard. The scene is an artist's delight.

"Look, wild horses!" cries a man on the lower deck. He is pointing at three blobs on a strip of marsh between the bluff and the water.

I train my binoculars on them—a gray and two sorrels, grazing contentedly on the marsh grass. Other passengers hasten to starboard.

"Now I can say I've seen wild horses," says a trim woman in designer jeans and leather jacket.

"Wait 'til you get on the island. You can actually step in wild horse doo-doo," says a tall man by her side, a black New York Yankees cap on his head.

———————

The boat moors to the wood-and-concrete Dungeness pier, which juts out over the Cumberland River on the island's south end. Fiddler crabs scurry into holes in the bank. Ranger Gissella Burgos—slim, dark-haired, smiling in her dark green uniform—meets the vessel.

A few minutes later, she is leading thirty of us up an allée of huge, bearded live oaks. She walks backwards, facing us, deftly sidestepping the horse droppings. The Timucuans were the first to occupy Cumberland, she explains. "That's TIM-mew-kwans," she says.

A wild sow and five piglets trot across the path directly ahead of us.

"Ooh, look, little piggies," the woman in the designer jeans says. "Aren't they cute?"

"Don't say that," Burgos admonishes, half-serious. "Pigs destroy the vegetation. They are bad for the island. They are an enormous problem. They are all over the place. We try to hunt them, but it doesn't seem to help."

Something rustles in the bushes—an armadillo. "They're everywhere, too," Burgos says.

We walk past the Carnegies' private cemetery, enclosed by a fence and a Tiffany gate. It is off-limits to park visitors so the family can retain its privacy, Burgos explains. It has marble benches and is well maintained, but it is kept in a semiwild state because the family wants it that way, she adds.

She points to a colony of saw palmettos, whose fan-shaped fronds look like strutting tom turkeys. She says Indians used palmetto berries to make potions for a number of ills, including prostate problems. A doctor among us says that a scientific study in a recent *Journal of the American Medical Association* issue showed that the berries indeed have curative powers. "That's interesting," Burgos comments. The Indians also used palmetto fronds for mats, baskets, and roofing, she says. She points to a young cabbage palmetto. Its "heart," she says, is a gourmet's delight when chopped up and mixed in salads. Indians boiled it in bear fat for porridge. Unfortunately, cutting out the heart kills the young tree. Next, she calls attention to a yaupon holly, or cassina, an evergreen shrub laden with caffeine. The Timucuans made a bitter concoction from it—a holy drink—that caused them to vomit. Hence the shrub's scientific name: *Ilex vomitoria*.

The oaks and wild shrubs give way to a magnolia-shaded esplanade. Lucy Carnegie ordered the magnolias planted, Burgos says. At the end of the magnolia-shaded way loom Dungeness's eerie ruins, the weathered bones of the Carnegies' first mansion on Cumberland. While we're staring at the remnants, Burgos urges us to imagine Dungeness in its glory—lavish parties, weddings with champagne-bubbling fountains, wealthy young sportsmen prancing about in riding habits, a grand piano tinkling out a waltz.

The walk ends at the Park Service's maintenance shop, which was once the spacious carriage house for Dungeness. "This is a beautiful island full of history," Burgos concludes. "If it weren't for the Carnegies, who preserved and protected it, we might not have it."

———•—•———

On our own, my wife, kids, and I stop at the old cemetery at Dungeness—not to be confused with the Carnegies' graveyard—where Revolutionary War general Light Horse Harry Lee was buried after he died on Cumberland in 1818. His bones are no longer here, having been disinterred in 1913 and laid to rest at Washington and Lee University in Virginia. The lichen-covered tombstone of Harry's original grave still stands in the little cemetery.

Then my son shouts and runs and slides pell-mell down the steep bluff to the nearby creek. A pair of dolphins is snorting and cavorting in the water, probably chasing mullet stranded there at low tide. My wife and daughter join him. They stand at the creek's edge in awe of the frolicking creatures.

For that, I decide that the fifty-six dollars for coming here was worth it.

———•—•———

Strolling northward on the beach at a leisurely pace, I'm ahead of the wife and kids by a football field's length or more. I glance back at them. My wife and son are bent over the edge of a tidal pool, peering into the shallow water and pointing at something there. My daughter is picking up yet another sand dollar. She wants several small ones to make a bracelet. Shell collecting is perfectly okay, the ranger told us. That's not so, though, with arrowheads and spear points and pottery shards. They are cultural artifacts that belong to the government. If you pick one up, it must be handed over. The Park Service also asks that you note where you found it, as the information might be useful to archaeologists.

No other humans are in sight. Then I make out a dot far down the beach that could be something living—perhaps a person or a horse. I focus my binoculars on it and see an equine form moving toward me. In a surprisingly short time, the roan-colored creature and I approach. By the anatomy dangling under his belly, it's plain he is a stallion. I am not a good judge of horses, but he looks in decent shape. He passes me and gives me a sideways glance, as if to say, "What the hell are you gawking at?" Mindful of the ranger's warning that the animals rear and kick, I give him a wide berth.

There is plenty of other life to keep me company. Tiny beach creatures scurry over the sand. Mixed flocks of shorebirds stand, flap, and wheel at the surf's edge. I pick out herring gulls, ring gulls, willets, common terns, sanderlings, Wilson's plovers, and semipalmated plovers. And there, mixed in with a flock, is a piping plover, a small, sandy-colored bird resembling a sandpiper. I can add it to my birding list. The plover is on the endangered species list, in part because of high fashion. Nineteenth-century hat makers used tons of piping plover feathers to decorate women's hats. The bird also was gourmet food, showing up on restaurant menus as "Plover on Toast." Such a useful little bird was easily killed, and its numbers plummeted.

I look back and can't see the family. They have left the beach, taken the boardwalk over the dunes to the dock, where we will catch the return ferry. I continue walking. I told my wife that I wanted to see the remains of some old Cuban refugee rafts that washed up on Cumberland in the

1990s. Whit Foster said that when he was driving Ted Kennedy up the beach for the wedding in 1996, Kennedy asked that they stop and look at the rafts. Norbody knows what became of the Cubans who crafted the crude rafts to escape to America.

I am truly alone now. Solitude. No doubt, this is the way the beach appeared to the Indians and the first Europeans. A woman friend told me once that she likes to trudge along Cumberland's empty beach pretending she can see and hear Timucuans, Spanish soldiers, Jesuit monks, Scottish Highlanders, black slaves, and the leisurely rich, walking and talking among themselves on the sand. I try imagining that, but it doesn't work for me.

Instead, I breathe deeply of the clean, moist air. I listen to the surf and gulls calling to the wind. I feel beneath my feet the powdery sand.

O N   S O U R C E S

THE PEOPLE, PLACES, AND EVENTS in this book are real. In the several cases where there is more than one version of what took place, I have tried to rely on what I deemed the most accurate versions. There are several versions, for instance, about how Lucy Coleman Carnegie first became aware of Cumberland Island and how Eli Whitney came to be at Mulberry Grove.

I relied heavily on Joyce Seward's superb oral-history project about Cumberland Island for much of my material. I also relied on historical documents and records on file at Cumberland Island National Seashore; the Georgia Department of Archives; the Georgia Division for Historic Preservation; the University of Georgia Library; the University of Florida Library; the University of Pittsburgh Library; the Yale University Library (the Whitney papers); the St. Marys Public Library; the National Park Service's regional office in Atlanta; and the *Atlanta Journal-Constitution's* News Research Department. And my own notes compiled over years of reporting on issues concerning Cumberland Island proved of considerable use.

I used information from legal records on file with the Camden County

Courthouse, the United States District Court, the National Park Service, and the National Oceanic and Atmospheric Administration.

Four very helpful books were *Robert Stafford of Cumberland Island: Growth of a Planter* by Mary R. Bullard (University of Georgia Press, 1995); *Caty: A Biography of Catharine Littlefield Greene* by John and Janet Stegeman (University of Georgia Press, 1977); *Andrew Carnegie* by Joseph Frazier Wall (University of Pittsburgh Press, 1989); and *Portrait of an Island* by Mildred and John Teal (University of Georgia Press, 1981).

A C K N O W L E D G M E N T S

I OWE A GREAT DEBT OF THANKS to the many people whose names appear in this book. I am especially grateful to Carol Ruckdeschel, and Whit Foster for taking me into their homes on Cumberland.

In addition, I am much indebted to a lot of other folks: Don O'Briant at the *Atlanta Journal-Constitution*, who supported me early on; Paul Winegar and John Mitchell of the National Park Service; Robert Coram, who gave good advice; the staff at the Georgia Department of Archives; the St. Marys Library staff; and Joyce Seward, a National Park Service volunteer whose superb oral history of Cumberland Island National Seashore was invaluable.

I also wish to thank Joe Tanner, Patricia Barmeyer, and Bill Harlan for helping to open doors to various sources on Cumberland; Lonice Barrett, Duane Harris, Barb Zoodsma, Brad Winn, and Ken Thomas at the Georgia Department of Natural Resources; Allison Steely, Francine Dyer, Karen Lockridge, and my wife, Laura, who read portions of the manuscript; the late Mary Miller, Cumberland's unofficial historian; and Greg Paxton of the Georgia Trust for Historic Preservation.

Finally, I want to thank the staff at John F. Blair, Publisher. Without great publishers, there would be no great writers.

I N D E X

Carnegie, Thomas M. III, 160, 162-63
Carnegie, Thomas M. IV, 163, 218, 221
Carnegie, Virginia Beggs, 135-36, 159
Carnegie, Will, 96-98, 128
Carnegie, William Coleman, 104, 138-43, 159, 162, 285
Carter, Amy, 173
Carter, Jimmy: and Bobby Rischarde, 188; and Carol Ruckdeschel, 24, 208, 209; and Charles Fraser, 224; and Jessie Bailey, 189, 192, 197; and Jane Yarn, 222; and John Pennington, 16; as governor, 240; love of the island, 13; story about island, 19
Chimneys, The, 86, 218, 219, 329
Christmas Creek, 39, 176, 177, 185, 186, 189, 191, 192, 196, 257
Civil War, 13, 68, 77, 79, 80-81, 84, 88, 99, 175
Cleland, Max, 33, 322, 325
Cockburn, George, 64-65
Coleman, William, 99, 100, 102, 103
Cook, Bobby Lee, 253-55, 260
Copp, Belton, 72, 78, 79
Coram, Robert, 17, 246, 276
Cornelison, John, Jr., 86
Count de Perigny, 147-48
Cumberland Island Hotel, 91, 93, 176-78, 199, 266
Cumberland Island National Seashore: author's visits to, 3, 358; beach driving, 7, 264, 320-21; condemned land, 212; driving on Grand Avenue, 3, 308, 345; feral hogs, 290-91, 305, 335-38, 361; feral horses, 4, 7, 304, 325, 330-35, 354, 363; ferry, 32, 358-60; formation of, 229, 230, 212, 257, 316; historic preservation, 10, 32, 327, 328; history of Grand Avenue, 58, 61, 91, 93, 138-39, 177; island's

future, 9; rules of driving on Grand Avenue, 7, 32, 251, 319, 320, 323, 325; visitation, 245-46, 355; wilderness area, 11-12, 32, 68, 319-321, 323, 325, 326
Cumberland Island Museum, 24-25, 347
Cumberland Island Preservation Society, 319, 321, 327

Davis, David, 348,
Davis, Denis, 11, 12, 31, 246, 270
Davis, George, 113, 295
Davis, Robert, 253, 256
Defenders of Wild Cumberland, 30-31, 316, 326, 328
Douglass, Gloria, 287
Dungeness (Carnegies): Andrew at, 105; construction of, 69, 93-95; demise of, 156-57, 162, 166-67, 168-69, 295-96; employees at, 182, 198; expansion of 107-9; life at, 4, 122-25, 129-33, 176, 216, 281; under the Park Service, 244, 328, 362
Dungeness (Catharine Greene): Caty's children and, 63, 64-65, 68-69; Caty's death, 67; construction of, 57-61, 71, 72; garden, 109; Phineas Nightingale and, 81-82; ruins, 88, 91, 92-93
Dungeness (Oglethorpe), 45-46

Ehrenhard, John, 45, 84-85, 86, 305-6

Ferguson, Janet "Gogo": and artists' retreat, 30-32, 315, 316, 355; and Carol Ruckdeschel, 13, 15, 30; and J.B. Peeples, 295, 297, 298; and Park Service, 11, 27-29, 29-30; her life today, 31; Greyfield Inn, 26, 300; memories, 10, 25-26, 186, 197, 292; Miss Lucy, 303, 311-12; Kennedy-Bessette

Georgia Rose, 270-71; lawyer for heirs, 218; on wilderness area, 320

Morrison, L.C., 351-53

Mulberry Grove, 49-53, 55-56, 60, 62

National Park Foundation, 228, 240, 241, 242, 248, 265

National Park Service: artists' retreat, 29, 30, 31; and Candlers, 33; and Carnegies, 221, 226, 227; and future of island, 353-54; and Carol Ruckdeschel, 213, 260; and Miss Lucy, 230, 272, 273; land negotiations, 7, 8, 248, 249; Plum Orchard, 10, 243; retained-use arrangements, 241; wilderness area, 319; wild pigs, 338

Nature Conservancy of Georgia, 313, 321, 322, 325-26

Neuhauser, Hans, 236, 317-18

New London, Conn., 72, 83

New York Yacht Club, 122

Nightingale, John C., 55, 62

Nightingale, Phineas, 66-68, 73-74, 80, 81-82, 91, 175

O'Byrne, Charles, 348

Oglethorpe, James, 43-45, 162, 175, 229

Olsen, Oley, 190-91, 193, 194, 195-96, 197, 200

Owen, Norman, 9

Page, William, 108, 117-18, 133, 148, 216

Peeples, J.B., 294-98, 305, 310, 336-37

Pennington, John, 16, 17, 209-11, 266

Perkins, Coleman, 230, 266

Perkins, Curtis, 127, 216

Perkins, Florence "Floss" Carnegie, 104, 120-21, 127, 148, 154, 159, 168, 215-18

Piehl, Tom, 240-42, 250, 265-66, 271

Plum Orchard: and the Johnstons, 163-65, 170-71, 218, 226, 229; artists' retreat, 15, 29-32, 315, 340; author's visit, 3; construction of, 110, 143-47; deterioration, 234; donation of, 243, 327; employees at, 200, 201-2; future of, 354-55; mail delivery, 117; Marguerite Bernardey, 75; memories of, 285; Park Service, 9-11, 243, 244, 325, 328; timber cut, 271; today, 171-74

Radziwill, Anthony, 348

Ricketson, Margaret "Retta" Carnegie, 104, 107, 143,150, 218, 249, 277, 279

Ricketson, Oliver Garrison, 143, 249, 277, 279

Ricketson, Oliver Garrison, Jr., 277, 278

Ricketson, Oliver Garrison III, 256

Rischarde, Bobby, 183-89, 192, 198, 322, 329

Rischarde, Della, 183-89

Rockefeller, James Stillman "Pebble," Jr., 8, 164-65, 166, 250-54, 255, 262, 291-92

Rockefeller, James Stillman, Sr., 159, 225

Rockefeller, Nancy Carnegie, 150, 159, 178, 217-18, 219, 224-26, 249, 251-52, 270, 299

Rose, Georgia Rockefeller, 270-71

Ruckdeschel, Carol: and Gogo Ferguson, 13, 15; and wilderness area, 319; artists' retreat, 30-33; Hal Wright, 315-16; her cabin, 5-6, 324, 347; historic structures, 328-29; her story, 16-25, 203-24; Grover Henderson, 249, 259,